The Triumph of Prudence over Passion

THE
TRIUMPH
OF
PRUDENCE over PASSION:
OR, THE
HISTORY
OF
MISS MORTIMER
AND
MISS FITZGERALD.

By the AUTHORESS of EMELINE.

IN TWO VOLUMES.

VOL. I.

DUBLIN:

Printed (for the Author) by S. COLBERT, No. 136, Capel-ftreet, oppofite Abbey-ftreet.

M,DCC,XXXI.

Title page from *The Triumph of Prudence over Passion*, vol. I

THE TRIUMPH OF PRUDENCE OVER PASSION;
OR,
THE HISTORY OF MISS MORTIMER AND MISS FITZGERALD

Elizabeth Sheridan

edited with an introduction and notes by
Aileen Douglas and Ian Campbell Ross

FOUR COURTS PRESS

Set in 10.5 pt on 12.5 pt Bembo for
FOUR COURTS PRESS LTD
7 Malpas Street, Dublin 8, Ireland
www.fourcourtspress.ie
and in North America for
FOUR COURTS PRESS
c/o ISBS, 920 N.E. 58th Avenue, Suite 300, Portland, OR 97213.

First published 2011
Paperback reprint 2017

A catalogue record for this title
is available from the British Library.

ISBN 978-1-84682-663-4

Printed in Ireland
by SPRINT-Print, Dublin.

Contents

The Literature of Early Modern Ireland series

Previously published in the series:
Faithful Teate, *Ter Tria*, ed. Angelina Lynch (2007)
Henry Burkhead, *Cola's Furie*, ed. Angelina Lynch and Patricia Coughlan (2009)
Richard Nugent, *Cynthia*, ed. Angelina Lynch and Anne Fogarty (2010)
William Dunkin, *The Parson's Revels*, ed. Catherine Skeen (2010)

Early Irish Fiction, *c.*1680–1820

Also published in the series:
[Anon], *Vertue Rewarded; or, The Irish Princess*, ed. Ian Campbell Ross and
    Anne Markey (2010)
Sarah Butler, *Irish Tales*, ed. Ian Campbell Ross, Aileen Douglas, and Anne
    Markey (2010)
Thomas Amory, *The Life of John Buncle, Esq.*, ed. Moyra Haslett (2011)
John Carey, Lady Mount Cashell, Henry Brooke et al., *Children's Fiction,
    1765–1808*, ed. Anne Markey (2011)

Forthcoming in the series:
Charles Johnstone, *The History of Arsaces, Prince of Betlis*, ed. Daniel Sanjiv
    Roberts (2012)

Preface

Irish prose fiction of the long eighteenth century has only recently begun to receive the attention it merits. While such names as Swift, Goldsmith and Edgeworth have long been familiar to readers of Irish (and British) literature, many other writers – born, educated, or living in Ireland – produced a substantial and imaginatively varied body of fiction from the late-seventeenth to the early-nineteenth century. This series aims more fully to indicate the diversity and breadth of Irish literature in the period 1680–1820 by providing critical editions of a range of exemplary works of prose fiction. In so doing, it will indicate the role the early novel played in inventing Ireland for readers at home and abroad, while offering new perspectives on the literature and history of these islands.

Each title in the series will contain a carefully-edited text, together with a critical introduction, a select bibliography, and comprehensive notes, designed for scholars and students of Irish writing in English, of the English novel, and all those concerned with Ireland c.1680–c.1820.

Aileen Douglas
Moyra Haslett
Ian Campbell Ross

Acknowledgments

The editors gratefully acknowledge financial assistance from the Centre for Irish-Scottish and Comparative Studies, Trinity College Dublin and from the Irish Research Council for the Humanities and Social Sciences.

For their assistance, the editors gratefully thank Moyra Haslett; Anne Markey; Christopher Fox; Michael Richardson and Jamie Carstairs, both of the University of Bristol Library; Charles Benson and the staff of Early Printed Books, the Library, Trinity College Dublin; and the staffs of the National Library of Ireland; the Hesburgh Library, University of Notre Dame; the Newberry Library, Chicago; the Bodleian Library, Oxford; and the British Library.

The editors wish also to thank their friend, the late Dr Siobhán Kilfeather (1957–2007), latterly of the School of English, Queen's University Belfast, for many engaging conversations about *The Triumph of Prudence over Passion* and early Irish fiction generally, that took place, variously, in Princeton; South Bend, Indiana; New York; Dublin; and Belfast. We are saddened that she did not live to see the publication of this volume, or to take her intended place, together with Moyra Haslett and ourselves, as a general editor of the series.

Francis Wheatley's *The Dublin Volunteers on College Green, 4th November 1779* (1779–80) is reproduced by permission of the National Gallery of Ireland.

The frontispiece illustration of the title-page of the first volume of the first edition of *The Triumph of Prudence over Passion* (1781) is reproduced by permission of the Board of Trinity College Dublin.

Introduction

On Saturday, 8 December 1781, the enterprising Dublin bookseller Stephen Colbert, who had recently moved his well-stocked circulating library to new premises at 136, Capel Street, advertised in the *Dublin Evening Post*:

> The *TRIUMPH of PRUDENCE over PASSION, or the History of Miss Mortimer and Miss Fitzgerald*, an original Novel, in a series of Letters, 2 vols. 4s. 4d. sewed, 5s. 5d. bound—This production, the principal scenes whereof are laid in Dublin, displays new and genuine sentiments, an easy familiar stile and judicious interesting remarks. The STORY abounds with affecting incidents, and is calculated to afford rational amusement.[1]

The previous year, Colbert had advertised an earlier work *Emeline: a Moral Tale*, by the same author, then identified as 'an Irish Lady'. It offered, he declared: 'Many circumstances ... that interest, at this Juncture, the IRISH Nation'.[2] The two fictions were published at a time of considerable political ferment: in 1780 public agitation in Ireland had forced the British government to abolish restric-

---

1   *Dublin Evening Post*, 8 December 1781. That *The Triumph of Prudence over Passion* was printed 'for the author' was not unusual in the period, even for established writers; Charles Churchill published his poetry in this way, and the first volume of Henry Brooke's *The Fool of Quality* (Dublin, 1765) was 'Printed for the AUT[H]OR' by Dillon Chamberlaine. Following the original notice by Stephen Colbert, *The Triumph of Prudence over Passion* was subsequently included in a list of 'New Books' sold by William Gilbert, of 26 Great George's Street, Dublin, in a series of advertisements in *The Dublin Evening Post*, beginning on 12 January 1782; the list included six further titles: another anonymous novel, *The Fortunate Sisters* (1782); the comedy, *A Trip to Scarborough* 'by [Richard Brinsley] Sheridan' (after Vanburgh's *The Relapse*); Samuel Croxall's successful *The Fair Circassian* (first published in 1720 but enjoying a revival at the Theatre Royal, Drury Lane), Robert Jephson's drama *The Count of Narbonne* (after Horace Walpole's *The Castle of Otranto*), Isaac Jackman's farce *The Divorce* (1781), and a new edition of Robert Dodsley's well-known *Collection of Poems*, first published in 1748.

2   *Dublin Evening Post*, 18 March 1780. No copy of the Dublin edition of *Emeline: A Moral Tale* is known to survive. The title page of *The Triumph of Prudence over Passion* (Dublin, 1781) identifies its author as also having written *Emeline*; both works were subsequently published in London by William Lane, best known as founder of the Minerva Press, using the same sheets in the case of the later novel. Lane's editions were published under different titles: *The Fairy Ring; or, Emeline, A Moral Tale. By a Lady* (London, 1783) and *The Reconciliation; or, The History of Miss Mortimer and Miss FitzGerald. In a Series of Letters. An Hibernian Novel* (London, 1783).

tive commercial legislation and concede 'free trade' to Irish merchants, and there were growing demands – eventually acceded to in 1782 – for increased independence for the Irish parliament in Dublin. This was the context that allowed Colbert to pitch the works at a local audience, enticing prospective readers with a view of fiction as an innovative space in which questions of national and personal identity might be negotiated (the London edition of *The Triumph*, suggestively re-titled *The Reconciliation*, appeared only in 1783, the year *after* England had bowed to the constitutional demands made by the Irish legislature).

As the advertisement of *The Triumph of Prudence over Passion* as 'an original novel, in a Series of Letters' indicates, however, prose fiction is a distinctive kind of representation, with its own distinctive formal qualities. The description of the work's 'easy familiar stile' immediately suggests the highly influential and much-imitated epistolary fiction of Samuel Richardson, especially *Pamela; or, Virtue Rewarded* (1740), the moral efficacy of which Richardson explicitly connected to the novel's style.[3] *The Triumph of Prudence over Passion* shares with *Emeline* thematic concerns with female experience and with political and moral authority. The author's earlier work is a charming and highly unusual fairy-tale in the course of which the orphaned adolescent heroine travels alone through unknown lands, becoming by tale's end a wife, a mother, and a wise ruler. *The Triumph of Prudence over Passion*, by contrast, locates identical thematic concerns in a very precise place and time. Set between November 1779 and December 1780, the novel is characterized by quite distinctive political views that link the state of the Irish nation closely to the position of its women, powerfully endorsing liberty for both. The novel matches this celebration of independence as a political and social value with a notable departure, in formal terms, from contemporary fictional conventions.

In all, *The Triumph of Prudence over Passion* consists of 53 letters from five different characters, but the greater part of the correspondence is that between the witty, spirited heroine Louisa Mortimer and her closest female friend, Eliza Fitzgerald. The plot of the novel is driven by various courtships, the most prominent being that between Eliza and her childhood friend Charles Skeffington. Their relationship, however, is imperilled when Charles becomes the object of the scheming Englishwoman Caroline Freeman who, desiring Charles for herself, exploits his predisposition to jealousy to separate him from Eliza. After various machinations in Dublin and London, Miss Freeman is eventually exposed and, following multiple misunderstandings, the pair are eventually reconciled in the idyllic landscape of the south of France. The beautiful young widow Emily Rochfort, sacrificed in her first unhappy marriage to family interest, accepts the proposal of Eliza's cousin, James Fitzgerald. In the third and most exotic match, Louisa's cousin, Gertrude St George, becomes the wife of

---

3   Samuel Richardson, *Pamela; or, Virtue Rewarded*, ed. Thomas Keymer and Alice Wakely (1740; Oxford: Oxford University Press, 2001), p. 3.

the Count of Roussillon, a soldier in an élite French regiment, thereby permitting the action of the novel, like most of its characters, to re-locate to France in
the second volume. A notable departure from novelistic convention occurs,
however, in relation to the work's most carefully elaborated character, Louisa
Mortimer. Louisa writes by far the greatest number of letters and, placed at the
work's centre, holds together its various relationships. Yet, at the end of the
novel, and in a complete reversal of contemporary (and modern) readers' expectations, Louisa not only remains unmarried but also re-affirms her dedication to
the 'single state'.

Louisa Mortimer's unconventional self-determination is of a piece with the
novel's other unexpected qualities: national, formal and thematic. The novel's
Irish settings were far from unprecedented, with national locations being
employed from as early as the 1660s. Such settings were not always well received
outside of Ireland, however. When published as *The Reconciliation* in London, in
1783, the work was noticed in *The Critical Review,* whose critic expostulated:
'This is entitled an Hibernian novel, but without any apparent reason for that
appellation'. *The Monthly Review* gives a clearer idea of what was expected of an
Irish novel in the period, decrying the absence of 'blunders—those happy and
truly laughable blunders, fortuitously struck out "beyond the reach of art;"
which have for so long been characteristic of Hibernian conversation, as to
become proverbial'.[4] If *The Triumph of Prudence over Passion* did not comply with
English readers' expectation of Irish fiction, then it is equally striking that in a
decade when reviewers regularly dismissed all new fiction, especially epistolary
novels involving female correspondents, as vapid and predictable, *The Triumph
of Prudence over Passion* is neither of these things. Its eloquent testimony to the
value of rational female friendship is found as much in the wit and irreverence
with which the novel's female characters communicate, as in the substance of
what they have to say. Through their letters, the characters reflect on how they
understand their positions as friends, lovers, children and Irishwomen, drawing
on their observations of the world around them, and reaching back into history
to find suitable comparisons for the situations in which they find themselves.
Strong-minded, self-conscious and occasionally acerbic, but also aware of others
and affectionate in disposition, the young women exchange views on the characters and inclinations of those close to them, the proper limits of parental
power, the necessity for female education, the nature of private and public
virtue, and differences in national temper. Louisa and Eliza assume to themselves
the ability and right not only to communicate the incidents of daily life but also
to take extensive views on issues of national importance. There is nothing,
Louisa declares, 'like shewing one's authority now and then' (p. 39). By virtue
of the fact that Louisa's and Eliza's 'communications of unreserved friendship'
(p. 36) demonstrate their concern for, and capacity to engage with, experience

---

4 *The Critical Review,* 55 (1783), 74; *The Monthly Review,* 68 (1783), 457.

in both its private and public dimensions, and because they write to each other in such an intelligent and penetrating manner, this fictional work in epistolary form legitimizes female expression. That the young women's views are confined to the privacy of their personal correspondence ensures that they can remark upon, and challenge, the gender constraints of their society, while still maintaining a proper decorum.

The novel begins when Louisa Mortimer, fulfilling her promise to write to Eliza, newly departed from Dublin, initiates the correspondence with an eye-witness account of one of the best-known scenes in late-eighteenth-century Irish political life: the gathering of the Volunteers on College Green on 4 November 1779. The Volunteers were a part-time military force, the original purpose of which was to protect Ireland from invasion while regular troops were fighting in the American war, but which rapidly took on a quite different political significance. Throughout the eighteenth century, various restrictions imposed by the Westminster parliament had protected English commerce by prohibiting direct trade between Ireland and other countries. The Volunteers rapidly took up the demand that these restrictions be lifted, supporting 'free trade' between Ireland and the colonies. When they gathered in Dublin at the statue of William III in College Green on 4 November, the anniversary of William's birthday and a day traditionally assigned for loyal demonstrations, the armed Volunteers used the opportunity to make menacing demands for 'a free trade or else'. The sentiments of delight Louisa, as an 'enthusiast in the cause of Liberty and my country', expresses at this 'most glorious sight' inaugurate one of the novel's major themes. It is entirely characteristic of the novel's handling of epistolary form that this striking patriotic sentiment is immediately followed by the more self-mocking 'I had wrote thus far yesterday, and should perhaps have expatiated for some time on the love of our country, but that I was agreeably interrupted by the arrival of an unexpected visitor' (p. 32), indicative both of Louisa's ability to make fun of even her own most cherished ideals, and the novel's characteristic movement back and forth between domestic space and the public sphere.

Neither in 1781 nor when the novel was published two years later in London, as *The Reconciliation*, was the identity of its author revealed. Here, for the first time, the editors attribute *The Triumph of Prudence over Passion* to Elizabeth Sheridan (1758–1837), daughter of the novelist Frances Sheridan (1724–66) and the actor, educationalist and theatrical manager Thomas Sheridan (1719?–1788).[5] Elizabeth was the youngest of the four Sheridan siblings who survived infancy, the most famous of whom was the dramatist and politician Richard Brinsley Sheridan (1751–1816), but all of whom were published writ-

5   The only other attribution of the book occurs in Rolf Loeber and Magda Loeber, with Anna Mullin Burnham, *A Guide to Irish Fiction, 1650–1900* (Dublin: Four Courts Press, 2006), p. 1151, where the novel is attributed to Maria Ruxton, on the sole basis that her name is inscribed in the Trinity College Dublin Library copy of the Dublin edition of the novel (OLS B-8-539,540).

ers: Charles Sheridan (1750–1806) was a historian and pamphleteer, Alicia Sheridan, later Alicia Le Fanu (1753–1816), a playwright, and Elizabeth Sheridan herself a novelist.

That Elizabeth Sheridan's name is almost wholly unfamiliar to readers is owing to the ways, at once curious and revealing, in which her works were published, both during – and after – her lifetime. Today she is known mainly for the lively, informative writings of the 1780s belatedly published only in 1960, under the potentially misleading title *Betsy Sheridan's Journal*.[6] Though a record of her daily life, the 'journal' in fact consists of letters written by Elizabeth in England to her sister Alicia in Ireland, gathered periodically into 'packets' for dispatch. Though known in the family as 'Betsy', the author habitually signed her letters 'Elizabeth Sheridan', sometimes abbreviated as 'E. S.'. Elizabeth Sheridan's acute observations on the glittering high society, and elevated political circles, in which her brother Richard then moved, the details she provides of the drama surrounding the incapacity of King George III and the regency crisis precipitated by it, along with her wry reflections on her own status as an unmarried woman and the difficulties of life with her curmudgeonly but much-loved father, make the *Journal* a distinctive and valuable record of a particular kind of late-eighteenth century female life.

More than a decade after the writing of the letters that comprise the *Journal*, Elizabeth Sheridan, then in middle age, would also publish two novels, *The India Voyage* (London, 1804) and *The Sister* (London, 1810), but she did so, using her married name, Mrs H. Le Fanu. A further novel, *Lucy Osmond*, published anonymously in 1803, has also been attributed to Elizabeth Sheridan, but the attribution is not authoritative.[7] In addition to the above, Elizabeth Sheridan in 1817 or early 1818 wrote a memoir, intended for publication, concerning the elopement in 1772 of her brother Richard with the singer Elizabeth Linley, who was to become his first wife. While this narrative would eventually find its way into print, it would do so not under the name of Elizabeth Sheridan, or of Mrs H. Le Fanu, but under the names of her brother's biographers, Thomas Moore and, later, William Rae.[8]

6 [Elizabeth Sheridan], *Betsy Sheridan's Journal*, ed. William LeFanu (London: Eyre & Spottiswoode, 1960), hereafter cited as *Journal*.

7 William Chamberlaine, whose father was a maternal uncle of Elizabeth Sheridan, referred to her as 'the elegant authoress of "*Lucy Osmond*" and "*The India Voyage*"' when lauding the publications of her daughter, Alicia, in the *Gentleman's Magazine* in June 1824. However, *Lucy Osmond* has been also been attributed to Elizabeth's daughter, Alicia, who subsequently became a prolific novelist herself, though she was only thirteen at the time of the novel's publication. She would also describe her acknowledged novel *Strathallan* to readers as her 'first attempt'; see Alicia Le Fanu, *Strathallan* ed. Anna M. Fitzer (1816; London: Pickering & Chatto, 2008), p. 2.

8 Writing in August 1818, Thomas Moore commented that Elizabeth Sheridan 'made some remarks upon Watkins Life [1817] with the view of refuting his falsehoods, but had since given up the idea of publishing them', *The Letters of Thomas Moore*, ed. Wilfred S. Dowden, 2 vols

There are, then, a significant number of texts of varied kinds – novel, memoir, letters – authored by Elizabeth Sheridan. The present attribution of *The Triumph of Prudence over Passion* to Sheridan is made in the absence of direct documentary evidence but with a great deal of circumstantial and textual evidence in its favour, including correspondences in form, language, themes and imaginative motifs across her work.

Unlike her older siblings who were born in Dorset St. in Dublin, Ann Elizabeth Sheridan, named in honour of the daughter of the novelist Samuel Richardson, was born in Henrietta Street near Covent Garden in London in 1758. When Elizabeth was six, the family moved to France in an attempt to evade Thomas Sheridan's creditors and settled in Blois, on the Loire. According to their father, the children took to France and were soon speaking French with greater ease than English. It was in Blois that Frances Sheridan died in 1766, at the young age of 42. For a time, Charles, Alicia and Elizabeth remained in France, while Thomas returned to Dublin to attempt to settle his affairs. Subsequently, the family moved to London, and later to Bath. In 1771, Thomas Sheridan returned to Dublin to act at the Crow Street theatre and in hopes of gaining a patent to establish another playhouse in the Irish capital, leaving his young family in Bath. While he was away, in March 1772, the twenty-one year old Richard Brinsley Sheridan, and the eighteen-year old Elizabeth Linley, eloped to France. Alicia and Elizabeth, at just eighteen and fourteen years of age, were drawn into the affair, Alicia even aiding the couple with some of the housekeeping money. The sisters were then left alone to endure a period of intense anxiety, during which Richard, on his return to England, fought two duels, in the second of which he was very seriously wounded. According to Elizabeth's narrative, the respective fathers of the fugitives, ignorant of the fact the pair had secretly wed in France, compelled them, on their return to England, solemnly to promise never to marry.

The elopement was a significant factor in the bitter, enduring rift between Richard Brinsley Sheridan and his father, from which Elizabeth, who lived with her father for extended periods, particularly suffered. Partly as a result of the ensuing notoriety, Thomas then took the two young women with him to Ireland, where they spent the 1770s. For the most part, the family lived in Dublin but Thomas Sheridan's theatrical success in Cork in 1773 led to a stay in that city and a trip to the lakes of Killarney. Three years later, the family made a further excursion to Munster, accompanied on this occasion by St John Jeffries, an improving landlord and an enthusiastic Volunteer. It was during these years that Elizabeth transcribed many of her father's educational works.[9] In 1781, Alicia

(Oxford: Clarendon Press, 1964), I, p. 461. Moore drew on this narrative for the *Memoirs* of Sheridan he published in 1825, but it is reproduced extensively in William Rae's *Sheridan* (London, 1896), pp 162–209.

9   Alicia Le Fanu, *Memoirs of the Life and Writings of Mrs. Frances Sheridan* (London, 1824), p. 317.

married Joseph Le Fanu, a member of a noted Huguenot banking family, leaving Elizabeth to keep house for her unmarried brother Charles, who would become under-secretary for the military department in 1782, with an official residence in Dublin Castle. The arrangement was not a happy one, and Elizabeth bitterly resented her status as a dependent female. The periods between September 1784 and September 1786 and July 1788 and March 1790 are the best documented of Elizabeth's life, for living in England with her father, she recorded her experiences in her letters to Alicia in Ireland. The same letters also evidence how painful to Elizabeth was her father's excision of Richard from the family, and apprise Alicia of troubled attempts to effect 'a reconciliation' – attempts which occasionally rebounded on Elizabeth's head.[10] Thomas Sheridan died at Margate, en route for Portugal, in 1788. In 1791, Elizabeth married Henry Le Fanu, a military man and the brother of Alicia's husband, and her daughter – also Alicia – was born in 1791. While Henry was a dashing figure, the marriage was 'not prudent' and the couple experienced considerable financial uncertainty.[11] Henry died in 1821 while Elizabeth lived on to the age of eighty, dying in 1837 in Leamington Spa. A memorial erected to her in the churchyard there noted that 'Through a long and blameless existence she enforced the purest principles of religion and morality, both by writing and example'.[12]

Maternal absence and the need to attempt to compensate for it; unprotected adolescents confronting dangerous adult situations; young lovers separated by solemn vows extracted by intractable father figures; the pain of family dissension and the deep desire to effect reconciliation: taken singly, any of these elements might seem the generic stuff of late-eighteenth-century fiction, but together they form a striking and unusual sequence. Elizabeth Sheridan's biography was decisively shaped by the early loss of her mother and the obduracy of male members of her family, the unhappy effects of which are expressed both in her memoir and in her correspondence. Her acknowledged fictions, like *Emeline* and *The Triumph of Prudence over Passion*, are repeatedly marked by absent mothers, and a male tendency to endanger family harmony. In *The Triumph of Prudence over Passion*, Louisa Mortimer is an orphan, while her cousin Gertrude loses her mother at fifteen. Similarly, the heroine of *The India Voyage*, Julia, is separated from her parents in London, where she befriends Mrs Desmond, who lost her mother 'just as I entered my fifteenth year', and learns the story of Miss Hervey who lost her mother at six and whose father 'knew not how to guide a female'.[13] In deference to her father, Louisa takes a solemn vow which '[no] power on earth' (p. 71) can dispense and which separates her from her lover; *The India Voyage*'s interpolated tale of the young French woman, Adelaide, involves vows 'registered in heaven' that separate her forever from her lover, Mortimer, who

10 *Journal*, p. 27.

11 T.P. Le Fanu, *Memoir of the Le Fanu Family* (Manchester: privately printed, 1924), p. 62.

12 *Gentleman's Magazine*, 8 (1837), 585.

13 Mrs H. Le Fanu, *The India Voyage* (London, 1804), I, p. 116; II, p. 107.

eventually effects a 'reconciliation' with his estranged wife.[14] Letters between Louisa Mortimer and her admirer Harry Maunsell, in the closing sections of *The Triumph of Prudence over Passion*, are dominated by their efforts to save the threatened relationship between the childhood friends, Eliza and Charles, siblings as much as lovers, which end happily with the couple's 'reconciliation'. In the same novel, however, troubled love affairs give rise to fears of male violence through dueling. What Louisa stigmatizes as 'that most horrid custom' (p. 174), was also something of anguished concern to Elizabeth Sheridan, following the two duels fought by her brother, Richard Brinsley, in 1772, in the second of which he was, as noted, severely injured.

The recurrence of these and other motifs, both major and minor, throughout the work of Elizabeth Sheridan are remarkable in themselves. Equally striking are the lexical and formal similarities between *The Triumph of Prudence over Passion* and Sheridan's later, acknowledged work. With regard to the former, a marked fondness for using phrases of (sometimes erratic) French in the middle of English sentences is as characteristic of the *Triumph of Prudence over Passion* and the author's later novels as of Elizabeth's letters to Alicia – and indeed of the correspondence of the Sheridan family more generally. 'Entre nous', author and characters confide alike, when exchanging gossip or discussing the current 'go[û]t'; they pay their 'devoirs', while much is either 'a-pro-pos' or 'mal-a-propos' ('a-pro-pos' – 'a porpoise' in Richard Brinsley's laboured variation – seems to have been a family joke among the Sheridans).[15] The regular use of 'adieu' in signing off letters is common both to *The Triumph of Prudence over Passion* and *The India Voyage*. In English, very specific lexical choices are common to Elizabeth Sheridan's letters and her later fiction, as well as to *The Triumph*. Among terms of approbation and censure in relation to women, for instance, 'elegant' is regularly employed; an impertinent young woman is condemned as 'absolutely disgusting' in the novel, while Elizabeth characterizes a former lover of her brother's as 'truly disgusting' in a letter.[16] 'Delicacy' is a singularly important social quality across Sheridan's writings and is almost always used as an attribute of mind and character rather than as a purely physical reference. Likewise, 'handsome' is a term much employed and used identically in discriminating the relevant attractions of Irish and English women in both *The Triumph of Prudence* and Elizabeth's letters. Likeable male characters in *The Triumph*, *The India Voyage*, and *The Sister* are introduced as 'amiable', though in both *The Triumph* and *The India Voyage*, female characters ascribe to men in general the mocking appellation of 'lords of creation'. In novels and letters alike are to be found variants of 'damp my spirits', 'cast a damp', or 'throw a damp'. There are several instances where relatively unusual words are consistently used in the same contexts across the novels and become indicative of

14 *India Voyage*, I, p. 212.
15 'To his sister Elizabeth', 13 September 1772, in *The Letters of Richard Brinsley Sheridan*, ed. Cecil Price, 3 vols (Oxford: Clarendon Press, 1966), I, p. 42.
16 *Journal*, p. 133.

a more general sentiment or complex of feelings. For instance, in *The Triumph of Prudence over Passion* the solemnization of marriage is an 'awful day' (in the now nearly obsolete sense of inspiring 'awe') and in *The Sister*, an 'awful business'. Similarly, in both *The Triumph* and *The India Voyage*, 'repine' is used in the context of obedience to parental wishes. In the former novel, we read 'but how few could follow your example! in so intirely subjecting their passion to their reason, as not even to repine at obeying your father' (p. 74); while in the second, the heroine writes of her reluctant accession to her parents' plans for her: 'Yet let me not indulge this repining strain, which seems to cast blame where love and veneration alone are due'.[17] Orthographical choices across Elizabeth Sheridan's correspondence and the novel are also suggestive: staid (stayed), 'chuse' (choose), 'chearful' (cheerful), 'ballance' (balance). *The Triumph of Prudence over Passion* was regularized by the publisher to some extent but, 'printed for the author', the regularization was often carelessly done, so that authorial preferences appear to survive.[18]

Like many other fictions of the period, *The Triumph of Prudence over Passion* is an epistolary novel. Unlike many such fictions, however, the letters of which it is composed combine elements of the formal letter and the journal, each letter made up of sections often written late at night, and in the intervals between social engagements, exactly as Elizabeth would write her letters to Alicia. 'Stealing' time to write is a refrain of the correspondents, while extending the writing of individual letters over several days, and writing prior to receiving responses to previous letters, are alike signs of their shared sense of 'laying aside ceremony in our correspondence' (p. 39). These formal elements persist in *The India Voyage*, the first of the two novels Elizabeth Sheridan published under her married name. While epistolary fiction was the dominant mode in the 1780s, by 1804 it was a good deal less fashionable, to the extent that her choice of form seemed to Mrs H. Le Fanu to require justification:

> The author of the following sheets, has adopted the epistolary, or, rather, the journal style; as it appeared to her more favourable to the development of character than the narrative; and, as that is more the object of the work, than extraordinary events, or fanciful descriptions, she trusts her plan will not on that account (whatever it may on others) meet with an unfavourable reception.[19]

Accordingly, the heroine of *The India Voyage* adds each day to her letters to her intimate friend, Harriet, before sending them from London to the country: 'I

---

17 *India Voyage*, I, p. 5.

18 It is important to note that William LeFanu's *Betsy Sheridan's Journal* offers a cut and modernized text of Elizabeth Sheridan's letters; the original manuscripts are held in Cambridge University Library and available as a microfilm, consulted in the National Library of Ireland, p. 2595.

19 *India Voyage*, II [np].

shall, as you wish it, write you a few lines daily, and send my paper when it is full'.[20] As this novel blurs the distinction between epistolary fiction and the journal form, so too does *The Triumph of Prudence over Passion*, just as Elizabeth Sheridan employed elements of the journal – daily additions – with the regular dispatch of packets to Alicia in Ireland. Other structural devices of the *Triumph of Prudence over Passion*, particularly in progression of plot and its management of interpolated elements also reappear.

It is especially striking that while the plots of both novels are furthered by the viewing of letters by third parties, the setting-off and general presentation of narratives within the journal form of the novels are remarkably similar. In the first volume of *The Triumph*, Louisa Mortimer finishes a letter to Eliza before beginning the interpolated narrative headed 'Count de ROUSSILLON, and Miss S. GEORGE', as she intends to give the story 'a sheet of paper to itself' (p. 43), concluding her tale with the words: 'I hope you will acknowlege yourself under uncommon obligations to me, for sitting up half a night to write a love-tale for you' (p. 50). In the second volume of *The India Voyage*, the heroine also relates a love story, once more set in France, which she presents as 'a little volume', set off from her usual correspondence.[21] The novel likewise contains a second interpolation, 'The Narrative of Miss Hervey', which is presented in the same way. Moreover, in each novel, responses to the interpolated narratives contribute to the verisimilitude of the whole by drawing attention to the fiction-like qualities of what has just been read, thereby giving the framing letters the effect of the real: 'it is quite a little novel' (p. 51), Eliza writes emphatically of Gertrude's tale, while in *The India Voyage*, the narrator is enjoined to 'complete your novel'.[22]

While there are marked structural parallels between the anonymously published *Triumph of Prudence over Passion* and the acknowledged *India Voyage*, the sexual and civic politics of the earlier novel also have much in common with those of its immediate predecessor *Emeline*, as well as with the slightly later views expressed by Elizabeth Sheridan in her letters to Alicia. In *Emeline*, the young heroine accepts that popular consent is fundamental to just rule and that a breach in the 'mutual contract' frees the subject from allegiance. The politics of *The Triumph of Prudence over Passion* are distinctly patriot, arguing that it was unconstitutional for the parliament at Westminster to make laws for Ireland to which the Irish (that is, the Protestant nation) did not consent. Eliza matches Louisa's enthusiastic support of the Volunteers – 'a most glorious sight' (p. 31) – in the novel's opening letter later praising her brother as 'a staunch patriot' and hoping that 'none of my family will ever be otherwise' (p. 52). Her views on independence cause her to assert that 'the King cannot confer any honour equal to that of being an honest man, and a steady patriot' (p. 52). Such sentiments echo the views of various members of the Sheridan family relating to the gaining of

20 *India Voyage*, I, p. 13. 21 *India Voyage*, I, p. 231.
22 *India Voyage*, I, p. 220.

Irish legislative independence in 1782 and especially in relation to the patriot politician whose name remains associated with the Irish parliament of these years: Henry Grattan. Elizabeth writes to Alicia describing Grattan as their father's 'hero', while Thomas himself declared that Grattan's life was 'of more importance, not only to Ireland, but to the general interests of the British Empire than that of any one man living'.[23] Richard Brinsley Sheridan was, as Elizabeth enthusiastically commented 'a very warm friend to the Irish', while his older brother, Charles, was the author of a celebrated pamphlet on Poynings' Law which argued against the power of the English parliament to pass legislation applicable to Ireland without Irish consent.[24]

The Triumph of Prudence over Passion, then, articulates a political position very close to that espoused by other members of the Sheridan family, Thomas, Charles and Richard Brinsley, between 1779 and 1781, and Elizabeth Sheridan in her letters of the mid-1780s. Yet while Elizabeth speaks warmly of Richard Brinsley's love for Ireland and the political views frequently shared by him and by Charles at the period, the relationship between the Sheridan siblings was far from uniformly harmonious. In her letters, Elizabeth often challenges what, on one occasion, she scathingly described as Charles's 'favorite doctrine of Male and Female souls'.[25] Similarly, indignation that men do not always consider women to be rational creatures, and irritation at the prerogatives men assume, are marked features of the letters of Louisa Mortimer. In her letters, Elizabeth challenges more than her brother Charles, as when she offers a wry and withering dismissal of one man at a London social gathering as 'grand diseur de rien and at the same time as Male creature laying violent hands on a considerable share of the conversation', indicating her characteristically cool ability to puncture male pretensions.[26] Yet, assertive as she undeniably was in writing to her sister, Elizabeth manifests her uncomfortable awareness of how society viewed women without means when she wrote of 'the difference the world makes between a man of talents and the women of his Family unless these are at least independent'.[27]

In *The Triumph of Prudence over Passion*, both Louisa and Eliza are staunch in their defence of female rationality, and denounce a male tendency to claim that good sense and reason are limited to their sex alone: 'good-sense is one of the things they would willingly make us believe they have an exclusive patent for' (p. 38). Contemplating with amazement the phenomenon of intelligent men who marry uneducated women, Louisa attributes it to male insecurity. The choice, she opines, is due to the hope that 'their own superiority in wisdom and knowledge may appear to greater advantage by the contrast, and some of them, I am sure, dread a competitor in those things' (p. 43).

23 *Journal*, p. 61; NLI, Lefanu Papers, p.2596.
24 *Journal*, p. 58; Charles Sheridan, *A Review of the three great National Questions relative to a declaration of right, Poynings' law, and the mutiny bill* (Dublin, 1781).
25 *Journal*, p. 46.
26 *Journal*, pp 46, 40–1.   27 *Journal*, p. 44.

The author of *The Triumph of Prudence over Passion* values reason but only when tempered by sensibility. So, male and female characters alike are commended for possessing both reason *and* feeling – 'a good head, and a good heart' (p. 37) – while Elizabeth Sheridan praises possession of an 'excellent heart and a fine understanding'.[28] However, the novel expresses reservations in relation to the contemporary cult of sentiment, suspecting that those who pride themselves most on their fine feelings may in fact be the least useful members of society, and cautioning that overt displays of feeling can often be duplicitous. Louisa Mortimer, reflecting on Eliza's useful philanthropy, comments that her friend is 'not one of those who fancy they are possessed of superfine feelings, yet never feel for any one but themselves, and are so apprehensive of hurting their spirits, that their dearest friends, if in sickness or affliction, must find some one of less feeling, and more humanity, to perform the tender offices of friendship' (p. 115). The same complex of feelings appears in Elizabeth Sheridan's correspondence where she declares 'there is scarce any emetick more powerful to my stomach than an affectation of sensibility where I know the heart to be truly selfish'.[29]

Though understanding human nature to be comprised of both reason and feeling, *The Triumph of Prudence over Passion* is, nonetheless, acutely aware of how individuals may be deformed by the gendered expectations of society. Elizabeth Sheridan not only shares the frustration concerning certain prejudices relating to female character expressed by the letter-writers of *The Triumph of Prudence over Passion*, she expresses that frustration in a markedly similar way, using humour and sardonic wit to deflate erroneous views. In addition, both the novel and Elizabeth's letters employ a wit that is playful, rather than satiric, in nature, most strikingly when dealing with subjects that might otherwise be too painful to broach. Louisa Mortimer, in particular, is adept at deflecting misery with a joke: 'I think if Charles does not mend his manners, you shall marry Mr. Hamilton; that is, if I do not; for I fancy I should like him for myself, by your description of him, but we will consider of these matters hereafter' (p. 38). Elizabeth would respond in similar fashion to a reference by Alicia to her own admirer, Henry Le Fanu: 'and Harry *says nothing* about coming home. I see how it is, I am thrown off and you are keeping him for someone else, but to be even with you I am determined not to accept of one of the numerous offers which I shall certainly meet with here'.[30] Louisa is no respecter of pieties. She expresses herself with an arresting directness, as when she opines of Emily's husband that 'the greatest favour he could confer on her was his dying' (p. 32). In the private space of her correspondence with her sister, Elizabeth Sheridan is similarly outspoken; so, when she informs Alicia that a former lover of her brother's is, 'thank God', gone to Brussels, she adds: 'I should not be sorry to hear that she was drown'd

28 *Journal*, p. 39.
29 *Journal*, p. 48; for Elizabeth's amusingly acerbic critique of the 'sentimentalism' of her cousin William Chamberlaine, including the curt phrase 'You know how I hate Sentiment', see *Journal*, pp 183–4.   30 *Journal*, p. 45.

on her way thither'.[31] The tone of Louisa Mortimer's letters, like that of Elizabeth Sheridan's, forces the realisation that female propriety in the late-eighteenth century is a nuanced concept, and that even perfectly proper women used the possibilities of private correspondence, real as well as fictional, to express themselves in an outspoken and direct manner quite at odds with the reserve demanded by contemporary conduct books.[32]

Less controversially, the heroine of *The Triumph of Prudence over Passion* clearly derives enormous enjoyment from a range of acceptable female interests to which Elizabeth Sheridan too devoted considerable attention: an enthusiasm for play-going, a taste for playing cards (defended in Elizabeth's case against Alicia's censure), a delight in gossip, and a developed interest in fashion. Louisa's knowledgeable account of the style and materials of Gertrude's wedding clothes (and her sense that her correspondent is eager for each detail) is matched by equivalent descriptions in the *Journal*, again provided in the expectation that every detail will be relished by the recipient.[33]

The Triumph of Prudence over Passion cheerfully represents the lighter side of female lives, but, as the title indicates, this is also a serious work, the roots of which lie deep in eighteenth-century moral thinking with regard to human nature. Both 'prudence' and 'passion' are in this context extensive terms: prudence is associated with reason and duty; passion allied not only to sexual desire but to visceral emotions of all kinds. Prudence is the virtue that fits the individual for society; passion, by contrast, impels the individual towards the inappropriate satisfaction of personal desire. In Sheridan's work, the struggle between these powers is psychological and internal and it occurs in relation to more than one character. Louisa Mortimer insists that a 'proper education' enables individuals to 'controul our passions when we are accustomed to give way to them, in opposition to our reason' (p. 55), though in the course of the novel both Charles Skeffington and Eliza Fitzgerald must struggle, he with his jealousy and she with her fears, before the prudence of each eventually triumphs. Meanwhile, the adverse effects of giving way to passion are dramatized through the character of the conniving English woman, Caroline Freeman. Having dismissed Louisa as one who 'conducts herself with the same prudence you might expect from her grand-mother', Caroline gives the reign to her own 'headstrong inclinations' and when these are frustrated she dies, after 'violent hysteric fits … a martyr to her own ungovernable passions' (pp 158, 170). More than twenty years later, in *The India Voyage*, Sheridan revisited the fundamental agon between passion and prudence. The heroine, who has fallen in love with a married man, is urged not to sacrifice herself 'to the cold dictates of prudence and propriety', but her resolve

31 *Journal*, p. 195.
32 See, for example, the section 'Conduct and Behaviour' in Dr John Gregory's immensely successful and much-reprinted *A Father's Legacy to his Daughters* (6th ed.; Dublin, 1774), pp 13–14.
33 See *Triumph*, p. 122; *Journal*, pp 26, 40, 58–9, for instance.

to make the sacrifice is strengthened by her insight that the man she loves would, although he returns her feelings, 'despise the woman whose affections were not completely under the control of reason'. This novel too, contains the warning figure of a character whose desires are frustrated and who dies from the 'ungovernable violence of her passions'.[34]

The relationship between reason and passion is an important general theme in eighteenth-century fiction but it had a particular and personal relevance for Elizabeth Sheridan through the work of her mother, Frances. A clear expression of the tension between prudence and passion occurs in the early work by Frances Sheridan, *Eugenia and Adelaide* (written *c*.1740), where the heroine is commended on the grounds that her 'prudence and good-sense will shortly teach you to overcome a childish and ill-placed passion'.[35] Contemporaries read the same author's much-admired oriental tale, *The History of Nourjahad* (1767), as demonstrating that it is in 'the due regulation of the passions, rather than on the outward dispensations of Providence, that true happiness or misery depends'.[36] In Frances Sheridan's compelling *Memoirs of Miss Sidney Biddulph*, the heroine accepts, out of a sense of duty, her mother's view that there is a fatal bar to her marriage to the man she loves, Orlando Falkland. Becoming wife to the respectable but cold and dull Mr Arnold, Sidney lives out, in exemplary fashion, the life her age, at its most severe, demanded of her, only to find her virtue rewarded by her husband's cruelty and sexual infidelity, leading to Samuel Johnson's famous remark: 'I know not, Madam, that you have a right, upon moral principles, to make your readers suffer so much'.[37] Here, the triumph of prudence over passion has catastrophic effects, for the heroine and for others.

For Elizabeth Sheridan, an emphasis on the relationship between prudence and passion was not just a literary influence but part of her matrilineal inheritance. In 1804, on first publishing under her married name, Elizabeth wrote to a relative of her daughter's literary ambitions, 'I think her natural abilities much superior to my own, and she had advantages which I never had, at least, that of the uninterrupted attention of an attached and rational mother'.[38] The loss of the mother is deeply embedded in all of Elizabeth Sheridan's works, not only in the number of motherless characters they contain but also through the strong maternal figures the fictions repeatedly create. The capacity of the orphaned girl to come to mother not just herself but others, and to do so in a fashion that unites

---

34 *India Voyage*, I, pp 185, 230; II, p. 265.

35 *Eugenia and Adelaide* (London, 1791), I, p. 183; the novel was written by Frances Chamberlaine at the age of fifteen, after her brother had taught her to write, against the express wishes of their father, the Revd Philip Chamberlaine, but only published a quarter of a century after her death.

36 Le Fanu, *Memoirs*, p. 295.

37 James Boswell, *Life of Johnson*, ed. R.W. Chapman. A new ed. corrected by J.D. Fleeman (1791; Oxford: Oxford University Press, 1970), p. 276.

38 *Gentleman's Magazine* (June, 1824), p. 582.

the private and the public, is certainly shown in *The Triumph of Prudence over Passion* but still more clearly symbolized in the extraordinary matriarchal fairy-tale *Emeline: a moral tale* (1780).

On her fifteenth birthday, Emeline, the eponymous heroine, finds her parents dead. Given a diamond key by a fairy, Emeline discovers that it opens a small door hidden in an arbour. Tested in the course of various adventures, which involve sailing alone across a body of water, Emeline reaches land and learns that she is the child of the dispossessed monarch of the place. The troubles of this kingdom are owing at least in part to the fact that the King has been insufficiently guided by the Queen, the 'delight of the people', whose influence would have allowed her husband to avoid 'the misfortune that happened to him'.[39] In this land, relations between ruler and ruled are firmly based in laws of contract, as Emeline is told prior to her restoration:

> you may be assured, it is your duty to study their happiness, and whenever you cease to do that, you lose all title to their obedience; for the compact being mutual, a failure on your side, frees the subject from allegiance.[40]

Once married to the prince of a neighbouring state, Emeline and her husband live as 'shining examples, both in public and domestic life'. They have two daughters, the elder of whom, we learn, inherits her mother's extensive dominions; the younger her father's 'little sovereignty', each governed secure from 'foreign and domestic enemies: for they reigned in the hearts of a FREE PEOPLE'.[41]

Emeline transforms vulnerability into sovereignty as the orphaned girl not only becomes a just and rational queen bound by the laws of contract but also successfully nurtures her daughters so that they too, in turn, will rule wisely. *The Triumph of Prudence over Passion* shares with the earlier work an emphasis on the ability of the orphaned child to mother both in the public and domestic spheres but it places this ability not in a fairy-tale dream world, but in a very precise historical and geographical location: late-eighteenth century Ireland, at an especially charged moment of its history. The novel's central character, Louisa Mortimer, can be seen as a tribute to Elizabeth Sheridan's long dead mother Frances embodying, as she does, several of the characteristics for which Frances was renowned: her 'colloquial powers' and directness, united with a charm that elicited considerable male admiration.[42] While *The Triumph of Prudence over Passion* may be read as restoring the lost mother by bringing her to life in fictional form, it also represents the daughter's notable transformation of her matrilineal literary inheritance. As a young writer, it was through re-writing her mother's literary concerns that Elizabeth Sheridan authored herself. In *The*

39 *The Fairy Ring; or, Emeline: a moral tale* (London, 1783), p. 92.
40 *Emeline*, p. 95.   41 *Emeline*, pp 134–5.
42 Le Fanu, *Memoirs*, p. 200; Boswell, *Life of Johnson*, p. 275; Moore, *Memoirs*, I, p. 11.

Triumph of Prudence over Passion, the issue at the heart of *Memoirs of Miss Sidney Biddulph* – that is, the proper extent of filial duty – is recast into the heroine's striking insistence on her personal autonomy.

In 1781, the year in which *The Triumph of Prudence over Passion* was published, Elizabeth Sheridan was twenty-three, the same age as the novel's heroine, Louisa Mortimer. Louisa's father is lately dead, while her mother had died before the heroine reached maturity. Of the three main female figures in the novel, only one, Eliza, has a parent living: her ailing mother. Despite her comparative youth, Louisa is already guardian to the even younger Gertrude. While both she and Eliza give each other advice and support, Louisa is notably stronger, warning Eliza against sinking into low spirits and strengthening her resolve when Eliza's lover manifests signs of jealousy. She even goes so far as to say that she cannot 'consent' to Eliza becoming the latter's wife 'till we are quite sure he has recovered his rationality' (p. 63).

The fairy-tale *Emeline* extends its heroine's maternal power into the public realm. If, in *The Triumph of Prudence over Passion*, the young women's claims are circumscribed by the exigencies of real historical time and place, and so constrained by the novelistic demands of *vraisemblance*, the fiction still asserts the importance of women as participants in the public sphere:

> How some of the wise heads would laugh at a girl pretending to give an opinion in politics; it is not, I believe, a very usual subject for young ladies to correspond on; but I know you have been taught to think, the welfare of our country is of as much consequence to women as men. (p. 85)

Both Eliza and Louisa are staunch patriots, each able to contextualize her political convictions by reference to classical models, Eliza at one point declaring herself to be 'as public spirited as any Roman Matron, in the most virtuous ages of the commonwealth' (p. 36) while Louisa envisages the pair making noble figures in history 'as Spartan wives or mothers' (p. 39).[43] In fact, as the historian Mary O'Dowd has argued, the early 1780s was an especially propitious interval – albeit one of short duration – for female visibility in Irish public life, as women seized the opportunities presented by the agitation for free trade and parliamentary independence, to make apparent their stake in the public sphere.[44]

Moving characteristically between the public and the private realms, *The Triumph of Prudence over Passion* does not only make a case for female rationality;

43 Eliza's reference to herself alludes to Thomas Sheridan's version of Shakespeare's *Coriolanus*, performed in 1755 at the Theatre Royal, Covent Garden and in 1756 at the Smock Alley Theatre in Dublin, and published as *Coriolanus; or, The Roman Matron* (London, 1755 and Dublin, 1757), while Louisa's comparison of herself and Eliza to Spartan wives or mothers recalls Oliver Goldsmith's *The Grecian History* (Dublin, 1774), p. 23 (see nn to pp 36 and 39 below).

44 Mary O'Dowd, 'Women and Patriotism in eighteenth-century Ireland', *History Ireland*, 14:5 (Sept.–Oct. 2006), 25–30.

it also foregrounds male abeyance of reason, most obviously in Charles Skeffington's sexual jealousy. The eventual reconciliation between Charles and Eliza is represented, by Louisa, as a political setting to rights after upheavals in the civic sphere. Recognizing Charles's 'just sense' of his 'high crimes and misdemeanors', and exercising royal prerogative, Eliza signs an 'act of oblivion', so permitting the pair to embark on their long-projected marriage (p. 166). In contrast to *Emeline*, however, the novel presents female sovereignty as metaphor, and leaves the reader in no doubt that the actual position of women, especially married women, is a compromised one. Of all the young women prominent in the novel, Louisa Mortimer alone remains unmarried at the novel's close. Her refusal of Harry Maunsell, her devoted admirer, is explained by the solemn promise she has given her father. Louisa confides to Eliza that her friendship with Harry 'is the softest, most pleasing sentiment, that can possibly be imagined; and the reserve that must take place (if he was married) of the delightful confidence that now subsists between us, would leave a vacuum in my heart' (p. 78). Despite these feelings, she wishes, for Harry's own sake, to see him marry another, insisting that 'the single state is really most suitable to my inclinations' (p. 76). Louisa's refusal, which makes the conclusion of the novel so striking, given the multiple marriages it contains, is expressed quite explicitly in terms of the vows of the marriage ceremony. The celebrant of Eliza's wedding:

> espoused the cause of his sex so far, as to insist on her pronouncing the word obey, pretty audibly: now had I been in her place, that of all words never should have passed my lips; I whispered that to Harry first opportunity; he replied, smiling, he would venture to take me even on them terms, if I would say I loved: No, said I, for if you would dispense with my promising obedience, I should fear you meant to enforce the doctrine by some more powerful argument: he called me some fond name, saying, he must be a brute indeed that would desire me to comply with any thing that was disagreeable to me. (p. 173)[45]

The relationship of private to public, and women's relationship to power, is a complex matter in the novel. Louisa's refusal of Harry Maunsell is owing to the unconditional vow she has made her father, and can therefore be seen as acceding to patriarchal power. Louisa's further refusal to repine at this promise, despite the acknowledged intensity of her feelings for Harry, is presented as evidence of the way her reason governs her passions. Paradoxically, her compliance with patriarchal demands is seen as proof of her reason – even though the

45 In *The India Voyage*, one character's discovery of her suitor's unworthiness causes a tearful admission that he 'does not now stand in the light of a man, whom I could willingly promise to love, honour, and obey'; when the heroine of the same novel is being 'pressed on all sides to fix a day' for her marriage she has nothing to plead 'but the reluctance we poor females feel, at resigning our few short days of power and liberty, and at once, to vow love and *obedience* till death' (II, p. 247).

requirement for such a solemn promise is never satisfactorily explained in the novel. The paradox dissolves, however, if one realizes that Louisa's solemn promise, apparently given at her father's behest, saves her from having to utter the word 'that of all words never should have passed [her] lips': the 'obey' of the wedding service. According to eighteenth-century law, in the well-known formulation of William Blackstone's *Commentaries on the Laws of England*, the woman upon marriage loses her independent legal identity, and is subsumed into that of her husband, becoming 'one person in law'.[46] Louisa refuses marriage because she recognizes its fundamental public nature, and has no desire to enter into the compromised legal definition it would confer upon her, maintaining a strong inclination towards the autonomy she enjoys in the single state.

While the title-page of the renamed London edition of *The Triumph of Prudence over Passion* declared it to be 'an Hibernian novel', such later national tales as Sydney Owenson's *The Wild Irish Girl* (1806), and Maria Edgeworth's *The Absentee* (1812) allegorize the attempted reconciliation of Ireland and Britain – that is, the political union between the two – by means of the marriages with which the fictions conclude. The political concerns of *The Triumph of Prudence over Passion*, and its conflation of the sexual and the political, encourage us to read Louisa's single state as a metaphorical assertion of Ireland's determination to assert her independence. It is not by chance that the novel's most negative character is the English woman Caroline Freeman, who intrudes into Dublin society, abuses the norms of hospitality, and disrupts the courtship of two of the novel's most important characters, through her guile and duplicity. In the course of the novel, Louisa makes several unflattering observations on the English as a 'selfish, illiberal people' and darkly opines that whatever England is forced to grant by Irish public opinion or the threat of force will have to be jealously guarded. Her suspicion that 'a little time will shew what dependance we can have on their affection ... for no doubt they will dissemble till they are sure of carrying their point' (p. 85) is couched in similar terms to her observations on male suitors who, once the wedding is over, reveal their oppressive natures (p. 173). Louisa is determined to remain single because only in that state does she have a real legal identity and exercise full consent; what she claims for herself she also wishes for her country.

The Triumph of Prudence over Passion appeared at a heady moment in Irish history. By means of the political commentary of the novel's young women, the author ventriloquizes a refusal to be confined to domesticity and makes an eloquent case for female involvement in the life of the Irish Protestant political nation of the 1780s. That nation, and anything it might have offered women, was short-lived, coming to a decisive end with the passing of the Act of Union in 1800. By that juncture, Elizabeth Sheridan had, unlike her resolutely independent heroine, entered into a personal union of her own. When she chose to acknowledge a published work, as she did in 1804, it was as Mrs Henry Le Fanu.

46 William Blackstone, *Commentaries on the Laws of England* (Oxford, 1765), I, p. 430.

A note on the text

The text of the present edition follows, as closely as possible, that of the first edition of *The Triumph of Prudence over Passion: or, The History of Miss Mortimer and Miss Fitzgerald*, using the Trinity College Dublin copy, OLS-B-8-539,540. Emendations to copy-text are listed on pp 196–7.

The first edition of *The Triumph of Prudence over Passion* was printed for the (anonymous) author, in two volumes, by Stephen Colbert of Capel Street, in Dublin. The title-pages of both volumes bear the date MDCCXXXI [that is, 1731] for MDCCLXXXI [that is, 1781]. The novel was first advertised in the *Dublin Evening Post* on 8 December 1781. In 1783, the novel was reissued in London, again in two volumes, using the same sheets, but with a different title-page, as *The Reconciliation; or History of Miss Mortimer and Miss Fitzgerald*, by William Lane, of Leadenhall Street.

THE

TRIUMPH

O F

PRUDENCE over PASSION:

O R , T H E

HISTORY

O F

MISS MORTIMER

A N D

MISS FITZGERALD.

By the AUTHORESS of EMELINE.

IN TWO VOLUMES.

VOL. I.

DUBLIN:

Printed (for the Author) by S. COLBERT, No. 136,
Capel-street, opposite Abbey-street.
M,DCC,XXXI.

THE
RECONCILIATION;
OR
HISTORY
OF
Miss *MORTIMER*,
AND
Miss *FITZGERALD*.

An Hibernian Novel.

IN TWO VOLUMES.

By an IRISH LADY.

VOL. I.

LONDON:

Printed for W. LANE, *Leadenhall-Street.*

M D CC LXXXIII.

THE

HISTORY

OF

Miss MORTIMER,

AND

Miss FITZGERALD.

Miss MORTIMER, to Miss FITZGERALD.

LETTER I.

Nov. 4. 1779.*

ACCORDING to my promise, made this morning at our parting, I shall dedicate all my leisure moments to my dear Eliza, and amuse her with the little
occurrences, or observations of the day, just as they present themselves to my
pen; I say, just as they present themselves, by way of giving you warning, that
you are not to expect much order or method in my Letters: but I fancy our
former correspondence may have given you some idea that my style is not
renowned for either. However, if you are diverted,* that is the chief point with
me, for I have my fears that great part of your time will pass but heavily, as I am
very apprehensive your mother's health will suffer by going from a very warm
house in town,* to a very cold one (surrounded by ponds and lakes)* in the
country, at this dreary season, you know what bad effect it had on her last
winter, though the weather was uncommonly mild; and I really think it was
very unnecessary for her to run any hazard, as the chief purpose of her going
could have been accomplished as well, had she staid in town; it is, I allow, a very
laudable custom* to be kind to the tenants, to entertain them, and make them
happy at the approaching season; but I think, as she is so delicate, Mr.
Skeffington* might as well have done the honours of Christmas to your tenants
as his own, since it must be done in his house, your's being sett.* I hope, however, my fears may prove without foundation, both for her sake and yours; for
then I know you will be happy any where with her, and another person that
shall be nameless.—You contrived mighty ill to leave town to-day, for by so
doing you lost a most glorious sight; a large body of our Volunteers* assembled,
to honour the memory of King William,* who made a very fine appearance, and
fired several vollies, even better than the Regulars,* who performed the same
ceremony an hour or two after. Every one looked delighted, except some few,

[31]

who want to be thought friends to Government,* but for me who am an enthusiast in the cause of Liberty and my country,* I was wonderfully delighted to see
our men of the first rank and property, as well as our most eminent citizens,*
voluntarily arming in defence of both: I think it warms one's heart, and I really
pity your lukewarm souls, who can see such a sight without emotion.—

November 5th.* I had wrote thus far yesterday, and should perhaps have
expatiated for some time on the love of our country, but that I was agreeably
interrupted by the arrival of an unexpected visitor; a thundering rap at the door,
threw all the family into consternation, as it was a very unusual hour for company: I, who sat by the window, stood up, and looking through the glass, saw a
post-chaise* and four horses up to their bellies in mud,* the postilions and servants all in black: the door was soon opened, and out stepped the prettiest young
widow I ever saw; I believe you will easily recollect this description suits but one
of our acquaintance; it was no other than our dear Emily: I flew to welcome
her, and in a minute a thousand questions were asked by each, without either
waiting for an answer: however, when we were seated, and began to be more
coherent, I told her she should be my guest, as I had spare beds for her and her
maid, and the men might go with their horses, for I had not room for them; and
if I had, she knew, I could not abide to run foul of a servant fellow every step I
took about my house: she smiled at the expression, but said, she had as little
liking to them as I, when they could be dispensed with, and that she would
gladly accept my invitation, that she might have as much of my company as possible while she staid. Gertrude, who, you know, is the mother of this family,*
no sooner heard this affair regulated, than she quitted the room to give the necessary orders; for that is a trouble she takes entirely on herself, and indeed she
makes a much better figure in the office than I should do, so I am mighty willing to indulge her in it. Emily and I being left quite to ourselves till tea-time,
you may imagine we had no lack of chat; I found the business that hurried her
to town was to administer to her husband's will; it seems her tender care of him,
during an illness of six months, touched his conscience, and by way of amends
for the very unkind treatment he had given her, all the while she was his wife,
he made a will, to which he appointed her Executrix, and left her the interest of
a large sum of ready money during her life, in addition to her jointure,* and
some part of the principal at her disposal: she is also to be guardian to the child,
and have the care of the estate; I know no one more capable of managing it for
the child's advantage: the man certainly meant well at last, but I think the greatest favour he could confer on her was his dying; for her own fortune is so large,
that she only wanted to be allowed to enjoy it in comfort, and what he has left
her, will, I am sure, be no great addition to her happiness, for I know few that
value riches less than she, nor none that make a better use of them. Lovely as she
was when last you saw her, you can scarce have an idea of what she is now! She
is of the middle size, elegantly formed, and has a feminine sweetness in her air
and manner, that is easier imagined than described; her weeds become her amaz-

ingly; and there is a langour in her countenance, contracted during the two unhappy years she was a wife, so peculiarly suited to her habit, that it interests one, you cannot think how much, in her favour. I cannot with any degree of patience reflect on her being sacrificed to a man, with whom it was impossible she could be happy, merely because his estate and her father's were contiguous: it is astonishing to think, that such ridiculous motives can actuate rational creatures, in the most material circumstances of life: I cannot say I should have been quite so obedient as Emily was; for a child has a natural right to a negative voice,* when it concerns the happiness of her life. I do not mean by that to justify all the pretty masters and misses who in direct opposition to the will of their parents, as well as to every dictate of reason and discretion, are daily performing the tragedy of, All for Love; and indeed, it usually turns out a very deep tragedy to them;* for whatever they may think before marriage, they soon after discover, that a competency,* according to their rank in life, is absolutely necessary to matrimonial felicity: but I think in chusing a husband for a girl, her friends should be careful to fix on one, whose qualities of mind and temper, are such as would be capable of inspiring her with that tender esteem, which, according to my notions, is much more likely to be lasting than fierce flaming love; for that being more a passion than a sentiment,* is, like all other violent passions, very apt to subside, and leave no traces but what are unpleasing.

I took the opportunity of Emily's being out on business, to finish my letter for the post, as I think you will be uneasy if I defer it longer. I hear her carriage stop, so shall conclude, for as her stay will be but short in town, I would not wish to leave her when she is at home; she is come up and bid me say a thousand kind things for her, to dear Eliza: Gertrude expresses herself much in the same manner. But I hope you have more conscience than to expect I should impart all they say: I shall therefore leave you to suppose them; and subscribe myself,

Your's,

in sincerest friendship,

LOUISA MORTIMER.*

Mrs. Fitzgerald and Charles know how much I esteem them; so I need not trouble you to tell them.

LETTER II.

Miss FITZGERALD, to Miss MORTIMER.

Castle-Skeffington, Nov. 7. —*

YOU cannot imagine, Louisa, how much I was disappointed this morning, when the servant returned from the post-house without a letter from you! I suppose I looked vexed, for Charles, who just then come into the room, asked what occasioned my chagrin, and when he heard, observed, you had promised to write; but those who relied on women's promises, would generally find themselves disappointed; and added some unfavourable reflections on female friendship; this affronted me, and I told him, if men were but half so sincere in their friendships, there would be a good deal less deceit and fraud in the world than there is at present: he saw I was warm,* and taking my hand, said, my dear Eliza, you seem angry, sure you cannot suppose I was serious, for you know I have the highest respect for Miss Mortimer, and if I had not, I would not willingly say any thing to offend you; I really did but joke, and thought you would take it as such: I accepted his apology, and we became friends again.

But are not you surprised at my warmth on such a trivial matter, and what might well be taken as a jest? I allow it must seem so to you; but I was displeased with, and had reason to think he was more serious, than, on recollection, he chose to pretend. You must know, I have discovered in him a propensity to jealousy, which has alarmed me most exceedingly, as it may be productive of great unhappiness to us both. But to tell my story with some method, I must inform you, that at the last Inn we lay at, we were joined by a Mr. Hamilton, a young man of large fortune in the county of Derry,* who being alone, Charles invited to sup with us, and we esteemed him no small acquisition to our company; for he has had a liberal education, is just returned from his travels,* and makes such observations on the laws, customs and manners of different nations, as do credit to his understanding, and promise fair for his being an ornament to his own country. You may think such a companion made us all very chearful, and I, who delight in such subjects, drew him on to give us a little description of the most material places he passed through, which he did in such easy, elegant language, that when he retired to his chamber, he left us full of his praises, that is, my mother and I, for Charles had grown very grave, and very silent for some time before; when my mother observed it she asked the cause, and he attributed it to a head-ach, upon which we separated for the night, in hopes rest would relieve him. In the morning he seemed quite recovered; Mr. Hamilton joined us at breakfast; politely regretted that he was to take a different road, and gave Charles a pressing invitation to his house, where he should be in less than a month, as he was to stay about that time on a visit to a relation in this country: Charles promised to go, on condition he would return with him. This point being settled, and breakfast over, he attended us to our carriage, where taking a very respectful leave of my mother, and a very gallant one of me; we all set out on our different journeys, and reached home in the evening without meeting any other adventure.* I took notice that Charles was at times very thoughtful, and though I had a small suspicion of the cause, I still hoped I was mistaken, till I was put out of doubt this morning, by Kitty, who, while she attended me, said, she thought it her duty to inform me Mr. Skeffington had asked her several questions concerning my opinion of Mr. Hamilton, whether I had talked of him, when she was undressing me last night, and in short was so inquisitive, that the girl, who you know, has not much penetration,* perceived he was jealous. I was very sorry he had exposed himself, and very much vexed that he had talked in such a manner to my servant, which was in effect making her a spy over me; besides that, if she was ill disposed it was putting it in her power to tell lies, and make mischief, for sake of a bribe he offered her, to tell him the truth; his behaviour hurt me greatly, and was the cause of my anger at what he had said this morning, which otherwise I should not have thought worth notice; however, his being so concerned at displeasing me, and the particular attention he has paid me all day, shew how anxious he is to be agreeable to me, and makes it impossible for me to retain any displeasure against him; I flatter myself my conduct will cure him of that unhappy propensity; but I will be very sure it has before I think of being united to him. I have no doubt but tomorrow's post will bring a letter from you, and will leave this unfinished till then, though it is already of a reasonable length; but, for my own part, I think letters of friendship can never be too long, nor those of business too short.

Nov. 8th. As I expected, this post has brought a letter from you, in which you fully account for the delay, the arrival of such a welcome visitor, is sufficient apology; I am however well pleased she gave you an opportunity of dispatching your epistle next day; for I think my patience would not have held out another post, and I should have joined Charles, in exclaiming against the fickleness of woman. It was very mal-a-propos* of Emily, not to come into town 'till the day I left it; for I should have great pleasure in seeing her easy and happy; and though it is a shocking thing to say, yet she certainly never could be either while Mr. Rochfort* lived, as an unkind husband must destroy any woman's peace: I am glad for his own sake he had the justice to acknowlege her merit before his death; however, he was of such an unhappy temper, that had he recovered, I doubt not, he would have relapsed into his former caprice and ill-nature, I am no great friend to second marriages; but I think Emily would be very excusable should she make choice of one with whom she's likely to be happy; for she is now at an age very subject to tender impressions, and the time she passed with her husband, can only be reckoned a time of slavery:* Whatever state she chuses, I hope she will enjoy all the happiness in it she so well deserves: thank her and Gertrude for their kind remembrance of me; and tell them no one loves them better. I shall not be so unreasonable as to expect you will be a very punctual correspondent while your guest is with you, as she is not to stay long; but I flatter myself, when you can steal half an hour, you won't forget your promise.——O! but I was quite unlucky in leaving town the day I did; for besides missing Emily, I lost seeing the Volunteers, which I am very sorry for, as I think them a most respectable body, and you know I am as public-spirited as any Roman Matron, in the most virtuous ages of the commonwealth,* I mean; for I would not chuse to compare myself to a Roman, after they were governed by the Emperors, because that Government was the cause of their being degenerated, and sunk in luxury and corruption;* so you see I have no small opinion of myself, at least of my public virtue;* and whatever others may think, I am satisfied, if women were taught disinterested love for their country, there would be more patriots* amongst the men than there are at present, for several obvious reasons; particularly that, as there are few of them that don't wish to recommend themselves to our favour, they would be very cautious how they acted in their public capacity, if they knew our contempt would be the consequence of their apostacy. No doubt the ancients were of this opinion; for you may find, in the most glorious times of Greece and Rome,* the women were just as warm in their country's cause, as the men: and history has applauded them for it; though now people affect to think those things above our capacity, and indeed the present mode of education* for our sex is so very trifling, that I fear there is some truth in the supposition.

When I am writing to you, my pen, I think, runs on of itself,* and I know not when to stop it; so pleasing are the communications of unreserved friendship! the hour for the post going out reminds me, it is time to conclude. It is probable you will hear from me very soon again, as I don't intend standing on ceremony with you, especially while Mrs. Rochfort is in Dublin.

My mother and Charles are perfectly grateful for your esteem; you know what a favourite you are with them both.

Farewel, dear Louisa,
Ever your's,
ELIZA FITZGERALD.*

LETTER III.

Miss FITZGERALD, to Miss MORTIMER.

Nov. 10. —

COUSIN James Fitzgerald* came here yesterday, to stay with us till he sets off for Dublin, to attend Parliament,* which will be to-morrow, and I could not think of letting him go without a line to my dear Louisa, as I know the first visit he makes in town will be to you: for I assure you, you stand very high in his opinion; and let me tell you, all the young ladies in the country set a great value on themselves, if they can obtain his approbation; for, as you have often observed, he has a good head, and a good heart,* and is esteemed accordingly. There is few of our gentlemen that would not wish him for a son-in-law: but though he makes himself perfectly pleasing in women's company, and likes being among them, no one seems, as yet, to have made any impression on him. I bid him guard his heart against the fair widow, but he is no way apprehensive, he says; however, I insist on it to him, that Mrs. Rochford will overcome all his sensibility* at first sight, though I am far from believing what I say, as I am certain when he attaches himself to any woman, it will be from conviction that she possesses the beauties of the mind, even in preference to those of the person, which are the only motives to those who fall in love at first look; a foundation that promises no great permanency in the passion; for I look on it as a proof either of a very weak mind, or uncommon susceptibility; or perhaps a mixture of both, and in any of the cases, great fickleness is to be expected.

I wrote to you so lately, that I have now nothing material to impart, except that I hope Charles's good sense has conquered his late tendency to jealousy; for I have not seen the least symptom of it since, though there has been several agreeable young men to visit us, within these few days; this hope has given infinite satisfaction: for I confess his affection is necessary to my happiness, yet I never could think of being his wife should he continue in that unfortunate disposition.

We are to have visitors to-morrow; a Mr. Boyle* and his daughters; they came to this neighbourhood just before I went last to town, I paid my compliments to them, but leaving the country two days after, I did not see them since, so I cannot say much about them: if they should prove agreeable they will be an acquisition, as they are but a short walk from us. I believe I told you, Bell-Park* was left to Mr. Boyle by his uncle, who was a delightful old man: I hope his relations may be as pleasing. In my next, you shall have my opinion of them. My mother is pretty well as yet; I shall be very happy if she does but continue so till we get to town again, for it alarms me much to have her ill here.

My dear Louisa knows how much I love her.

ELIZA FITZGERALD.

LETTER IV.

Miss MORTIMER, to Miss FITZGERALD.

Nov. 12. —

IT is impossible for me to steal a moment since I wrote last, to tell my Eliza how much I am concerned at the defect you have discovered in Mr. Skeffington's temper; it may cause you a deal of uneasiness, for it is seldom cured. I depend but little on your hopes of his having conquered it, for you are a partial judge, being so prejudiced in his favour; besides people are apt to believe what they wish; but when you all come to town, I shall have a watchful eye over him, and will not let you deceive yourself in a point so material to your happiness. I doubt that you will think yourself much obliged to me, though I am sure you ought, for you must allow, a woman in love stands in need of a friend to see things in a proper light for her, as she is utterly incapable of seeing with her own eyes, when the beloved object is any way concerned. I think if Charles does not mend his manners, you shall marry Mr. Hamilton; that is, if I do not; for I fancy I should like him for myself, by your description of him, but we will consider of these matters hereafter. At present I want to tell you, I received your last epistle by your very agreeable letter-carrier, who delivered it himself the day after he arrived in town. Emily was out when he came, but I asked him for the evening, and then introduced him to her; he admires her as every one does, but as to any thing more, I do not take his heart to be very vulnerable. Do you know that a handsome widow, of eighteen,* is too great an attraction for a sober, sedate spinster to have in her home.

I am absolutely fatigued with entertaining all the fine fellows that come here since she has been my guest. They pay me the compliment of their visits, but I am not so vain as to take them to myself, for I know if she was not here, I should not be honoured with their company above once in a month, and indeed I think it often enough in all conscience to be troubled with them, for my spirits are quite wearied with the incessant peal of nonsense they think it necessary to ring in the ears of every woman of this side forty: after that age, I fancy one would be pretty free from them. To be sure some of them could not talk sense, but I should be glad those that can, would be convinced that women are rational creatures as well as themselves.*

I really think the generality of young women have more solid sense than the young men; at least, it is so in the circle of my acquaintance. But this is ENTRE NOUS:* for should it be known I thought so, the whole Male Sex would be up in arms against me at once, because good-sense is one of the things they would willingly make us believe they have an exclusive patent for. But I, who hate monopolies,* cannot help putting in a claim to share of the commodity for self and Co. to speak in the trading style,* which is mighty convenient when one is in haste, though so laconic.

You are a good girl in laying aside ceremony in our correspondence; it would be quite barbarous to insist on an answer to every letter, now my time is not my own; it is very well if I can give you a short acknowlegement for two or three at a time.

Emily will, I fancy, stay longer than she at first proposed: some business has occured that cannot be soon concluded. True it is shocking enough to date a woman's happiness from the death of her husband; but if husbands will be brutes, they must expect both their wife and her friends will wish them dead. Emily behaves with the utmost propriety; never speaking a reproachful word of Mr. Rochford, for tho' one must think she is pleased at her release, it would not be decent in her to say so. I like your political sentiments, they exactly coincide with my own: I see no reason why women should not be patriots; for surely, if tyranny and oppression* are established in a country, they are more liable to suffer from it, both in their persons and properties than men, because less able to defend themselves: it, therefore, concerns them much, to use all their influence in opposing it; and doubtless that influence is more powerful than people are aware of; they should, therefore, be taught to use it for the good of mankind, both as it relates to individuals, and the community at large. What a pity you and I were not born in ancient Greece! we should have made a noble figure in History, as Spartan wives or mothers.*

Yes, I was surprised at your warmth, before I knew the cause, and for that matter, I am surprised still: for you are such a soft, gentle, soul, so formed for the tender passion, that I did not think it was in nature for you to be displeased with your beloved two minutes together; especially when his crime proceeded from his too great affection for you. I am glad, however, to find you are getting a little spirit; I often advised you to it, and you see what effect it had: your anger brought him out of his airs in an instant, whereas I will venture to say, your tenderness would not have done it in a month. Nothing like shewing one's authority now and then; it makes one appear of consequence, and is absolutely necessary to keep down the domineering temper of those lords of the creation.*

I am going with Emily and Gertrude, to spend the evening with a friend. Oh! I have a secret to tell you of Gertrude; it is a love affair too, therefore just fit for your ear: how was it she never made you her confidant. I cannot tell it now, as they wait for me.

Adieu, dear girl,
Your's,
LOUISA MORTIMER.

LETTER V.

Miss FITZGERALD, to Miss MORTIMER.

Nov. 14. —

ACCORDING to promise, I go on writing to my dear Louisa, without wait-ing for an answer: I do not, however, want to pass it on you as a great obli-gation, for I think I could not exist any time without communicating to you all the little incidents that occur, and constitute part of my happiness; but I will acknowlege, hearing from you, is a material addition to it.

I informed you in my last, Mr. Boyle and family were to be with us next day; they came much earlier than is usual with strangers, to shew us, as he said, they wished to be on a friendly footing, and hoped we would follow the exam-ple, which we did the very next day, for we were pleased with each other: we did not part till after supper,* nor would they quit us, till we promised to return their visit so immediately. I wished for you often, you would be infinitely charmed with Mr. Boyle, who is a true born Irish-man:* generous, hospitable and humane; accompanied with a quality for which our country-men are not much renowned. That is, such a prudent œconomy* as prevents him from out-running his fortune, though every thing in his family is in the genteelest style of life, and he is continualy doing good-natured or charitable actions; but he does not throw away his money; nor do his daughters think it beneath them to attend to the management of houshold affairs. He is mighty chearful, and has, I think, all the good disposition of his uncle. His daughters are rather pretty, the youngest most so, and she knows it; she is about eighteen, her sister two years older. Miss Boyle pleases me best, for she is sensible and agreeable, without any airs. Miss Harriet has a good understanding, improved by reading, but she has a degree of affectation that spoils her, when she lays that aside, which she can do, she is very pleasing. I believe it is the effect of a foolish vanity on account of her personal charms; and I am surprised that one whose mind is so amply endowed, should fall into such a weakness; but probably a few years will cure her of that folly, and she will then be an amiable woman. I am very happy in having them for neighbours, as there is not a young person of my own sex in any of the fam-ilies very near us, except one, and she is as unfit a companion for a rational being as any vegetable in her garden,* which is the only thing in life she seems to have any knowlege of. Unfortunately for the poor girl, she will have a very large estate, and her mother thinks it unnecessary she should have any thing else to recommend her. I really pity the poor thing; for, no doubt, she will, some time or other, find her ignorance a great inconvenience to her. What ill-judging people they must be, who can look on money as a good substitute for all the useful and agreeable qualifications of the mind.

I will lay this by for a while, in hopes of hearing from you; besides the Miss

Boyle's are come in to tea, and I dare say, I shall have no more time for writing this evening.

November 18th. I guessed right when I said I should have no time for writing that day. The young ladies were easily prevailed on to stay supper, as their father was not expected home till next day, he was gone some miles off to see a friend. We had also some gentlemen that Charles had brought home with him, and we were a very chearful happy party: my mother was quite delighted, for you know how happy she is to see me pleased: and I had the satisfaction to find that her presence was no restraint on the young folks. Indeed it need not, for though she is elderly and not healthy, she does not forget she was once young herself: and therefore endeavours to promote innocent mirth in youth, which, as she says, is the proper season for it; and she is loved and respected accordingly. I am sure her advice would have much greater weight with them, than that of any of your formal peevish old ladies, who having lost a relish for amusements themselves are continually preaching against them, be they ever so innocent, or moderately pursued.

The gentlemen staid* here till this morning, and we had a good deal of company in the forenoon, some of them staid dinner.

Yesterday we all spent an agreeable evening at Bell-Park, by invitation; both the ladies are proficients on the Harpsicord,* and have sweet voices; and one of our gentlemen played enchantingly on the flute;* so we made up a little concert, and the cards were laid aside, except Mr. Boyle, who challenged my mother at picquet,* and was not a little pleased at beating her, because she plays the game infinitely superior to him.

I have just received your epistle; how could you be so teasing as to say you had a secret to tell me? and then leave me to puzzle my brains about it, perhaps for this week to come: you suppose every one to have as little curiosity as yourself; though you know it is a legacy descended to us from our grandmother Eve,* of which very few have not a large share.

I have thought of all the young men that visit you, but cannot recollect that Gertrude ever shewed the smallest partiality for one of them; though I know some of them admired her much: who can it be? I may as well bid you adieu, for I can neither think or write of any thing but this secret; so you need not expect to hear from me again till you tell it me.

Your's,
ELIZA FITZGERALD.

LETTER VI.

Miss MORTIMER, to Miss FITZGERALD.

Nov. 17. —

I HAVE retired to my chamber rather earlier than usual, that I may acknowlege the receipt of my dear Eliza's last favour; and gratify her curiosity, which, I find, is at the highest pitch.

I really did not think of distracting your mind so much, when I mentioned Gertrude's affair, as it would not have had that effect on me; and when I considered, that I had no right to disclose another person's secrets: I determined to tell you my scruples on that head, and leave you in ignorance till time should discover it. However, your letter made me alter my mind, and Gertrude being present, I shewed it to her, and telling her I had thoughtlessly given you a hint of it, asked her permission to inform you of the affair. She smiled at your eagerness to know the event, and said, it would be a pity to deprive me of such an agreeable correspondent on that account, as she was sure it would be safe with Miss Fitzgerald: and she believed you would make allowances for the weakness of her heart, your own was so susceptible. So you see, my dear, your tenderness is very visible, though you flattered yourself no one perceived it but me.

As to this love tale, you may guess, it was mere accident discovered it to me; for as you observe, I have very little curiosity. But if I had ever so much, it could not have been excited in this case, because I had no suspicion: and thus it happened.

A few days before I wrote to you last, I was to have company in the evening; and when I was dressed, stepped into Gertrude's chamber to ask her some questions; she sat with her back towards me, so lost in thought, that she never heard me, though I was near enough to see. She held in her hand a miniature picture of a beautiful youth, in the uniform of the French military,* on which her eyes were intently fixed. You cannot imagine what an aukward situation I found myself in, when I saw she had not heard me. I felt as if I had purposely stolen on her privacy, though I was conscious I had not, but it must appear so to her. I therefore, thought, if I could go out unperceived, it would save us both a deal of confusion; and was turning about to do so, when the rustling of my gown against her chair, roused her from her reverie, and startled her so much, that I thought she would have fainted: I am sure I looked very silly myself, but thinking it best to take no notice of what had passed, I asked the question I came about, and then saying I supposed she would soon be ready to come down, I left her to recover herself from the flutter into which I had unintentionally thrown her.

She did not come into the drawing-room, till some of the company were come, and I could observe, her spirits seemed quite distressed; but she exerted herself to conceal it, and as she is naturally rather serious, it passed unnoticed by every one also. I paid more than usual attention to her, that she might see I was not offended at her reserve: for I am certain, it proceeded more from bashfulness than want of confidence in my friendship. Though she lived so long in France, she still has that amiable modesty, which is there called, MAU VAIS HONTE;* but which in my opinion, is quite becoming in a young girl, though it is now reckoned a capital offence against all the rules of good-breeding to be capable of blushing.* And it is part of the business of French dancing-masters, to cure their pupils of that vulgar propensity, and substitute an assurance, that will enable a Miss of fourteen to come into a room full of company with a broad stare, as if she meant to defy them to put her out of countenance. An undaunted woman of any age, is, I think, shocking, but in a young creature it is absolutely disgusting; besides, setting a girl above shame, is breaking through one of the strongest barriers of female virtue: and we see daily examples of it in England, where the fashionable mode of education* has introduced a levity amongst the women, that even out-does their neighbours on the Continent. I much fear we shall catch the infection; for where the intercourse is so frequent, it will be next to a miracle if the contagion does not spread; and I have long observed, that neither the manners nor morals of my country people are at all improved by a jaunt to England.*

You will say I have wandered far from my subject; but I intend giving Gertrude's story a sheet of paper to itself, that your patience may not be put to such a trial, as being obliged to go through so much of my letter to come at it.

I congratulate you on the acquisition of such agreeable neighbours, and hope they will come to town, that I may endeavour to rival your mother in Mr. Boyle's good graces; for I should like of all things, to have a flirt* above fifty, and I suppose he is that age at least. And besides that, I would try to cure Miss Harriet of her affectation,* which, by your description, is the greatest defect she has. Well, there is none of us perfect; so we must take human nature as we find it, and make allowance for its frailties: it is best to laugh people out of their follies, and be severe on their vices.

I know who your female vegetable is, it was the happiest idea you ever had, for you could not chuse a more suitable appellation. I am by no means surprised that her mother should think a large estate required no other qualification, because she herself had no other; and to be sure her father is of the same opinion, as it was all he thought necessary in a wife. Is it not amazing that any man of sense, can make choice of a woman to pass his life with, that has not a sufficient understanding to make her an agreeable companion, even for an hour? yet one sees such wives every day; and the poor things think they are of great consequence, and have answered all the purposes of their creation, if they can scold their servants, and swarm the house with children, though they are totally incapable of instructing their children in any one thing that is proper for them to know. I have no doubt but the men chuse them, that their own superiority in wisdom and knowledge may appear to greater advantage by the contrast, and some of them, I am sure, dread a competitor in those things.

I should have a bad opinion of your visitors, if they disliked your mother's company. A woman of her disposition, though not very young, cannot be a restraint on any one, unless they wish to behave improperly. Good night, I must begin my story, which will keep me up an hour longer, and I feel I shall be very sleepy before it is finished.

Your's, affectionately,
LOUISA MORTIMER.

Count de ROUSSILLON,* and Miss S. GEORGE.

GERTRUDE came into my chamber next morning just as I was rising; and telling Sally she would assist me to dress, as she wished to be alone with me; the girl withdrew, and with much hesitation and visible confusion, she began, saying; the discovery I had made the day before, distressed her more than she would express, lest I should imagine her reserve proceeded from want of confidence in my affection for her, which she earnestly assured me, was not the case: she should think herself very ungrateful if it was. But indeed, cousin, said she, blushing to death, the truth is, I could never get resolution enough to tell you.

I had entangled myself in such an affair while I was so very young—Here I interrupted her, to clear myself of any design, to pry into her secrets, and requested she would not think herself under any obligation to disclose them, if it gave her the least pain. She knew me too well not to be convinced I spoke truth; but said, she had long wished to break it to me, and now, that accident had done that for her, she would take the opportunity of opening her whole mind to me.

You already know my aunt St. George's ill health obliged her to reside above two years at Montpelier;* during that time, Gertrude contracted an intimacy with a young lady of her own age, daughter to the Count de Roussillon, whose chateau* was in the neighbourhood. Her mother also became acquainted with the Count and Countess, who were very polite, and even friendly to any genteel strangers, who frequented the town: our friends received uncommon civilities from them; for they insisted on their passing great part of their time with them, which made their stay very agreeable, especially to Gertrude, who found a most pleasing companion in Mademoiselle Adelaide;* she often heard the young Count mentioned in the family, particularly by his sister, who spoke of him with all that fond partiality, which the ties of blood and affection are apt to create; and frequently wished his return, that she might introduce him to her pretty Irish woman,* by which appellation Gertrude was known at Montpellier: she had been more than a year there, before the young gentleman, who was at the Military Academy,* came home.

He arrived one day, rather unexpected, and a messenger was immediately dispatched to bring my aunt and cousin to the Chatteau, to rejoice with the family on the occasion. Adelaide presented Gertrude to him, with a thousand kind expressions in her favour; and told him, she loved her better than any woman in the world: a French man could not say less than, he would love her as well as she did, which was really the answer he made: and it seems it was prophetic; for he very soon shewed an attachment to her, but it passed unnoticed, as it would there be thought unpolite in a young man, not to behave with some degree of gallantry to a girl, who was so often at the house. He was only a year older than his sister, and there was a remarkable similitude both in their persons and dispositions, which was exceedingly amiable: the first created admiration, the latter esteem. No wonder, the unguarded heart of my young cousin, fell a victim to the charms of mind and person, united in this agreeable foreigner, whose constant study it was to render himself pleasing to her; and the perfect amity that subsisted between him and his sister, gave him continual opportunities of recommending himself to her favour, in which, I find, he succeeded so well, that when he declared his passion to her, she was, before they parted, brought to acknowlege, she would have no objection, if the consent of their parents could be obtained.

When she related this circumstance, she seemed ashamed at having so soon confessed her sentiments to him; but told me, it happened one evening that the beautiful serenity of the sky invited Adelaide and her to take their Guitars* to a delightful arbour in the garden, by which a gentle rivulet murmured. There they were entertaining themselves with some of David Rizzio's most plaintive Scotch airs,* when the young Count joined them: and while the pleasing effects of the soft melody was still powerful in her heart, he made his declaration, and his sister pleaded so earnestly in his favour, that she could not refuse to their joint solicitations, the acknowlegement of sentiments which her prudence told her she should have concealed.

The old gentleman having an employment at court, was then attending the King at Versailles,* and the young folks agreed, not to mention it to their mothers, till his return, when his son was to ask his approbation, which he had no idea would be refused, as Gertrude was a great favourite with him, and her fortune and connexions were such, as he could not object to.

Their time rolled on in uninterrupted scenes of happiness and content during three months that the Count remained at court; but his return dashed all their prospects of felicity; and the disappointment was the more sensibly felt, because it was unexpected. It was, however, a chastisement they in some measure deserved, for allowing their affections to be so strongly engaged, before they knew that their parents would approve it.

Louis (that was the youth's name) could not mention it to his father, the day he came home, but determined he would defer it no longer than the morning. That evening the Count sent for him to his study, and after informing him, he was appointed to a company in the Count D'Artois' regiment,* said, he had still better news, which was, he had agreed with the Marquis de Bretagne,* to conclude a marriage between him and that nobleman's only daughter; who, as he knew, was a most amiable young lady, the King himself had been so kind to propose it, and the Marquis and he had joyfully consented to it, as it would be a still stronger cement to the friendship that had so long subsisted between them.

This discourse was like a thunder clap to the young Count; and for some minutes totally deprived him of utterance; during which time his father went on, enumerating the many advantages that would attend his alliance with a family so powerful at court, not to speak of the fortune she would bring him, which was much larger than his estate, (though a good one,) entitled him to expect; and concluded, by bidding him prepare to set out for Versailles in two days to make his acknowlegements to his Majesty for his goodness to him, as well in that affair, as in promoting him, before he had ever joined his regiment; (for it seems he has had a commission since ever he was born, which the late King, who was his godfather, presented him with on that occasion;) and also, to pay his compliments to the young lady; for they meant to celebrate the marriage as soon as the necessary preparations could be made.

By that time the old gentleman had ceased speaking, his son had recovered the use of his speech, and ventured to say, he was sorry they had gone so far, before they knew that the young lady would be disposed to accept of him; and hinted the difference of religion, as an objection to the match; for his family are Protestants; but his father who could not bear the least contradiction, flew in a violent passion at his raising any difficulty, and told him, the thing was determined, and nothing should make him recede from his word, or affront the Marquis, by mentioning such a frivolous obstacle: and sternly ordering him to take care that he acquitted himself properly in his addresses to the lady, he flung out of the room, and left poor Louis in a state of mind not be described. Unable to fix on any rule of conduct for himself, he went to his sister's apartment, to whom he related the cause of his distress. Adelaide, who tenderly loved her brother, and had a sincere affection for Gertrude, was much affected at the disappointment of their fond hopes, but too well knew her father's determined temper, to hope to move him, by telling him the true state of his son's heart, which she judged would at present only exasperate him; she therefore advised he should carefully conceal it from every one, but the young lady herself, to whom he should reveal it in confidence; and if she deserved half the praises she had heard given her, she would spare him the indelicacy of refusing her, as well as the pain of disobliging his father. She was surprized he made light of the difference of religion, because he was strongly attached to his own, and said, she thought it an unsurmountable obstacle, even if his heart had no pre-engagement: he assured her, he did not mention it merely to raise an objection, but because it was his sentiments; that people of different persuasions could not be happy in marriage, as the education of their children would be a continual source of uneasiness; and as Mademoiselle was reckoned very sensible, he had hopes she would be of the same opinion.

He then requested his sister would break the matter to Gertrude, in the best manner she could, and procure him an interview with her the next day; she promised to do so, and having consoled him greatly by her conversation, he retired from her apartment, much more composed than when he entered it.

Next day Adelaide ordered her carriage, saying, she would call on Gertrude to take an airing with her, which she often did, and the Countess bid her engage Mrs. St. George too, to come and spend the day with them, which she accordingly did: and my aunt having some morning visitors, promised to be at the chateau by the time they returned from their airing. Adelaide, who was well pleased she did not offer to go with them, as soon as she found herself alone with Gertrude, informed her as cautiously as she could, of what had passed between Louis and his father, and with all the tenderness of friendship, pointed out to her, the reason they had to expect the lady would refuse him; but to prevent her being any way alarmed, assured her, from her brother, that though he held himself bound by duty, not to marry without his father's consent, nothing could ever prevail on him to think of any other woman.

Gertrude says, she received this intelligence with more fortitude than she thought she was possessed of; but the truth is, her pride was hurt, that any man should think it necessary to conceal his attachment to her: she therefore told Adelaide, it would give her much concern to be the cause of any misunderstanding between the Count and his son, to prevent which, she would advise him to marry the lady that was chose for him. As for her, she never would have encouraged his addresses, had she thought it probable there could be any objection; but since there was, her rank in life set her above forcing herself into any family against their consent; (are not you proud of her spirit?)

Adelaide seemed surprised at her manner of receiving news which she thought would greatly affect her; but no doubt, quickly penetrating into the real cause, she took her hand, and said, my dear Gertrude intirely misconstrues my meaning; I can safely affirm, that every one of our family would think themselves honoured by a connexion with you: the misfortune lies in my brother not having declared his attachment to you before my father went to Paris; he left home supposing his son's heart disengaged; and, at the King's desire agreed to marry him to the daughter of his dearest friend; that, surely, cannot be looked on as an affront to you. I acknowledge my father's fault is obstinacy, he never will retract from a resolution once taken, and expects unlimited obedience from his children, in such a case. Your own good sense will shew you the impropriety of mentioning the affair to him now; especially when we have fixed on a scheme very likely to succeed, without provoking my father. Let me then beseech you, not to add to the inquietude my poor brother labours under, by expressing a displeasure he really does not deserve from you.

Gertrude, who could not but assent to the truth of what Adelaide said, promised she would not; but was determined in her own mind, not to be prevailed on to enter into any private engagement with him, which she doubted not he would propose at the interview she had consented to give him. It being near dinner-time,* they returned to the Chatteau, where they found my aunt and a widow lady of the neighbourhood. The day passed off not so agreeable as usual; for the Countess and Adelaide were low-spirited at parting with Louis so soon; and he and Gertrude, you may think, could not be very lively: so that my aunt and the other lady were the only unconcerned persons, and kept the rest from being quite silent. After they had taken their coffee, the three old ladies and the Count sat down to quadrille,* and the three young folks went into the garden, and entering their favourite arbour, sat down to enjoy the pleasing scene, and listen to the sweet warbling of an infinite variety of birds, that inhabited the trees around them: the soft notes charmed them for a while to silence; but the young Count could not long defer the subject next his heart; and told his tale so pathetically, that Gertrude could with difficulty refuse a promise he endeavoured to draw from her; but she thought it too humiliating to engage herself to wait for a man, whose father would, perhaps, never consent to their union. She, therefore, did refuse it, though he solemnly swore, never to marry any other woman, while she remained single.

She had intended to return his picture, and demand her's which he had, [they were both of his own drawing*] but his distraction was so great at parting with her, that she thought it should be barbarous to mention it; and I dare say, was well pleased to have any excuse for keeping the dear resemblance.

The farewel was, no doubt, very tender on his side; and, I believe, a little so on hers', notwithstanding all her discretion. However, upon the whole, she certainly behaved heroically, if we consider her youth, for she was but fifteen; and that she really loved the man, his merit and the pains he took to win her heart, is sufficient apology. She determined not to tell her mother, lest she should be uneasy on her account, and she had come to a resolution, not to let it prey on her spirits, but wait patiently to see how matters would turn out.—

He set off with his father very early the next morning, and the first account she had from him, was in a letter to his sister, wherein he informed her, he had waited on the lady, but had no ocasion to make her his confidant, for knowing the motive of his visit, she, with a pleasing frankness, told him, he might spare himself the trouble of declaring it, for there was an insuperable objection to their union; which was, his Religion. She had been educated in a Convent, where she had imbibed all the uncharitable doctrines of Popery:* and said, she hoped he could not take it amiss if she told him, she could not think of risking her salvation by marrying a Heretic; for in this case, she thought it best to speak plain, that he might know her resolution was fixed.

He said all that was proper on the occasion, and left her with a heart quite at ease; but found it necessary to conceal his satisfaction, when he came into his father's presence, to whom he related her answer. The Count had scarce patience to hear him out; taking it for granted, the fault was intirely his, as he had, at first mention of the affair, made that objection. He was in an absolute rage; and though Louis gave him all the assurances possible, that the lady had pronounced her refusal before he had well spoke, it was to no purpose. He forbid him to appear in his sight; and next day sent him an order from the King to repair to his regiment, and not presume to leave it without his Majesty's particular permission.

He was then preparing to obey this unwelcome command; and as it was very uncertain when he should be able to plead his own cause, he requested his sister to be his advocate with her fair friend, and if possible, to keep up an interest for him in her heart.

He soon after wrote to her under cover to his sister, which he still continues to do, though she never answers his letters, except by messages in those she writes to Adelaide.

I have seen his letters; they are sensible and well-wrote, but full of those passionate exclamations, with which FRENCH love-letters always abound, but which in our language sounds very ill; at least I think, Ah! Oh! and Alas! have a mighty bad effect in an English letter. But to proceed with my story: the war breaking out,* my aunt determined to set out for Ireland, and Gertrude did not at all regret quitting France, as the Countess and Adelaide were soon to go to Paris, where the Count's employment obliged him to reside during the war. The parting was very painful to the young friends, who promised a mutual correspondence, as often as opportunity would permit: and it is still continued, though Adelaide was married very soon after she went to Paris, to a man of large fortune, M. de St. Veriolle. Her father's displeasure against his son, is not yet removed, nor can they prevail on him to get leave for him to come home to see them before the regiment embarks, which is now under orders for America.*

Though Gertrude would not give him a promise, I believe he is quite as secure of her as if she had, for she is now her own mistress,* and seems not the least inclined to encourage any other. She never told her mother a word of it; indeed it was useless to give her any disquiet about it; as the cold she got on her journey occasioned such a rapid decline of her health, (before very precarious) that as you know, she did not survive above two months after her coming home.

Having always lived with my father, since her widowhood, and after his death with me, she requested Gertrude should remain in my house till she was married, if agreeable to us both, which she hoped it would be; for though Gertrude was by her father's will to be of age at sixteen, yet she thought that too young for a girl to be left to her own direction, and as I was a few years older, and had more experience, she wished Gertrude would be always advised by me, whose affection for her, she was sure, she might depend upon. You know it has been my study to make her happy: I thought her rather serious for her age; and wondered she had not got some of the French vivacity, as she went amongst them while a child. I did not then suspect her heart had learned a lesson which is apt to give a thoughtful turn to the most sprightly temper.

She seemed very apprehensive of losing my good opinion, by informing me of this affair, as she was perfectly sensible her conduct in it, would not bear to be scrutinized by any unprejudiced person. I freely blamed her for giving him any encouragement, without first acquainting her mother, and bid her observe, that all the uneasiness she had suffered since, was in consequence of that one deviation from the path of duty; had they both consulted their parents in proper time, it is most probable there would have been no obstacle to their happiness. I praised her, however, for her discretion in the other circumstances, particularly refusing to contract herself to him; and she was quite happy that I approved any part of her conduct. I hope you will acknowlege yourself under uncommon obligations to me, for sitting up half a night to write a love-tale for you. I now leave you to read it, for my eyes are just closing.

Ever your's,
LOUISA MORTIMER.

LETTER VII.

Miss FITZGERALD, to Miss MORTIMER.

Nov. 20. —

I HAVE just received my dear Louisa's packet of the 17th Inst.* and do indeed acknowlege myself much obliged to you, for sacrificing a night's rest to gratify my curiosity. Could I have had a notion the story would run to such a length, I should not have been so unreasonable as to ask you to communicate it, but I thought it was something that had lately occurred, and would be related in a few lines. Instead of that, it is quite a little novel;* and has afforded me an hour's pleasing amusement. I sincerely hope it may end happily for Gertrude and her agreeable French-man.

Your observations were very just: she was certainly wrong in concealing it from her mother at first; however, I could make a thousand excuses for her, and to tell truth, I fear had I been in her situation, I should not have been above half so prudent. I think she must have had an uncommon share of resolution to refuse his request at their last meeting: but no doubt, being so nearly related, she has a tincture of your philosophy: nothing less could enable her to resist the solicitations of the man she loved, when consistent with virtue. I own it was perfectly prudent; and I think she deserves great praise for it. But you will grant it requires a degree of fortitude seldom to be met with in so young a person, to act up to our duty in every respect, on an occasion where the heart is so much concerned. For my part, I am thankful I never had any such trials. As I have great doubts of myself, for I know I am but too susceptible of tenderness, though I hoped no one had made the observation but you, who are acquainted with the inmost recesses of my mind; for though I have been so fortunate as to place my affections just where my friends wished, I should be sorry to deviate from the paths of delicacy* in my behaviour; which I really think would be the case if my attachment to Mr. Skeffington was visible to strangers: but I flatter myself, Gertrude being an adept herself, has more penetration in these matters than the generality of people. I am satisfied at her discovering my susceptibility, as it procured me her confidence; and she may be sure, I shall make all the allowance for her weakness (if it deserves that name) which I should hope for myself in like case; being in some-what of similar circumstances, usually makes one follow the Christian Doctrine, of doing as we would be done by;* though I am sorry to say, we are but too apt to forget that best of all Rules, where we do not think the situation is ever likely to be our own.

Be sure inform me whenever there is news from France; for I shall long to hear if the Count lets his son go to America without seeing him: if he does, I shall hate him, it will betray such a want of paternal affection.

Tell Gertrude, when I go to town I will expect to see the letters, now that we are all En Confidance;* I dare say you must both have felt aukward enough, when you made the unexpected discovery; though she that is so well acquainted with your disposition, must at once acquit you of any design to pry into her secrets: but accident sometimes leads one into situations extremely disagreeable, and which makes one seem to themselves as if they had done wrong, though conscious they did not mean it so; which I am sure was altogether your case. The accident will be of use to Gertrude, for now the ice is broke, she will not be ashamed to consult you on the affair, when she has occasion for advice. After the hint you had given me, I should have scarce admitted your qualm of con-science as an excuse for withholding the rest of the story; so you did well to get permission to tell it; yet I must acknowlege, that without that permission, you had no right to divulge it; and there was no fear but you could recollect that, for I never knew you to deviate from the right path: or if you did, it was but momentary, and you recovered your step immediately. Why do not I always think so justly? especially when your example has been continually before me; for you have acted according to the rule of right, as long as I have remembered you; at least as long as I have been capable of judging.——

You did not mention Emily in your last, nor cousin James, but once since he went to town; he writes to Charles often, but their correspondence is chiefly on political affairs;* so we have all that sort of news from him. I need not tell you he is a staunch patriot;* indeed I hope none of my family will ever be otherwise, for there is something so unnatural in deserting the interest of our country, that I could not have a good opinion of any one that was guilty of it; besides, it is such a meanness of spirit in a man of family, to submit to be made the tool of any Administration,* that I could not help despising such a one, if he was my brother; I think the King cannot confer any honour equal to that of being an honest man, and a steady patriot: Court favours are no longer desirable when they cease to be the reward of merit; Charles is of the same opinion; so I do not fear he will be disgraced by any when he is a Senator.*

I have often wondered what could be the reason that the very young ladies of this age were so amazingly undaunted when first brought into company, but I did not then know it was a science they were made to study under their danc-ing-masters; I am obliged to you for the information, for while I thought it was natural to them, I cannot but say, it gave me very great disgust;* now I know it is acquired, I am in hopes some of them may have a little modesty in their hearts, though they are ashamed to shew it. But I agree with you, that taking pains to eradicate the natural bashfulness of the sex may be of very bad conse-quence to their virtue; and certainly a girl that keeps genteel company, will of course learn an easy behaviour,* without being taught an impudent stare.

What a pretty picture you have drawn of ignorant women, and a very just one too; it brought fresh to my memory some ladies of our acquaintance, who are, I think, the originals from which your piece is taken: I visit them as seldom as I can, because I am sure to be entertained with nothing else but the careless-ness of their waiting-maid, and the wit of their children: now, though I will allow the little creature's prattle may be perfectly entertaining to a parent, or even to a stranger if they were present, it will very seldom bear a repetition: however, I must acknowlege it is generally as sensible as any thing the mother could say; for a woman whose mind is uncultivated, scarce ever says any thing to the purpose. You are rather severe on the men who marry such women, yet there is no other way of accounting for their choice; and I have often observed, that men would rather pass their time with the meerest trifler of our sex than with a girl who is reckoned sensible, and has read a good deal; which is no great credit to their understanding, and a clear proof of their inconsistency; for they are ever accusing us of neglecting to improve our minds; yet where mental accomplishments are to be found, they seem afraid of the possessor. I am come to the end of my paper before I observed it, and have only room to subscribe myself,

Your affectionate,
ELIZA FITZGERALD.

LETTER VIII.

Miss MORTIMER, to Miss FITZGERALD.

Nov. 24. —

I SHALL now be more punctual in answering my dear Eliza's letters than I have been hitherto, for as Emily will be with me some time, I shall not think it necessary to confine myself to her so much as while I thought her stay would be very short; and she has requested I would not use any ceremony with her, indeed I never meant it in that light, but gave up my time to her purely to enjoy as much of her company as I could, because she meant to stay but two or three weeks; it is now probable you will find her in Dublin when you come, for her father and mother are coming up.

Mr. O'Neil had lately a sudden attack of the gout in his stomach,* it was soon removed, but has alarmed him so much, that he is coming to town for advice, and will stay the winter, for fear of a return of his complaint: there is not a good physician within many miles of his house, and only there was one attending at a neighbour's when he was taken ill, he might have died before he could get help: he never thought of that inconvenience while he was in health, but with the fear of death before his eyes, it appears very terrible to him.

Emily has taken lodgings for them very near us, it was a house he desired, but all the furnished houses were set,*—which she is not sorry for, because she could not have excused herself from staying with them if they had room for her, and she would much rather be with me, though no child can be fonder of parents than she is, but her father has some particularities, that makes it not pleasing to live with him; such as going to bed at ten o'clock, and expecting all his family to do the same; at least they must be at home at that hour, and cannot have company after it, as the doors are then locked, and the keys taken to his room. He makes no allowance for the alteration of customs and manners* since he was a young man; so if his daughter was with him, she could neither pay nor receive any but morning visits, unless she could prevail on the people to dine and sup at the same hours they did forty years ago.

Mr. O'Neil was an old batchelor when he married, and had got several oddities, (as people who live alone are apt to do) which he still retains, for his wife, though a very young woman, accommodated herself to his ways, by which means he never was broke off them, as it is likely he would have been, had she gone a little more into the gay world; but she was just the gentle temper of Emily, and feared even a grave look; it was all she had to fear, for he was not an ill-tempered man, as I have heard my father say, who blamed her for not bringing him off these peculiarities which makes men disagreeable that would otherwise be very pleasing. If ever I marry an old batchelor, I shall take pains to make him as pleasing as I can.

You observed I did not mention Emily, I hope you are satisfied now I have filled half my paper about her and her family. As to your cousin James, I knew he wrote to Mr. Skeffington, and concluded you must know more of him than I could, though he often favours me with his company, and I am always glad to see him, for I do not put him on a footing with some others that visit me, because one gets both information and entertainment from his conversation. If I am any judge in these matters, his heart is not quite so whole as when he came to town, not that he has given the smallest hint to the contrary; but his behaviour to Mrs. Rochford shews it very plain: the minute attentions, or as the French express it, LE PETIT SOINS,* are never thought of but by a lover. Any man of politeness will think of all the civilities which they know we expect from them; but none but a man in love will think of attending to every trifling circumstance that may occur. I never yet found myself mistaken in the observation; however, I would not have you mention it to Charles, lest he should hint it to Mr. Fitzgerald, who would know you had it from me, and there would be an indelicacy in it's coming from her friends: I would not caution you about it, only I know, you think Charles is all discretion, and to be intrusted with any secret; but I know the men all tell each other those sort of secrets.— I have teized* Emily a good deal on the subject, but she affects not to perceive his attachment; and when I tell her that is only to make him speak plain, she prims and looks so matronly, and so discreet, that I am obliged to be silent. She certainly does not dislike him; but I am convinced she would not at present listen to any man on that subject; she has too just notions of propriety: besides her unhappiness in marriage is so recent in her memory, that I think she will consider well, before she enters into the state again; was I in her place, I should have got a compleat surfeit.

I cannot accept of your compliment, because I feel I am by no means the perfect creature which your partial friendship has described me; though I am sure you only say what you have persuaded yourself to think; it does not, however, require such a share of philosophy as you seem to imagine, to enable us to controul our passions when we are accustomed to to give way to them, in opposition to our reason;* and I think myself infinitely obliged to my parents, for teaching me to curb them before they grew ungovernable: so that what you call philosophy, is purely the effects of a proper education, enforced, I acknowlege, by religious motives, since I have been capable of comprehending them; for though I am of a very chearful turn of mind, I can think seriously on subjects of importance.

Gertrude is highly flattered by your approbation, and says, she begins to be better reconciled to herself, since you and I think her conduct excusable. She bids me tell you, she will let you see the letters when you come to town, and all that she may yet receive from the Count; she expects to hear soon, as he will certainly write before he goes to America.

Harry Maunsel* surprised us just as we sat down to tea last night, I did not expect him, for I had a letter from his sister very lately, which mentioned his intention of going to Corke* on business; but it seems some pressing occasion has brought him to Dublin; and he says, will detain him great part of the winter. I find Charles and he correspond, and by some words he let fall, I am sure he has mentioned his uneasiness about Mr. Hamilton to him; if so, it is probable we shall discover his real sentiments, and whether, as you think, his reason has conquered his jealousy; but as yet, I have no time to enter into a conversation on the subject.

Harry, who has not seen Mrs. Rochfort since she was with me, a year before her marriage, was so struck with the loveliness of her countenance and figure, that I had some hopes she would rival me, and observed him closely to see if it was so, but have reason to think his admiration was nothing more than the pleasing effect which the first view of something very beautiful always has on the mind, but which, as it grows familiar to the sight, ceases to attract the attention. You will think it an odd expression, to say, I had hopes of being rivalled; however, for his sake, I sincerely wish it had been the case.

Is Charles as great a book-worm as ever? You should endeavour to wean him a little from his studies, as he is not to follow any profession; it is high time he should study the manners of the world, which he is really too ignorant of. I shall talk to Henry about giving him a little advice on that head, now I find there is such an intimacy between them.

Gertrude begs you will not make yourself uneasy at what she said of your susceptibility; for though that is very perceptible, your delicacy remains unimpeached, in which opinion I join, and think you a good, decent behaved girl, notwithstanding you are a perfect turtle in love and constancy.* I wonder how it is that Charles and you have continued to like each other so long; it seldom happens that a fancy of that kind, taken in childhood, subsists when the parties grow up: besides, from the manner you were reared together, I am surprised you did not rather mistake each other for brother and sister. Was I in your place, I should be a little afraid the whole stock of tenderness on both sides, would be exhausted before marriage; if it is not, I can only say you have an amazing fund of it.

I wish Christmas was over, that you might come to town; and on consideration I do not see any necessity there was for your going almost two months before, that you might be there at the time; but Mrs. Fitzgerald is so methodical, she does not like to break through old customs, and it is very fit you should comply with her inclinations, her actions are always governed by some laudable motive.

What a long epistle here is, with little or nothing in it; however, as I am in a scribling vein, it is likely it would be still longer, but luckily for you, who will have the fatigue of reading it, I must break off, for your cousin James and Harry Maunsell, are to gallant Gertrude and I to the play; and it is just tea-time, no doubt they will soon be here. Emily spent the day at her aunt's, you may think she does not as yet go to any public place, which has confined me a great deal. Our beaux are arrived; have only time to say, I am,

Dear Eliza's

very sincere friend,

LOUISA MORTIMER.

LETTER IX.

Miss MORTIMER, to Miss FITZGERALD.

Nov. 25. —

DEAR ELIZA,

A Conversation I had with Harry Maunsell this Morning, determined me to write directly, though I had dispatched a letter to you by last night's post; but as I think I have something interesting to say, I would not delay it a moment.

Harry was with me all the forenoon, and Emily and Gertrude being out shoping,* I had an opportunity to speak to him about the hint he dropt in regard to Mr. Hamilton. He immediately told me all he knew of the matter; he had it from Mr. Skeffington; and taking a letter out of his pocket, gave it to me to read. When I had finished, I went for your first letter, and read the account you gave me of the affair; then observing to him, how necessary it was to your happiness to be acquainted with Charles's real sentiments upon the occasion; obtained permission to take a copy of it for your perusal. Nothing but that consideration could have tempted him to give it; but I assured him, he might rely on your discretion, that you would destroy it as soon as read: you will easily see the necessity for so doing, and here you shall have the copy.

Castle-Skeffington, Nov. 10.—

DEAR MAUNSELL,

WE left Dublin on the 4th, as I informed you we should, and arrived in due time; but met with an adventure on the road, which has roused a latent spark of jealousy in my bosom, and given me so much uneasiness, that I could not sufficiently compose my mind to write to you sooner; though I never had more occasion for your counsel.

A Mr. Hamilton of the county of Derry joined us on the last night of our journey; he is, I must acknowledge, a most accomplished young man. Being lately returned from his travels, the conversation turned on the manners and customs of the places he had visited, which he described with so much understanding, and elegance of expression, that my aunt was delighted, and Eliza quite charmed, which gave me pangs I never felt before, and cast such a damp on my spirits, that I was incapable of taking any part in the conversation: every word she addressed to him was a dagger to my heart, and the particular attention he paid her, added to my uneasiness; for his person is really faultless, and his address perfectly pleasing; attractions sufficient to gain any woman, and alarm any man that loves as I do, and is not very partial to his own merit.

When he retired, the ladies were lavish in his praise, and Eliza observed, what an advantage Travel* was to young men of sense, as it enlarged their ideas, and gave them a knowledge of the world, which they could never obtain from books alone. As I took this observation to be intirely directed to me, who wanted that advantage, it confirmed my suspicions, and increased my ill temper; so that my gloominess was, I am sure, apparent, for I caught Eliza attentively looking at me several times, and my aunt taking notice of my silence, I was forced to pretend a head-ach, on which she insisted I should go to bed, and ever attentive to my health, ordered whey and hartshorn* to be given me; but knowing that was not a cure for my real complaint, you may guess I did not take it. I went to bed in a state of mind little short of distraction, and lay cursing the whole fickle sex and my own misfortune, in being so strongly attached to one of them, that I felt it impossible to tear her from my heart. The agitation I endured, at last fatigued my spirits, and threw me into a sound sleep: when I awoke, I found myself refreshed and composed; and on revolving impartially, every circumstance that had passed the preceding night, I was ashamed to acknowlege to myself, that I had not any one tolerable reason to assign for the suspicions that gave me so much disquiet. Convinced I had been in an error, I recovered my temper and my spirits, and met the ladies in my usual manner: my aunt congratulated herself on the success of her medicine, and Eliza, with a glow of pleasure on her check, rejoiced I was so much better.

Mr. Hamilton breakfasted with us, and gave me a very genteel invitation to his house, where he will be before Christmas; he regretted much we were so soon to part, and when we were ready, handed Eliza to the carriage, and took leave with such expressions, and such looks, as to me appeared a proof that she had made a strong impression on his heart, which again disconcerted me; but as she remained quite chearful after he had left us, I cursed my rising dissatisfaction, to prevent her suspecting the cause, but determined to take some method of discovering her sentiments towards him: I abhor myself for the meanness this distracting passion made me commit. I questioned her maid, and even offered her money to betray her mistress's secrets: she stedfastly denied ever hearing her mention Mr. Hamilton, except to her mother or me.

I soon saw the impropriety I had been guilty of, in exposing my weakness to this girl, and dismissed her, saying, I only wanted to try her integrity. This happened early in the morning after our arrival, and when Eliza came down to breakfast, I guessed from her serious air, when she spoke to me, that her maid had informed her what passed between us, and I was soon after convinced of it; for being disappointed of a letter she expected to receive from Miss Mortimer, I threw out some sarcastical observations on female friendship and sincerity, at which she immediately took fire, and expressed herself with so much warmth, that I who knew myself in fault, was glad to make an apology; and finding I could not bear her displeasure, spent the whole day in reinstating myself in her favour, which from her natural sweetness of temper, was not difficult to accomplish; and we are now on as good terms as ever, but I can perceive she watches me closely when there is any young men here, as if she wished to penetrate into my heart, and see if jealousy still lurked there; however, none of our visitors raise any emotions of that kind in my bosom, as I think they do not possess any superior degree of merit, and she has, beside been acquainted with them from her infancy, but I cannot be so easy in regard to Mr. Hamilton; for I feel that his presence would quite destroy my peace, yet I wished they would meet again, that I might know my fate, for I cannot bear suspence, though I dread the certainty. When she is present my suspicions vanish, and I am happy; but the instant I am alone, all my doubts return. Do, dear Maunsell, give me your advice and opinion. You that have loved, will, I am sure, pity my anxiety, even though you may blame me.

I have thoughts of pressing our marriage, which is delayed till I am of age,* on account of settlements;* if she consents, it will calm my fears, for I think I could not suspect her virtue if she was my wife; but I shall do nothing till I hear from you.

Your's,
C. SKEFFINGTON.

I believe this letter needs no comment to convince you, you were much deceived when you imagined he had conquered his foible; for it is plain, his good humour depended on Mr. Hamilton's absence.

Perhaps Harry's arguments may by this time have had some effect on him; for he says, he placed the improbability of your giving him any cause of suspicion in the strongest light he could, and as it really appeared to him; but advised him to make his promised visit to Mr. Hamilton, and bring him to the castle, that he might be certain he was cured of all doubts before he urged you to marry him; otherwise he would insure misery both to himself and you.

In his answer to Harry, he seemed ashamed of his folly, and promised to follow his advice; so we must suspend our judgment for a while: and I am more easy on that subject than I was, now I have a method of knowing his real sentiments; for I was very apprehensive you would be too willing to trust to appearances, and deceive yourself into an opinion that he was just what you wished him to be. He is in every other respect, a most estimable character, and wants only a little knowledge of the world to make him an accomplished young man.

I would, if I dare, advise his travelling for a couple of years, but I fear to give you pain by mentioning his absence for so long a time; however, if you cannot bring yourself to bear it, I would have you marry, and go abroad with him; I mean when you are quite convinced he is cured of this foolish imagination that has possessed him. Is it not very unaccountable, that he who is, on other occasions, rather too unsuspecting, should so suddenly grow suspicious where he has least cause? it must proceed from too humble an opinion of himself; if you could inspire him with but half so high an idea of his own merit as most young men have, he would never be jealous again, and that I believe is the only advantage that can spring from self-conceit.

Adieu, dear girl;
believe me,
ever your's,
LOUISA MORTIMER.

LETTER X.

Miss FITZGERALD, to Miss MORTIMER.

Nov. 28. —

M Y dear Louisa's letters of the 24th and 25th, are now before me; and shall begin with the latter, as it is wholly on a subject in which I am deeply interested.

I was a good deal distressed when I read the copy you sent me, for I could no longer doubt that I had been deceived in my hopes of his having laid aside his causeless jealousy, which affected my spirits not a little; and I should have been quite in the horrors,* only I was obliged to exert myself, being engaged to spend the day at Mr. Boyle's, to take leave, as the whole family are going to pass the Christmas with a sister of his near Belfast,* and the young ladies will go from that to Dublin with their aunt, to stay the remainder of the winter. They will be a material loss to me while I am here. We passed the day so agreeably, that my melancholy was insensibly dispelled, and things appeared in a better light, for I then recollected that Mr. Maunsell's advice and opinion had probably great weight with Charles, and would convince him of the folly of his suspicions, and I had some reason to think it had; for I have lately been in company at Belle Park with some very accomplished young men that I was not acquainted with from my infancy, which Charles seemed to lay a STRESS on, and he did not appear the least disconcerted, though one of them paid all his attention to me, and I did not discourage it, purely to try how Charles would bear it; it did not alarm him one bit, which I think a very good symptom: however, I shall soon be a better judge of the matter, for he had this morning a letter from Mr. Hamilton, reminding him of his promise, and appointing to meet him about twenty miles off, where he will be in two days, on his way home, and insists on Charles going with him. He says he will go, and sent an answer to that purpose by the servant; so that he will certainly meet him: but I find, he intends, if possible, to prevail on Mr. Hamilton to come and spend a few days here before he proceeds on his journey. I wish he may come, as that would put us all out of suspence, though I dread the certainty; for if the worst should happen, I fear I should but ill support myself. However, I will not anticipate misfortunes, as I think I have some reason to hope it will turn out well.

It is now time to return Mr Maunsell thanks for permitting you to copy the letter for me: I shall take care no bad consequence shall attend his kindness. I knew Charles and he corresponded, but never thought of mentioning it to you.

As to what you advise about Mr. Skeffington's going abroad, I am sensible it would be a great advantage to him; I know he wants it more than most young men, because he has pursued his studies with such unremitting application, that he really secluded himself from company and amusement a great deal more than was proper for his rank in life: but to you I will acknowlege, I cannot bring myself to think of it with any degree of fortitude; I cannot even reconcile myself to his going to England, though I know he must go in Spring; and if the idea of his being absent two or three months is so painful, what would two or three yeas be? My imagination is so fertile in creating trouble, that I should be miserable from the apprehension of dangers, which perhaps, he should never experience. I am really ashamed of my weakness, but cannot conquer it; if we should be ever united, I would have no objection to going with him; for I do not fear dangers to myself half so much as to those I love.

I shall be very happy to find Emily in Dublin when I return, which I hope will be soon after Christmas; for indeed the country is very dreary this time of year, and the air much too sharp for my mother, who begins to complain of the rheumatism, as well as for her daughter, whose constitution, you know, is but delicate.

I am glad Mr. O'Neil is to be in lodgings, that Emily may remain with you, which must be more agreeable to her, though I have no doubt of her affection to her parents, yet one would not wish to be confined to their particularities, when it would oblige us to give up all the rest of our friends.

It would give me great pleasure if your conjecture respecting cousin James's attachment to her should prove true; they are worthy of each other; and I do not know where either of them could have a better prospect of happiness. I shall not hint it to Charles, though I am certain he would not repeat it, if I desired him not, but I think there is a delicacy in these matters, where our female friends are concerned, that makes it improper to talk of them to men.

You deny that you are possessed of any degree of philosophy, and yet wish yourself to be rivalled; now, in my opinion, that is as great a stretch of philosophy as DIOGENES* himself could boast, though so renowned for self-denial. But there is something in the affair between you and Mr. Maunsel, that has ever been a mystery to me; yet as you always seemed desirous to avoid the subject, I was unwilling to ask any questions: that he loves you, cannot be doubted; indeed he does not endeavour to conceal it; and those little attentions which you yourself allow to be a proof, are very observable in him; for I think the smallest minutiæ that can be pleasing to you, does not escape his notice. You cannot have had any quarrel, because the most cordial friendship subsists between you; what then can prevent your union? I am at a loss to guess since there is no one to controul either of you.

Your wishing for a Rival, has drawn me in to ask questions that are impertinent; however, I beg you will not think yourself obliged to answer them; if it is in the least disagreeable to you, you have only to pass over this part of my letter in silence, and assure yourself I will never mention it again.

If Charles and I should ever be married, (which probably a few days will determine) I flatter myself our affection will never be exhausted; though I am not romantic enough to expect it will continue just what it is now, but I hope it will subside into a tender and lasting friendship, that will end only with our lives: and I think I have great reason to hope it will be so, as neither of us have the smallest degree of fickleness in our disposition, else it must have appeared by this time, which accounts too for our liking having subsisted so long; a circumstance that seems to surprise you; but I cannot so easily account for our not looking on each other as brother and sister, which might very well have happened from the manner we were brought up together; had that been the case, it would have occasioned no small chagrin to our friends; and if I should find it necessary to break with him, I dread the effect it would have on my mother, who loves him as if he was her child, and has no joy equal to the prospect of seeing me his wife; for which reason, I have never given her a hint of what has passed in regard to Mr. Hamilton, till I see how it ends; I wish you were with me, for my spirits begin to sink at the apprehension of what may happen when he comes, but I will call up all my resolution, as it is necessary to my peace to know for a certainty if Charles be likely to conquer his folly; for indeed I can give it no other name.

Let me hear from you very soon: you shall know how matters go on here, as soon as possible.

I long for Christmas to be over, that I may once more enjoy your company; not forgetting Emily and Gertrude.

Dear Louisa,
ever your's,
ELIZA FITZGERALD.

LETTER XI.

Miss MORTIMER, to Miss FITZGERALD.

Nov. 30. —

I REJOICE to find my dear Eliza has cause to hope matters will turn out to her satisfaction; and I am of opinion from what you tell me, that Charles is giving his reason fair play. What a deal of uneasiness he would have avoided, had he done so before!

I shall be very impatient to hear the event of Mr. Hamilton's visit; if he should come to the castle, which I really wish he may; because if there is the least spark of jealousy lurking in Charles's bosom, he will not then be able to conceal it so well, but the traces of discontent will be visible on his countenance, and you will know to what it is to be attributed.

I should be well pleased to be with you for the time, as I should be more at leisure to make observations than you will be, and less partial; but I hope you will consider your happiness is at stake, and not be blinded by your tenderness; it will be a folly to conceal the truth from me, as you know. Harry will hear it, and then I shall.

I have a high esteem for Charles, but love you still better, and cannot consent to your being his wife till we are quite sure he has recovered his rationality.

I am sorry you are losing the Boyle's; an agreeable neighbour in the country is a very material loss; but I hope it will determine your mother to come to town as soon as she possibly can, now you have no companion. I always think of the good any evil may produce, which lessens the ill greatly, at least makes it more supportable.

Mr. and Mrs. O'Neil arrived last night, and have brought their little grand-daughter: 'tis a beautiful infant, and as they tell me, the very temper of it's mother; she had left it at home under the care of a relation that lives with her, a genteel, discreet woman; but Mr. O'Neil had it at his house some part of every day, and when he was coming to town could not bear to be so long without seeing it; so brought the nurse and little one off. Emily, who did not expect it, was agreeably surprised; for she had often regretted leaving it, but she meant to return so soon, and besides that, was afraid of offending her father, who adores it. We had it here to-day for a while, Emily had it on her knee when Mr. Fitzgerald came in; after paying his compliments, the child attracted his notice; the resemblance is so striking, he knew it was Emily's, and took it in his arms to kiss it, when the baby, who is but just attempting to speak, called him Papa; it seems she calls all men so, but her mother's confusion is not to be described, and it was no way lessened by his saying, he should be happy indeed, if he had a title to that appellation; at the same time giving Emily a look infinitely more expressive than his words. She was struck intirely dumb; Gertrude had a smile full of meaning, and you cannot imagine any scene more ridiculous than it was, till I, in compassion, set them all laughing, by wishing the child was mine, that I might have such pretty things said to me; this set us talking nonsense, and gave her time to recover from the palpitation which his speech had given her; but I have a strong notion this trifling circumstance has opened the way for a more serious declaration from him, the first convenient opportunity: at present I am sure she will not accept him, for the reasons mentioned already, though I think he need not despair of succeeding in time; and indeed I join with you in opinion, that she could not have a fairer prospect of happiness with any man I know.

Gertrude has a smile in one eye, and a tear in the other; she had a letter from her swain this day, informing her, he had just got his father's permission to take leave of him, and was in consequence, setting off for Paris, where his stay would be very short, as they were in daily expectation of embarking, but says, he will certainly inform his father of the true state of his heart, before he leaves home, and will let her know the result. This is the most material part of his letter; the rest contains only love-like expressions of fear for what may happen during his absence, and soldier-like hopes of a speedy return, crowned with laurels.

You may guess, the account of his father sending for him, is very pleasing to her, but the thoughts of his going to America casts a damp on her spirits: she is the picture of an April day, alternate clouds and sun-shine, as each reflection happens to predominate. She begged I would tell you the news, as you were so kind to express a desire to be informed of any circumstance that occured.

I have not forgot your question about Harry Maunsell, nor do I intend to pass it over in silence; though I confess, it is a subject I have hitherto avoided: but I hope my dear Eliza does not look on my reserve in that particular, as any breach of the perfect confidence that subsists between us; for it's the only occurrence of my life in which I have not been quite open, and you must consider, the most material circumstance relating to it, passed while you were too young to be my confidant; and since that, I thought the less was said of it the better; for it has the appearance of vanity to talk of having refused a man; and looks too, as if one wished to prevent his marrying another; for certainly, it could not recommend him much to any lady he might address, to know he would not think of her, if he could have had me; and till very lately, I had no notion he would be so foolishly romantic, as to determine on living single, because I cannot marry him. But you must know, in that letter, which I believe I had from his sister, before she knew he was coming to town, she mentioned, she had great reason to think her sister-in-law, Miss Herbert, liked Harry; and she had some hopes that she was pleasing to him, as he paid more attention to her, than ever she had seen him pay to any woman, except one; and since his passion for that one was hopeless, nothing would be more agreeable to her than a union between him and Miss Herbert, who was both as to person and fortune, a desirable match for him,

I had another letter from Mrs. Herbert, by Harry, requesting I would endeavour to discover his real sentiments for her sister, as a circumstance had happened since her last, that made her fear he thought not of her in that way she had hoped, and at the same time left no doubt of her attachment to him; which was so very visible, she was sure he must have perceived it, though he would not seem to do so; which looked as if he did not mean to make any advantage of it. However, she begged I would use my influence, which, she says, is all-powerful, to prevail on him to think seriously of it: and even desired me to inform him of the lady's partiality towards him, which she thought might induce him to make her a return: at all events she said, I must insist on his being quite explicit; for if he will not comply with our wishes, it will be absolutely necessary to inform Miss Herbert of the state of Harry's heart, that she may recall her own, before it is too late.

I executed my commission with very bad success; for my influence joined to every argument I could employ were insufficient to persuade him to return the lady's passion, (which he said he had with concern discovered, just before he left home) and only drew from him a declaration, that as there was an insuperable bar between him and I, he was determined never to marry. I endeavoured to shew him the folly of such a resolution, but to no purpose; and when I found him so determined, I told him he should then be cautious how he gave any girl room to think she was agreeable to him; and he assured me, it was Miss Herbert's resemblance to me, both in person and manner, that attracted his notice; but he hoped I would acquit him of any design to gain her affections, when he knew he could make her no return; he should abhor himself if he could be guilty of such a dishonourable action; indeed I do not suspect him for it; vanity is not amongst his faults. I wish, for his own sake, he had less constancy; for I think an old batchelor the most forlorn being in the Universe, though an old maid may be quite the reverse; the domestic life being natural to women, they can manage their house and see company as well without a husband as with one, if not better; and if they dislike living alone, they cannot fail of a female companion, unless their temper is very bad; and in that case they could not be happy in marriage.

But all this while you will say, you are not a bit the wiser respecting this same said mystery between Harry and me: true, my dear, nor are you likely, till next post, for I am called down to company, and can only add, that I am,

Affectionately your's,
LOUISA MORTIMER.

LETTER XII.

FROM THE SAME TO THE SAME.

Dec. 1st. —

As I imagine my dear Eliza's curiosity is on full stretch for the delightful history of Henry and Louisa,* I take the first leisure hour to give it you, for I suppose I should be quite out of favour if I passed one post, and perhaps I might not have time to-morrow.

I believe you may remember that in old Mr. Maunsell's time the family spent every winter in Dublin, and as they were our next door neighbours, there was a great intimacy between him and my father; their example was followed by their children, and Patty* Maunsell and I (who were much of an age) were scarce ever asunder. Harry was but a year older than his sister; and as we were all children when our first acquaintance commenced, he was usually with us till he was sent to a public school, and I recollect when he came to take leave of our family, he could not be forced from me without the greatest difficulty; as for me, after shedding a few tears I was consoled for his loss; since Patty was still with me, I did not see him for three years after our first separation, as the ill health of his mother and mine took both the families to Spa,* where, and in France we remained about two years and a half when we returned, and had the misfortune to lose two of the best women in the world in a few months after. My mother died first, and I received all the comfort and attention from poor Mrs. Maunsell, that was in her power to give; for tho' she was declining fast herself, she let Patty stay entirely with me, till the first shock was over, and I began to be reconciled to my loss; she did not long survive, and when she found she could not live many days, she desired to see her son, who was accordingly sent for; when he arrived I was returning the melancholy compliment to Patty, assisting in her attendance on her mother, and endeavouring to comfort her for the loss she was going to sustain: my father being out of town on business, I could dedicate all my time to this friendly office; and indeed I never left her for a day, till his return, which was not for a month after Mrs. Maunsell's death. During that time, the childish affection which Harry expressed for me, before he went to school, seemed to be ripened into a more serious attachment: he did not in plain terms tell me so, but some body has said actions have a language,* and his were so eloquent as not to be mistaken; I did not however seem to perceive it, tho' I acknowledge I was far from being indifferent about him: you who know him will not be surprised at that, especially when I tell you, that joined to a mind as faultless as human nature could admit, he then, notwithstanding his youth, possessed all those manly graces of person for which you have so often admired him; add to that, we had parted children, and now met, when both our persons and manners were strikingly improved, and we at an age when the heart is but too open to soft impressions;

and being in the same house for a month we made a greater progress in each other's esteem, than if we had met on temporary visits for a twelve-month.

Soon after I went home Harry entered the college,* and while he was in it, his attendance on his duties, (in which he was very assiduous) kept the family longer in town every summer than was usual, by which means he had such constant opportunities of seeing me, that his passion never had time to cool, which probably it would have done, had we been separated just when it was beginning; unfortunately for him, that did not happen till he was going to travel in three years after, and by that time his love was proof against absence; yet he had so much prudence as never to make any declaration, or attempt to draw me into any engagement that might have involved us in difficulties; but before he set out, Patty took an opportunity of lamenting to me, that her brother was never likely to be settled to his mind during their father's life; for tho' the allowance he gave him, was ample for a single man, it would not support a wife, as the woman he would wish to marry ought to be supported, not could he think of offering himself to any one, while he was unable to make such a settlement as she had a right to expect; and his father had given him to understand he had done all he could afford to do, without stinting himself, which he would not do, nor would Harry permit him if he was inclined; for you know, Louisa, continued she, my father was always used to profusion, and is not at a time of life to be debarred of what he has been accustomed to; it is much fitter Harry should suffer for a time, tho' I am sure it is no small mortification to him.

I was very sensible this discourse was intended as an apology to me for his silence on a subject, which his behaviour gave me all the reason in the world to expect he would come to an explanation about, before he went abroad. I took no other notice of it however, than to join in opinion with her, that their father ought not to be put to any inconvenience; tho' I dare say my looks betrayed a consciousness of the intention of her speech, or at least, my not asking who the lady was, might convince her I guessed her meaning, and did not chuse to have it farther explained, which was the real truth.

Harry left us soon after, and as we were always on the most friendly footing, I did not hesitate to express a moderate concern at losing him for so long a time; he endeavoured in vain to restrain his passion within the bounds he had hitherto prescribed to it; the idea of parting was too strong for his prudence, and he took such a tender farewel as convinced me of the sentiments he entertained for me, more than a thousand vows and protestations would have done.

He wrote regularly to his sister, who always shewed me his letters while she was in town, and when she left it used to send them to me, by his desire, no doubt, as he knew I would be entertained with his account of the countries thro' which he passed; and beside that, I was always mentioned in a manner that would have been pleasing, even tho' my heart was quite unconcerned.

He had been about a year away, when I made a considerable conquest one evening at a drum;* a gentleman, that shall be nameless; (because I don't think it genteel to speak of those we have refused) stood at the back of my chair while I lost two or three rubbers,* and perceiving it did not ruffle my temper, wisely concluded I would make a most desirable wife, and paid a visit to my father with whom he had a slight acquaintance, and without farther ceremony made his proposals in form, not doubting my acceptance of an offer so advantageous, added to the powerful inducement of a title, and a very ancient family, (the latter joined to settlements that were far above my expectations) had great weight with my father, who being descended from the oldest families in England,* held a long pedigree in great veneration; but tho' I too have all due respect for those things, I thought something more was needful, and could not marry any man for the merit of his ancestors; and I could see no one agreeable quality in himself: beside that from what I had heard of his disposition, I thought it probable he might put his wife's temper to trials more severe than that of losing at cards, and tho' my patience held out against bad fortune, I could not answer for its being so complaisant to a bad husband; then his applying to my father, without first endeavouring to gain my approbation, disgusted me exceedingly, as it shewed he must either think my good opinion of very little consequence, or else he must have a large share of self-sufficiency, that made him take it for granted I could not refuse him: take it any way, there was so little delicacy in it, and so much the appearance of thinking he conferred a favour, that it was a pleasure to me to mortify his pride by rejecting him, which I did when he came in full confidence of being joyfully accepted, as I could see from the astonishment visible in his countenance, and which indeed was so great that he had not power to speak; so when I finished my speech, which was very laconic, I made my curtsy and withdrew, leaving my father to reconcile him to his disappointment.

What passed between them after I was gone I cannot say, but my father informed me that evening, his lordship had begged his permission to continue his visits, in hopes a little attention on his side might remove my objections, as he feared he had been too hasty, for it was usual for young ladies to expect to be solicited some time before they were required to give an answer. And I hope, sir, said I (with quickness) you did not encourage him: and why not child was his answer; such offers are not to be met with every day, and deserve at least to be considered before they are refused.

If that be all, sir, said I, he has nothing to hope from giving me time to consider, for I dislike the man, and never can bring myself to marry him: rather say, Louisa, said my father, you like another man, and are meanly waiting till he thinks proper to ask you. This unexpected attack confounded me a good deal, but as it really was not the cause of my present refusal, I soon recovered myself, and asked him who he suspected of having such influence over me.

He instantly replied, I believe your own heart will tell you, it is Harry Maunsell I mean; he is a young man I have a high esteem for, and if he has any thoughts of you, and had made a proper declaration of it before he went abroad,

I should have no objection; but as it is, if he was a prince, and you can be so abject as to wait his pleasure—you are no daughter of mine.

This unusual severity of speech from a father who had been always so indulgent, threw me into tears, which instantly softened him, and taking my hand, my dear; said he, I did not mean to distress you, but I cannot bear with patience that any man should think he may have you, at any time he finds himself at leisure to ask.

Convince me Harry is not the cause of your refusing his lordship's offer, and tho' I greatly approve it, I will immediately free you from his addresses: I assured him I could with great truth aver, he was not the cause, for my dislike proceeded from circumstances I had heard, and observations I had made of his lordship's disposition, which was really true, as I had often met him at the same house before that unlucky night when he took a fancy to me, but to put the matter out of all doubt, I gave a solemn promise never to marry Harry Maunsell.

My father seemed much pleased with me, resumed his wonted good humour, and I heard no more of my noble admirer, except that the lady of the house where I saw him, told me, it was with great difficulty he could be persuaded to resign his hopes of gaining me.

What a long winded tale is here!—I am so tired of it that I must defer the remainder to another opportunity. You have brought me into such a way of telling long stories to amuse you, that I shall begin to think myself an old maid, the symptom is so strong; and tho' it is a character I have a great respect for, and mean to shine in one time or other, I would not chuse to be one before my time.

I am now going to revive my spirits by a little party at Cards, so farewell till to-morrow.

LOUISA MORTIMER.

LETTER XIII.

THE SAME TO THE SAME.

Dec. 2.—

I GREATLY long to hear from my dear Eliza, as I expect your next will contain a full and true account of the effect Mr. Hamilton's visit, (that is supposing he came to the castle) had on Charles; and I dare say, before this reaches you, you will be quite as impatient for the continuation of my romance. I cannot deny but I felt some regret, when first I reflected on the restrictions I had laid myself under, but it proceeded chiefly from the pain I thought it would give Harry, when he should be informed of it; however, the pleasure I enjoyed in being freed from the solicitations of a man I disliked, soon reconciled me to it, but I wished much for an opportunity of telling Patty what had happened, that she might hint it to her brother, yet I could not think of writing it to her, as she had never spoke to me in plain terms on the subject, so I determined to let it lye till she came to town, when I thought it likely I might find means of introducing it; but in that I was disappointed; for before their usual time of leaving the country she was married to Mr. Herbert, which detained them some time, and just when they intended coming up, her father was seized with that illness which occasioned his death, after confining him to his room the whole winter, during which time Patty never quitted his House; and when he was gone her husband took her home, the season being then so far advanced, it was not worth the trouble of coming to town, for the short time they could have staid.

Mr. Maunsell's death hastened Harry's return, who arrived at Cork in May, which was about three months after, but his father having left his affairs in rather an unsettled state, owing to indolence in attending to his agents accounts, that business detained him in the country till winter; by which means I had time enough to be prepared for an interview, which I believe would have affected me a good deal had it happened a few months sooner, but by this time I was perfectly satisfied with what I had done. I was however a little fluttered when I saw his carriage stop at his own house, where he did not remain ten minutes before he paid me a visit, and though my father's presence a little restrained his tongue, his eyes plainly told me what he wished to say; company coming in he staid only till tea was over, as he saw it would be impossible to speak to me that evening, but next morning he came in, at an hour he knew my father would be out, and after many tender professions of joy at seeing me, offered himself and fortune to my acceptance, and begged my permission to make such proposals to my father, as he hoped would meet his approbation.

I hardly knew how to go about telling him a circumstance, that would at once dash all the hopes of happiness with which he had been so long flattering himself; but it must be done, and I accomplished it in the best manner I was able: it is utterly impossible for me to give you an idea of the agitation that appeared in his countenance while I spoke; I felt for his disappointment, and used every argument in my power to soften the severity of it; but he was for a time absolutely incapable of listening to reason. He execrated the man whose offers had been the occasion of my making such a promise, and cursed the family pride that had instigated my father to require it; in short, he said a thousand extravagant things, and railed himself out of breath before I could bring him to any degree of composure; at last I convinced him that as his behaviour to me had been always so particular that every one observed it, my father had great reason to think I was ill treated when he went abroad without explaining his sentiments, and of course it was natural for him to resent it, as it must hurt him much to have it supposed I was waiting any man's pleasure.

All his anger was then turned on himself, for not declaring both his passion and his situation in pecuniary matters, before he left Ireland; but he determined to clear it up to my father that he might be reinstated in his good opinion, though it could answer no other purpose, as the promise I made was solemn and unconditional, therefore could not be revoked.

I said all I could to persuade him to look out for some other woman, capable of making him happy, which would be the best method of blotting me from his mind, except as a friend, in which light I should ever esteem him; but my arguments had no effect, and though I thought a little time would change his romantic notions, I find he is now as determined as ever. When my father was acquainted with the nature of his silence, he expressed much concern at the obstacle that was between us, and said, if it would satisfy my scruples, he would willingly free me, as far as in him lay, but as I had shewed no reluctance in making the promise, he believed I could not easily be brought to think he could release me from it; but that Harry did not tell me, till I had given a final answer; which was, I did not think any power on earth could dispense with a solemn vow, unless it was taken by compulsion, and that was not the case with me. I therefore intreated Harry never to mention the affair again, and by that means he might bring himself to forget it. As to the first part, he said he should certainly obey me, but the latter he knew was impossible; it was too deeply engraven on his heart. I have often since, at his sister's request, pressed him to think of marrying, but though deprived of all glimmering of hope, his attachment seems stronger every time we meet; and you know we are very much asunder: but he really may sing, "His passion's constant as the sun."*——For me, I acknowlege, I have the most perfect friendship for him; and find it very flattering to be the sole object of attention, to a most amiable young man, whose love, I am sure, must be of the purest kind, since he can have no interest to gratify, nor the least expectation of gratifying his passion. I do not, however, at all, regret being debarred from marrying him; had I thought it a state capable of making me happier than I am, I should not have carried the Romance so far as to refuse some other young men, that you know addressed me, and who certainly had merit sufficient both to gain my heart, and keep it; I never had a high idea of matrimonial felicity: and I am sorry to say, the observations I have made amongst my married acquaintance has not altered my opinion. My notions of happiness, may, perhaps, be singular, and I do not wish to make converts to it; if many thought as I do, it would be of the worst consequence; there would be an end of all the tender relationships that bind mankind to each other, and the world would be one continued scene of discord and confusion: the institution is certainly good and capable of making us happy; but human nature is so perverse that we have ingeniously contrived to frustrate the beneficent intentions of heaven in that, as well as other things, and turned to our misery what was meant to promote our happiness, it is not however necessary that every one should marry, and I really believe Providence designed me for a single life, as it always appeared to me the most elegible, and, I am convinced, is most suited to my disposition; if every one considered their own temper, there would probably be fewer unhappy matches than we now see, but that is what we shall never persuade the generality of people to think necessary; so we must even let them go on, kissing one moment, and quarrelling the next, to the end of the chapter; and I have seen violent advocates for wedlock pass their whole life that way; but I suppose they thought it happiness, or they would not have so strongly recommended the state to others.

That my dear Eliza may enjoy more felicity in it, than has yet been the portion of any one I have met with, is the sincere wish of her

Affectionate,

LOUISA MORTIMER.

LETTER XIV.

Miss FITZGERALD, to Miss MORTIMER.

Dec. 5. —

I DELAYED writing to my Louisa these many days, for two reasons: first, till I had the whole of your interesting narrative: second, till Mr. Hamilton was gone, and I should be able to tell you, how we went on here.

Charles met him at the place appointed, and easily prevailed on him to pass a few days here, before he set out for home; he did not leave us till this morning, when Charles accompanied him according to promise, and is not to return this fortnight. You cannot imagine how solitary I seem without him: but to the material point, which I am sure will give you great pleasure.

He never shewed the least symptom of jealousy or uneasiness, the whole time Mr. Hamilton was here, though I could perceive, he scrutinously observed every look and word that passed between him and me, and I was well pleased he did, as it must tend to cure him of his suspicions, as far as they related to me; and Mr. Hamilton, I saw, avoided addressing himself so particularly to me, when Charles was present, as he would do at other times; no doubt, for fear of giving him pain; for he had heard, since first we met, how matters were circumstanced between us, and I dare say, guessed at Charles's foible from his behaviour at the Inn; else why that caution? for his address to me at all times, was only what might be expected from a man of politeness; though he had told me, he had heard of the intention of our family, with regard to Mr. Skeffington and me, just in time to recall his heart: I believe I looked rather simple; but I chose to take that opportunity of acknowleging my attachment, and answered, it was true, our parents had always intended us for each other, and happily for me, Mr Skeffington's amiable qualities, made my duty and inclination go hand in hand. He paid me some genteel compliments on what he called my ingenuousness, and said, Mr. Skeffington was, indeed, a happy man in meeting with a lady so far above the little punctilios of the Sex, as not to be ashamed to acknowlege the impression his merit had made on her heart. It was a compliment, however, that I did not deserve, for I felt very much ashamed at making the acknowledgment, and certainly would not have done it, but that I had reason to think he had some little liking for me; and if I was silent he might take it for encouragement; for though I never saw any thing like vanity in him; and there is few men ignorant of their own perfections, and I dare say, he is sensible that both as to person and accomplishments, he is such as might gain any woman's favour, who had no pre-engagement.

I told you I dreaded his coming here, though I wished it; but I had a thousand fears, lest Charles should be unable to command his temper, and therefore expose himself, and throw me into a very disagreeable situation; but as it hap-

THE TRIUMPH OF PRUDENCE OVER PASSION

pened, my fears were needless; he behaved very well, and we were all easy and chearful. Part of the time we had some other company, yet I wanted the Boyle's very much; they went to Belfast a day or two before I wrote last, and I cannot repair my loss while I am here; but my mother will go to town as soon as possible after Christmas.

I am now to thank you for giving up so much of your time to my amusement; and indeed your little Story affords both entertainment and instruction, in the manner you tell it; but how few could follow your example! in so intirely subjecting their passion to their reason, as not even to repine* at obeying your father, though we may easily guess it must have affected you much at the time: your good sense enabled you to bear a disappointment that most girls, at the age you then were, would have thought insupportable, the object considered: for certainly, Harry Maunsell's merit would be a powerful excuse for refusing to abjure all hopes of being united to him, when one knew it was a generous motive prevented him from explaining his sentiments. I cannot help thinking you have an uncommon share of Philosophy, though you will not allow me to say so; but as it is possible Harry has not so much, I pity him exceedingly: his resolution to remain single, is a convincing proof of the strength of his affection. I must, at the same time, acknowlege, it savours more of the Romantic than I should have suspected him, or any other young man of this age for.

Whenever I hear the Platonic system* disputed, I hope you will give me leave to produce you and your Swain, as a proof in favour of the Doctrine.

Your opinion has such weight with me, that I am heartily sorry it is so unfavourable to matrimony; for I know you consider a subject most deliberately before you form a judgment: and I am satisfied you would not determine against the state, if you did not think there was a small chance of happiness in it. I never could form the least idea how Mr. Maunsell and you were circumstanced, nor could I guess why you did not marry him: I plainly saw he was passionately fond of you; and to tell truth, I thought you had no dislike to him; therefore, could by no means guess at the cause of delay, when you had both been so long at your own disposal. Will you give me leave to blame your father? however indulgent in other respects, he was, surely, too severe in exacting such a promise from you, as the only terms on which he would free you from the addresses of a man you assured him you could not like, if you had never seen Harry. I think he might have depended on you for not doing any thing beneath the family you sprung from; for though you are not haughty, you have that proper degree of pride, which would prevent your bearing an indignity; therefore, he might be sure you would not accept of Harry or any other man, whose behaviour, when explained, would not meet the approbation of your friends.

Do not you think Patty was too close, when she told you, her brother could not marry while his father lived? and the reason of it, had she said plainly, you were the person who possessed his heart; it would have prevented the disagreeable consequence that ensued, because you could then have told your father, but in the manner she spoke, it would really have looked very vain to take it to yourself.

I am so sorry for Mr. Maunsell, that I am disposed to find fault with every one who was any way the cause of his disappointment.

I made a thousand reflections as I read, but will not, at present, trouble you with any more of them, except, that I cannot imagine how you kept it such a secret; for though I have heard many express their surprise that you did not marry him, I never yet heard a reason why you did not; and in general, those sort of affairs are very soon whispered about.

I am much pleased with what you mention of cousin James and Emily; he could not bring any one into the family that would be more agreeable to all his relations; I answer for them all, because I have heard it wished for amongst the old folks who knew her.

I sympathise with Gertrude, both in her joy and sorrow; I judge what she must feel at the idea of the Count going abroad, from what I should feel myself; but I hope she has more fortitude than I should have on such an occasion, else she must be very unhappy.

I am quite obliged to her for desiring you to tell me what occurred, and beg you will never forget to inform me when she hears from him, as I am really interested in the event on her account; sure his father cannot have any objection to the choice he has made.

If Charles should write to Mr. Maunsell, no doubt you will see the letter, and I believe I need not request you will let me know the contents, or procure me a sight of it, for I dare say, you would not wish to conceal any thing that is material to know.

Adieu, dear Louisa: believe me,
Affectionately your's,
ELIZA FITZGERALD.

LETTER XV.

Miss MORTIMER, to Miss FITZGERALD.

Dec. 12. —

A CONTINUAL round of company at home, and visiting abroad, this week past, prevented me from acknowledging my dear Eliza's last favour, which I was sorry for, as I suppose you are rather in the dismals* on account of Charles being away; but I hope you have too much sense to let such a trifle depress your spirits very much.

I am heartily glad Mr. Hamilton's visit passed off so well, especially as he really does admire you: you see how quicksighted jealousy is, for Charles perceived the impression you had made on him immediately, as he mentions, in his letter to Harry; if he writes on this occasion, I shall certainly inform you; but by what you say of his behaviour, I have great hopes he has recovered his reason; for I think he could hardly have dissembled his uneasiness during so many days.

I am happy in having amused you with my little story; as to the instruction I cannot say much about it; for was it public, probably more would condemn than approve my conduct: at least I am sure I should be held in abhorrence by all those who think LOVE an excuse for every act of imprudence or disobedience, they can be guilty of: but I do not take such merit to myself as you are willing to allow me, for not repining at what is past; I have no claim to your praises on that head, because the single state is really most suitable to my inclinations, yet notwithstanding it is more than probable if I had not made that promise, Mr. Maunsell might have prevailed on me to marry, against the conviction of my reason; but as that is now impossible, no other man is likely to have sufficient influence over my heart, to make me do any thing contrary to my judgment; so that instead of repining, I rather think I have cause to rejoice, that I have a certainty of passing my life in the state most pleasing to me. But you may, perhaps, think, it requires all the philosophy you talk of, to enable me to support the reproachful appellation of an Old Maid; it might be so formerly, but do not you remember, my dear, that Mr. Twiss* has kindly rescued us in this kingdom from undeserved contempt, by allowing the old maids of Ireland to be perfectly pleasing and agreeable; and since he acknowledges it, I think I have nothing to dread; for you know he allowed no perfection either in the country or the people, that he could possibly detract from. I doubt the Platonic system would not gain much by producing Harry as proof of it's existence; for I fear his passion is not so perfectly refined as that requires, though I grant you it is more romantic than what we usually meet with, indeed more so than is for his peace, because he certainly did not wish to live single, and has determined to do so, merely in consequence of his disappointment; it is a resolution I by no means approve, as I think he will be apt to repent it, or at least have cause to do so, when youthful passion has subsided, and he finds himself a solitary being in his own house, without any companion, and depending on the care of servants: if ill health should be the attendant on old age, as usually is, my arguments will then have all their weight in his mind, and he will be sorry he would not suffer himself to be convinced by them before it was too late.

You are so absorbed in compassion for him, that you do not take the least notice of poor Miss Herbert, whose hapless love I expected would have a large share of your pity.

I wrote Patty an account of my unsuccessful pleading in behalf of her sister-in-law; and as I was convinced it would be in vain to hope for any alteration in Harry's sentiments, I advised her to take the first opportunity of letting the lady know the whole of the affair between him and me, and his determination to remain unmarried, that she may withdraw her affections before they are so strongly fixed as to make the effort painful.

I have had an answer, wherein she tells me, she had let Miss Herbert into the secret of Harry's attachment to me, the day after she received my letter, some discourse happening between them which introduced it very a-pro-pos;* she says, she listened very attentively while she spoke; her colour frequently chang-ing, and now and then interrupted her with tender expressions of pity for his disappointment; at the conclusion she sighed heavily, and said, she wondered how any woman could dislike Mr. Maunsell, to whom he endeavoured to render himself agreeable; but when she heard it was quite otherwise, Patty says, her astonishment is not to be described: she could not conceive it possible, that any consideration even of duty, should have force to prevail on a woman that loved Mr. Maunsell, to give him up for ever.

Oh! madam, said she, had Miss Mortimer qualified the promise so as to leave it in her father's power to release her, they might have been happy; but now they must surely be wretched. Patty said, indeed, she knew no body happier; for my passions were so intirely under the government of reason, that I never suf-fered them to interrupt my peace. The tears stood in the poor girl's eyes, and she only said, such fortitude seldom fell to the share of our sex.

She was very ill the remainder of that day and the next, but when Patty wrote, was much better, and tried to be chearful, though it was plain it did not come from her heart: however, as she has very good sense, no doubt she will see the necessity of overcoming an attachment, that promises her nothing but uneasiness.

I am exceedingly sorry Harry could not, or would not, return this young lady's regard, as from the character I hear of her temper and disposition, I am sure they would have been happy. He himself says, she is deserving any man's affection, who had a heart to give.

If you must praise my heroism, let it be in wishing and endeavouring to per-suade him to marry; for that I confess, is a great degree of self-denial, since it would of necessity put an end to that agreeable intercourse, which at present contributes to my happiness: for the friendship I entertain for him, is the softest, most pleasing sentiment, that can possibly be imagined; and the reserve that must take place (if he was married) of the delightful confidence that now subsists between us, would leave a vacuum in my heart, that would ever remain; yet as his welfare is of infinitely more weight with me, than any gratification of my own; I have sincerely wished to see him cured of his unfortunate attachment: but here he is, and I must lay down my pen.——

Writing to Miss Fitzgerald, said he; yes. Then I have something for your perusal, which, perhaps, you would chuse to mention to her; and put into my hand a short letter from Charles, which he permits me to enclose, and which I shall leave you to read. So farewel, dear Eliza, says,

Your affectionate friend,
LOUISA MORTIMER

LETTER XVI.

DEAR MAUNSELL,

Hamilton-Hall, Dec. 11. —

YOU will see by the date of this, what good effect your advice had on me; since I am now in the house of a man, whom I could scarce bear the sight of when I wrote to you last, but the force of your arguments opened my eyes, and restored me in some degree to myself, at least so far as to enable me to consider the matter more dispassionately than I had yet done; and the result was, that I would pursue your plan, and, if possible, get Mr. Hamilton to the castle, and observe both his and Eliza's behaviour when together, by which means I could judge what foundation I had for my doubts, and also know if they were likely to be removed.

He reminded me by a polite letter of my promise to spend some time at his house before Christmas, and appointed me to meet him at a place he mentioned, to accompany him home; I went and easily prevailed on him to pass a few days with me before we set out for Derry;* accordingly we came directly to the castle, where he continued till the 6th when I accompanied him to this place, which is perhaps one of the most beautifully improved* spots in the universe, and during his absence has been kept by his mother in the same elegant order it was left by her husband.

But to return to my subject; by all the observations I could make while Mr. Hamilton was with me, I am still of opinion he admires Eliza; but as he heard after our first meeting how we were circumstanced, I am sure I have nothing to fear from him, unless he received encouragement from her behaviour, which I could not see the least reason to apprehend, so that I find myself at present very easy.

However, keeping your advice still in mind, I do not intend to mention hastening our marriage, till after my return from England, where business will call me in five or six weeks at farthest, but I do not know exactly how long I shall stay there; I suppose a few months will do to put matters on a proper footing, which are very indifferently managed by the present agent; and I think if I find Eliza entertains the same sentiments for me when I return, that she has always seemed to do, I shall be cured of those jealousies that have of late interrupted my peace, and will then press her to compleat my happiness, which will be very imperfect till I am certain I possess both her heart and hand.

I could not answer your last sooner, because I was quite undetermined how to act, (though in mine I had promised to do as you advised) till the opportunity of getting Mr. Hamilton to the castle so much sooner than I expected, determined me to follow your opinion, which I inclined to all a long, but I feared it would be a length of time before I could see them together, and I could not bear the suspence I was in long, for it was a state, I am convinced, infinitely worse than Popish purgatory.* Jealousy is the worst of fiends: Why is it an attendant on so sweet a passion as love? But you Maunsell are free from it, and yet I know you are a lover! It must then be a weakness in the mind, and if I cannot conquer it I shall be wretched; but I hope your assisting council,* joined to my own efforts, will effect a cure.

Mr. Hamilton calls on me to go with him a few miles on a visit.

Adieu, Dear Maunsell,
Your's,
C. SKEFFINGTON.

LETTER XVII.

Miss FITZGERALD, to Miss MORTIMER.

Dec. 15. —

My dear Louisa,

I HAD the pleasure of your's, with the inclosures, and am much obliged both to you and Mr. Maunsell for giving me the perusal of it: I shall return it with this. I cannot but say I had better hopes of Charles before I saw it than I have now, for you may observe he seems doubtful himself, that he shall be able to conquer his weakness, (as he calls it) from which I infer, he still finds it more powerful than he acknowleges, but as he wishes to be cured, I have hopes he will accomplish it; and if it depends on his finding me in the same sentiments on his return from England, I think I may answer for it.

I now see the folly of parents endeavouring to attach children to each other, before they know what their dispositions will be, for when the affections are strongly engaged it is not easy to withdraw them; though our reason may tell us we were not formed to make each other happy; at least I find it so, and fear I have a great deal of uneasiness before me. You I know would find no difficulty in doing what your reason dictated; but as Miss Herbert observes, such fortitude is not common in women; and I think I have even less of it than others.

That letter has quite depressed my spirits, which were not very good since Charles left us, and to make them worse my mother has been ill these two days; if she continues so, I shall be frighted to death: I wish we were safe in Dublin, there I should have the comfort of your society, which would enable me to bear any affliction better than I can do, when unsupported by your friendly council.

Though my regard for you and Harry took up all my thoughts when I wrote last, yet I assure you Miss Herbert was not without my pity; but as her liking was but of a short standing, I should suppose the disappointment cannot very greatly affect her for any time, though at first she may feel it severely, as she imagined him disengaged, and had no reason from his behaviour to expect any obstacle; however a beginning inclination may soon be conquered.

I do indeed, Louisa, allow you great praise for your whole conduct; particularly your endeavours to persuade him to marry; since that is what your heart is most repugnant to, and I own I cannot help being pleased at his determination, though I assent to your opinion in regard to old batchelors; but I think he must be happier even in that state, than married to one woman while he passionately loves another, and as that is the case, it would be a pity to take from your happiness without adding to his; for certainly in your present situation you enjoy more real satisfaction than any one I ever met with, and I begin to think you have chosen the right road to content; for that must be the surest way that does not depend on the caprice of another.—Why have not I resolution enough to

make the same choice? and put an end at once to all the anxieties I have suffered, since I came to the knowlege of Mr. Skeffington's temper; but your good
sense enables you to correct that too great sensibility, which is the thing will
ever prevent me from that happy repose, (if I may use the expression) that you
continually enjoy. That you, my dear girl, may long continue to enjoy it, is the
fervent wish of

Your Affectionate,
ELIZA FITZGERALD.

I have just got a letter from Charles, wherein he says he will be home the 20th
at farthest: he writes in the most tender manner, and expresses great impatience
to see me.

LETTER XVIII.

Miss MORTIMER, to Miss FITZGERALD.

Dec. 18.—

I AM sorry to find my dear Eliza's spirits are so very low, and request you will not give way to that encroaching disorder, which if not struggled against in time, creeps on imperceptibly, and gains such an ascendant over us that we will not endeavour to conquer it. I often cautioned you against encouraging that sensibility, which you allow interrupts your happiness, because I foresaw it would do so, and I know if you could make the trial, you might correct it as well as me; it is not the want of sense, but resolution prevents you; you had always a propensity to indulge melancholy ideas: for my part, I own I do not wish for such exquisite sensibility as should make me wretched; for as one of our female poets, (I do not remember who*) expresses it,

> "Nor ease nor peace the heart can know,
>   That like the needle true,
> Turns at the touch of joy, or woe,
>   But turning, trembles too."

Yet do not imagine I wish to stand unmoved at the joys or griefs of myself or fellow creatures; far from it,—but then I would chuse to feel them as a christian out;* I would not be beyond measure elated with one, nor distressed by the other: I would moderate my own afflictions by patient submission, and firm reliance on Providence, and I would endeavour to mitigate those of others, by affording either assistance or consolation as the case required, or my abilities extended; though tenderness of heart is certainly very amiable in a woman, it requires a proper degree of resolution, to prevent its degenerating into weakness, which it is but too apt to do; fortitude is as becoming in a woman as a man, and quite as necessary; for how very unfit must that woman be to offer consolation to her husband, her family, or friends in affliction, that suffers herself to sink under the most trifling disappointment; besides it betrays such a distrust in Providence, to depend on every untoward accident of life, as renders us very unworthy of any assistance from him, whom we are taught to hope will extricate us from our difficulties, provided we put a proper confidence in him, and endeavour to deserve his protection. Excuse me, my dear girl, for preaching to you, but I feel myself so interested in your happiness, that I cannot be silent when I see you likely to lose it, merely for want of a little exertion of that understanding with which heaven has liberally endowed you.

  Your mother is not, I dare say, in any alarming way; and for what relates to Charles, I do not think his letter need effect your spirits so much; for though I grant he is not yet perfectly cured, we may well hope he will, since he seems determined to use his own efforts for the purpose; but I have a great notion his absence, more than any thing else, occasions your melancholy; at least I hope so, for then his return will set all matters to rights. Do pray get out of your lachry-mals* before you write again; for I fear a few such letters as your last would infect me.—True, Harry is certainly better as he is, if he cannot conquer his passion; but what I contend for is, he might conquer it if he would try, for I believe passion of any kind may be subdued if we chuse to do it.

I will tell you why you cannot make the same resolution I have done, which you seem unable to account for; in the first place you are too much in love; and in the second, the single state is not your choice, nor indeed is it fit for you; you are much too timid to go through life alone, and therefore want some one on whom you can depend for protection in all the vicissitudes of human affairs. If any thing happened to separate Charles and you, it would be absolutely necessary for you to make another choice. Now you need not make any protestations against it, because I do not think it likely the thing will come to pass; but if it should, I would have you take a few months to consider, before you make any declaration of that sort.

I was interrupted by Gertrude, who walked in with a packet of letters in her hand, and pleasure sparkling in her eyes; they were from France, she said, and if I had time, would be glad I would read them before I finished my letter, that I might acquaint Miss Fitzgerald with the contents; I accordingly run them over; there is three of them, one from the count, one from his son, and another from his daughter, all on the same subject; the substance is, the count has been informed of his son's inclination, and quite approves it; is only displeased he was so long kept ignorant of it.

He has wrote in very genteel terms to Gertrude, hoping, that as she is still unmarried she will remain so a while longer if Louis has been so happy as to gain her esteem, as nothing would give him greater pleasure than a union between them; he says, his son cannot avoid going out with his regiment, and serving one campaign, for his honor is concerned, which he is sure she will think of sufficient importance to plead his excuse, for not throwing himself at her feet immediately, but promises to obtain leave for him to return as soon as the campaign is over, when he flatters himself, his behaviour in the field will render him still more worthy her favour.

The young man's letter is truly a love letter, expressing hopes and fears, griefs and joys, every other word, to the end of a large sheet of paper; and concludes with a request, that she will now indulge him with an answer; a thing she has never yet done, except in her letters to his sister.

Adelaide's joy I think is greater than her brother's, because less intermixed with fears: she mentions this happy change in her father, was brought about by his being at last convinced by the lady herself, that she really had refused his son; and she assured him she would have done so, had he been a king, and of a different religion from her own: this brought the count to hear reason, and he consented to see Louis, who immediately declared his attachment to Gertrude, and obtained his father's approbation, who said, if he had known it before he proposed the other match for him, it would have saved them all some uneasiness, as there could be no objection either to Miss St. George or her family, who he knew were people of rank.

This has quite satisfied our pride, which I assure you was up in arms, and we were determined to keep up a proper dignity, in case the old gentleman did not consent with a good grace: you may guess I encouraged her in that, as an affront of that nature was not to be put up with. So this love affair is likely to come to the same end which most love affairs do, I mean matrimony, that is if a cannon ball does not occasion a more melancholy catastrophe,* which I hope will not be the case, for Gertrude is a deserving girl, and I should be sorry to see her afflicted. I shall have an unspeakable loss when this young Frenchman takes her from me.

I have forborn to mention political transactions this some time, as I know you have the most material occurrences from Mr. Fitzgerald, and the public prints;* by them you are informed our commons have demanded a FREE TRADE;* I do not however give them the credit of it, except those few who have uniformly been actuated by love of their country; as for the rest they were impelled to it, by the spirit that at present pervades all degrees of people, and which they dare not set themselves against: the same reason will oblige England to comply, because she is not in a situation to refuse; but I am clear of opinion, that if we do not watch her with unremitting attention, she will, by some artifice, the first convenient opportunity, contrive to render every thing she grants of no effect, for they are selfish, illiberal people, and look with a jealous eye on every advantage enjoyed by their fellow subjects, either envying their prosperity, or looking on it as so much taken from them; like some individuals, who are as anxious to detract from other people's merit, as if they thought it would add any thing to their own. To repine at another's prosperity is a most odious disposition, even in private persons; but it is still worse, when it is the temper of a whole nation, because it then affects millions of people, who are connected with, or dependant on them; and who in consequence, are sure to be oppressed.

The uniform conduct of the English towards this kingdom, as well as to America,* justifies my opinion of them; and I dare say, a little time will shew what dependance we can have on their affection, that is, provided we give them an opportunity; for no doubt they will dissemble till they are sure of carrying their point.

How some of the wise heads would laugh at a girl pretending to give an opinion in politics; it is not, I believe, a very usual subject for young ladies to correspond on; but I know you have been taught to think, the welfare of our country is of as much consequence to women as men; and when public affairs are the general topic, to write on them is an agreeable variety, and at least as improving as intrigue or scandal, which the men generously allow us to talk of as much as we please, and indeed make no bad figure in such conversation themselves.

We go on here just as usual: cousin James as attentive as ever to our fair widow; and Harry Maunsell a constant attendant on your humble servant. If Gertrude had her young count here, three such swains would make us the envy of every female circle we frequented.

I observe when we meet Mr. Fitzgerald at a drum, which often happens, all eyes are cast on him and Emily, for the town has already made a match between them, and his behaviour confirms the idea, as it is really very particular.

These men, Eliza, with all their sense, have mighty little discretion in those sort of matters: we women have it all to nothing: now Emily behaves with the greatest composure and indifference, while your cousin is unable to conceal his chagrin if he cannot play at the same table she does, and yet I am sure she likes him.—What an unmerciful letter here is! I am half dead with writing.

Adieu,
LOUISA MORTIMER.

LETTER XIX.

Miss FITZGERALD, to Miss MORTIMER.

Dec. 26. —

MY dear Louisa's very agreeable epistle of the 18th had all the effect you could wish in restoring my spirits; for you point out the folly, and I may say, impiety of sinking under every trivial distress in such forcible language, that I grew ashamed of my own weakness while I read, and have ever since manifested such resignation and composure, though my mother is confined with the rheumatism, and Charles did not arrive till the 22nd, that I am sure you would be astonished at my improvement in your Philosophic Doctrines, joking a-part. I wish you were always near, to teach me to support disagreeable accidents with some degree of resolution: I fear I shall very soon stand in need of all your arguments on that head, as the time for Charles going to England advances fast, and there is little probability that my mother will be able to go to town before then, as she intended. But I will not anticipate uneasiness, if I can help it.

Yesterday, according to ancient custom,* Charles's tenants were entertained in the Great Hall, with roast beef and plumb-pudding; mine were treated in the same manner the day before, the Steward and House-keeper doing the honours of the table. My mother was not able to come amongst them, which was a great mortification to her; but I went, dispensed my usual present of a guinea to each of the young girls who was cloathed in her own housewifery;* and that, you may be sure, was every one that was present; but if on enquiry I found any of them so industrious as to help to cloath the younger children of the family, I added a second guinea, by way of encouragement to her, and to inspire the rest with emulation: a cap and ribbon to each of the little ones, makes them attend both to their book and their needle; and my approbation makes them all compleatly happy; for I often call in at each of their houses, when I take an airing, and then the mothers inform me how they go on at school, and I praise or chide them, according to the account I hear.

I pay for the schooling* of those whose parents cannot well afford it, because I think reading and writing* may be useful to them, if they should happen to be hereafter in any sort of business: besides, they can be better instructed in religion, if they are able to read the Bible.

Charles accompanied me into the Hall, and chatted with the old folks, while I was distributing my favours amongst the young ones. A large bowl of punch was brought in for them to drink my health, and one of the old men made me look very silly, by adding a wish, that their next meeting might be to rejoice on my ladyship's marriage with his honour: you may think I could not answer such a speech, but Charles relieved me by thanking him for his wish, and hoping he should see them very shortly on that happy occasion. The girls simpered, and their mothers smiled: I recovered from my confusion enough to say something kind to them all, and then left them to enjoy their mirth the rest of the evening; and diverted my mother with what had passed, who was rather inclined to be low-spirited at being unable to go down to them, for she used to take great delight in seeing them all so happy; and has made it a request, that I will never drop the custom, which I could easily promise, as it is quite agreeable to my inclination.

Charles's behaviour, since he returned from Hamilton-Hall, is just what it used to be, before he discovered any symptoms of that unhappy failing, which has this while past interrupted our peace; but I dare not flatter myself his present disposition will hold, as his letter to Mr. Maunsell shews, how doubtful he is about it.

I rejoice to hear Gertrude's little Novel is likely to conclude to her satisfaction; though to be sure, his absence will give her much uneasiness; but something may happen to occasion his return sooner than she expects; there may be a peace, or cessation, not that there is now any appearance of it; but she must hope the best. She will, indeed, be a great loss to you; you should think of some one to supply her place; for it will not be pleasing for you to be alone, nor you need not, as you have several young relations, who, I dare say, would like well to be with you.

Your bit of Poetry was happily chosen to illustrate your own sentiments; I am convinced you are perfectly right, not to let your sensibility run away with your happiness, and sincerely wish, I could follow your example, but fear I have not strength of mind sufficient for the purpose.

I am of your opinion, both as to our own Parliament and the English nation, and I find cousin James thinks as you do; for in one of his letters, he says, "There is no doubt but our demands will be granted, as it would be too dangerous to refuse them; but I am sure England will seize the first opportunity to render her concessions abortive."* I hope we may all find ourselves mistaken; yet I am afraid we shall prove too good politicians in that respect.

I know most men disapprove of women pretending to any opinion on these subjects;* but the men of your family and mine were above that vulgar prejudice, and took pains to make us capable of judging with some degree of precision; and I think we are obliged to them for it, since it enables us to converse sometimes on matters of importance, and not be always confined to trifles; a little of each is agreeable.

I wonder the men are not more discreet in their behaviour before strangers, for I should think it not pleasing to themselves to have their attachments public, before they know how they will be received: most men look on it as very mortifying to be refused, and would think themselves very ill treated if the lady should publish it; though they scarce ever fail of making it known to every body, they make very little use of their understanding on those occasions. James is a striking proof of it, for by what you say, a giddy lad could not be more foolish; and yet in every other circumstance of life, he is quite a pattern of propriety of manners; and it certainly is far from that to draw people's eyes on Emily, and set them telling of her second marriage, before she is out of her weeds: why do not you speak to him about it? but indeed, as it is a fault, or a folly (call it which you please) most of them are guilty of, I suppose they cannot help it.

Charles has just got a letter from England, which, he says, will hasten his departure; he talks of going in two or three days, and all your lessons are insufficient to make me hear it with any composure; all I could do was, to restrain my tears till he had quitted the room. I can only add, that I am your's,

with much affection,
ELIZA FITZGERALD.

LETTER XX.

Miss FITZGERALD, to Miss MORTIMER.

Dec. 27. —

WRITE to me, my dear Louisa, and comfort me if you can; for when you receive this, I shall be a wretched creature, as you will easily believe, when I tell you it will be delivered by Mr. Skeffington, on his way to England.

I wish you could inspire me with a little of your fortitude, to enable me to part from him with any degree of composure, for I fear to expose my weakness to my mother, who is very ill, and is, you know, greatly affected by every thing that afflicts me; so kind is this tender parent. However, as he does not set out till tomorrow, I will endeavour to conquer my folly before then, or at least to conceal it.

I once thought of persuading him to go through Scotland,* to avoid the danger of the sea between Dublin and the Head,* but on recollection I did not mention it, for it occurred to me, he would hazard his life as much in a long journey, this inclement season, in a very severe climate. Yet if the air does but move a blade of grass, my heart dies within me, at the idea of the ship's being dashed against the rocks; or what would be still worse, it's foundering at sea, for then he would have no chance of escaping. In short, I have a thousand fears, and from the terror I feel at parting, am half persuaded, we shall never meet again.

I wish he would not go, but I am ashamed to hint my wishes, as I know he has material business: it is very unfortunate for me, that I have been from my infancy used to his company, as it makes me unable to bear a separation with any degree of fortitude, though I know the necessity of it, and fear that necessity will often recur; but what one has been long accustomed to, grows habitual, and is not easily conquered.

My father's death, which I can but just remember, occasioned my mother's breaking up house, and going to live with her brother, whose wife being dead, they thought it would be more pleasing to both, as each had but one child, and they too young to be their companions; and the society of those to whom we are attached, by any tender ties, whether of blood or affection, is very desirable.

My mother and uncle found it so agreeable, that they continued together till death (as you know) deprived us of him about two years since.

The education of Charles and me took up the greatest part of their attention; and as they were both too fond of us, to bear us for any length of time out of their sight, they determined to employ proper teachers for us in the house, and have us instructed under their own eye; by which means we were continually together, and indeed, never wished to part, which, I believe, was the very thing our parents had in view. However, though I think a home education, where proper instructors can be afforded, is by far the most preferable for a woman; it has great inconveniencies with regard to men,* as it sends them into the world totally unacquainted with all its ways, and of course liable to be imposed on, by the first that shall find it worth their while to make a dupe of them, which is another of my fears, on Charles's account; for I know good sense, without a knowlege of mankind, is not sufficient to guard an unsuspecting mind, against the wiles that are practised by both sexes, to seduce the young and inexperienced into their nets.

But why do I teize you with my foolish fears? yet write to me, if it be but to chide my weakness; for I have no one here, either to console or advise me, and you know what a timid creature I am, and how very easily my spirits are depressed.

Adieu, my dear Louisa, believe me,
Ever your's,
ELIZA FITZGERALD.

LETTER XXI.

Miss MORTIMER, to Miss FITZGERALD.

Dec. 31. —

"Oh! what pain it is to part."———— *

WHAT a tragedy has my dear Eliza wrote on the departure of Mr. Skeffington: no Heroine of Romance ever lamented the absence of her Swain in more pathetic terms. How could the barbarous man think any business of sufficient moment to be preferred to LOVE and you? I hope, however, he has the excuse of not knowing how deeply you were affected at his going, which I am apt to think was the case, as I never saw him more lively than he was the few hours he passed with me, in his way through Dublin.

I beseech you, keep him in ignorance, if you wish to maintain any degree of consequence in his opinion; for men are as subject to vanity as women, and quite as ready to make a bad use of their power over the heart they are sure of.

Now for my part, such a thought would never have occurred to me, as not seeing him again, any more than the perils and dangers of a voyage from this to Holy-Head, which you have painted in such dismal colours, as would make one's heart ach, in anticipating the distresses of a shipwreck; if we did not luckily recollect, that the thing scarce ever happens. I thank heaven, my nerves are not of such a delicate texture; or my heart is not so tender as your's, else I should be wretched something more than three-fourths of the year; for about so long am I without seeing Harry: yet I bear it with great philosophy, and even think the pleasure of meeting, which we could not know without parting, far out-balances any uneasiness that may give; it is quite an Epicurism in Love,* of which you can have no idea, because you have not yet experienced it. Indeed I do not see how it is possible to keep an attachment alive for any length of time, without frequent separations; it would be quite as dull as being married to the man, to have him like a fixture in your house, never to be moved: but when he has been a while away, he has a thousand things to tell you; ten thousand soft professions of constancy to make; and in short, one feels such agreeable sensations, that when you come to enjoy that refined pleasure, you will agree with me, that being perpetually together, is the most insipid thing in the world.

I hope this reflection will make you submit with a better grace to the necessity of sometimes parting from this idol of your heart, as you probably must do it often, since his estate in England* will, no doubt, require his presence at least once a year, to see that justice is done, both to his tenants and himself: now he is nearly at age, you must expect he will attend to his own business. I should hope your good sense would prevent your wishing him to act otherwise; as the largest fortune cannot hold out against the neglect of its owner, but will, by degrees, waste away; and most probably fall into the hands of those to whose care it was committed: so that your own interest, which will shortly be connected with his, should keep you from encouraging him to indolence,* a fault which men of rank are too apt to fall into, with regard to their own affairs.

I shall conclude like all other preachers, by desiring you to consider what has been said, and I hope your next letter will convince me it has had a proper effect: give your reason fair play, and I am sure it must. Farewel, my sweet friend, says,

Your

LOUISA MORTIMER.

It being late, I was in such haste to conclude, that I forgot to take notice of one of your fears, though I think it the least groundless of any you mention; that is, the danger your cousin may fall into from his ignorance of the world. I confess, I think it more than probable his purse will smart for it, if he makes any stay in London, where all kinds of sharping* is brought to a degree of perfection, (if I may use the expression) that is yet unparallelled, and where a dangerous gloss is put on every vice. However, as he has good sense, and good principles, I hope he will come off with the loss only of a little money, and he will know more of mankind by the time he goes there again.

I am much concerned for your good mother's indisposition, and wish she was able to come to town, which would be a more eligible place for you both than where you are. It is a lucky thing that women have the privilege of writing long post-scripts, else the most material part of the letter would be often left out.

LETTER XXII.

FROM THE SAME TO THE SAME.

Jan. 2. —

I HOPE my dear Eliza has, by this time, suffered her reason to get the better of her foolish fears, and that she is enough composed to be ashamed of them. Foolish I must call them, because they were groundless, and conjured up by your own imagination, merely for an excuse to make yourself wretched. I could not help smiling at your giving me such a long account of the manner you were brought up together, as if I had been quite ignorant of it; but as you were making it an excuse for your being so unreasonably affected at parting, I suppose you chose to refresh my memory on every particular circumstance, that it might the better plead your apology, which was natural enough in you; when you must be sensible, you stood in need of every excuse that could be made. However, I take it for granted, you have e'er now, recovered your senses, which were certainly suspended for a while, and are capable of reflecting on the bad consequence of letting any passion get so powerful a dominion over you, as quite to overwhelm your understanding.

A man of sense, though it may flatter his vanity to be so extravagantly beloved, would not be much delighted to have his wife so miserable when he was out of her sight, as it would be a continual drawback on his enjoyments, if he had any regard for her; and a man that had neither sense or affection, would have it always in his power to make you unhappy.

Harry could not conceal his astonishment, when I read your letter to him.

Sure, says he, "Mr. Skeffington does not know how tenderly he is beloved, or he could not harbour such jealousies." But, added he, perhaps he may fear she is too susceptible, for that is sometimes the case.——

I leave you to consider whether it be prudent to give room to such an idea.

You will, I doubt not, hear from Charles in a few days, for he has as fair a wind as can blow; and to be sure he will write as soon as he lands at the Head. He begged I would advise you to get your mother to town, whenever she was able to bear the journey; for he cannot be easy till he hears you have left the castle, as he knows how lonely you must be, since you lost the Boyle's, and every one else will be coming to Dublin, when the Holy-Days* are over.

I promised to mention it to you, but told him, I was sure your own inclination would bring you the instant your mother could venture to move.

Harry and he walked out together, and had, I find, a deal of conversation on the old subject. He seemed convinced that reason did not warrant his suspicions; but said, Love or Jealousy had little to do with reason; and when he considered Mr. Hamilton's accomplishments, and knew that he liked Eliza, he could not help fearing she might think too favourably of him; but said he, if I find no alteration in her sentiments when I return, I think I shall be quite easy; so there it rests; and as it depends on that circumstance, I fancy you have nothing to dread.

Adieu, dear Eliza; let me hear how your mother is, and if there is any hopes of our meeting soon. I expect to find by your next you are again a rational creature.

Your's, sincerely,
LOUISA MORTIMER.

LETTER XXIII.

Miss FITZGERALD, to Miss MORTIMER.

Jan. 3. —

MY dear Louisa's very agreeable letter, shewed me to myself in such a ridiculous light, that I could not forbear laughing as I read it. I question, however, if it would have all the effect you wished, had not the same post brought a letter from Charles, informing me of his safe arrival at the Head, which, as it made my mind easy, rendered me more capable of attending to your arguments; and they are, I confess, unanswerable; but though my reason is convinced, I cannot conquer my folly, and fear I shall have frequent returns of what you call the Horrors, during Mr. Skeffington's absence; all I can promise is, I will endeavour to get the better of it, and may, perhaps, succeed in time, with a little of your assistance; if left to myself, I am sure I never shall.

You tell me, with what philosophy you bear Mr. Maunsell's absence, greatest part of the year; you might too, have reminded me, of the patience with which you resigned him at your father's desire; when your affection for him was at the highest, and I could only have answered, that to follow your example, required more fortitude than I am mistress of: but when I go to town, you shall read lectures to me on the subject, and I will be all attention, till I become what you wish me. I am sure it would be much for my own ease to be so, as it would relieve me from a multitude of disquiets, which I suffer from being incapable of correcting my too great sensibility; yet that it may be done, you are a convincing proof, and it will be a shame for me if I do not improve under the instruction of one whose precepts are enforced by practice.

You describe the pleasure of meeting a beloved object after a long absence, so feelingly, that it is easy to know you speak from experience; I wish I may find it so agreeable, but Mr. Skeffington's present disposition, makes it impossible to guess what our next meeting may produce: perhaps an eternal separation may ensue. If that should ever be the case, you tell me, it will be necessary for me to transfer my affection to another, as I am unfit to go through life alone. I grant I am; but can you, Louisa, expect I should ever love another, after being so cruelly disappointed in him, that has possessed my heart since I was a child? It is not possible; but you forbid me to make declarations; I hope I shall have no occasion.

———

January 4th.

I was yesterday obliged to quit my letter to entertain a neighbouring lady, who came to pass a day with my mother; and as she lives but six miles from us, she staid till it was too late for the post, so I deferred concluding till to-day.

I have just got your's of the 2nd, and am really ashamed of my own weakness, and of all the trouble I have given you in trying to preach me out of it. But sure you cannot be serious in saying you read my letter to Mr. Maunsell; I blush at the remark you say he made, and am ready to die at the thoughts of having given cause for it; but I will not believe you could be so unfriendly as to expose me, even to him. You who were so delicate in regard to Emily and cousin James, that you would not allow me to mention your observations to Charles, though they related only to James's growing inclination, and can you be less anxious where my delicacy is concerned? I once thought I had the first place in your friendship; and am more hurt than you can conceive, at the bare idea of finding myself mistaken; though as yet I am willing to flatter myself, you only wrote in that manner to alarm me: if so, you cannot be too speedy in telling me so, as I shall suffer much uneasiness till then.

I have the pleasure to inform you, my mother is a good deal better; but as to her going to town, I know not when she can attempt to travel. I shall be impatient for your next.

Your's,
ELIZA FITZGERALD.

LETTER XXIV.

Miss MORTIMER, to Miss FITZGERALD.

Jan. 5. —

NO, indeed, I did not expose my dear Eliza's weakness, my regard for her is too sincere; and if it was not, my partiality to my own Sex, would prevent my letting any of the fellows (not excepting Harry Maunsell) know that an attachment to one of them, could make a good, sensible girl, behave like a fool, on the trifling occasion of parting with him for a month or two. I only took that method to convince you, you were wrong, by the distress I knew you would feel on the supposition of its being known to any one but me. Do not, however, think, that what I said was merely my own words; for I assure you, I have heard Harry, as well as other men, make the observation, that people who are very susceptible, were usually very fickle also; being subject to tender impressions, for every pleasing object they meet with. Though I know you are an exception to this rule, yet if Mr. Skeffington happens to be of those sentiments, his jealousy is easily accounted for; not having an high opinion of himself, it is natural enough for him to fear a more accomplished person may supplant him.

If you think this likely to be the case, no doubt it will be a stronger motive with you to correct the too great tenderness of your heart, than any I could offer, and I hope we shall have no occasion to renew the subject.

Mr. Fitzgerald is become a violent favourite with Mr. O'Neil; they met here, (for the old gentleman frequently visits me) and James, artfully enough, accommodated himself to his opinions, which are rather singular; and so pleased him, that he received an invitation to call in and play Back-gammon* whenever he had an hour to spare. I believe he goes there two or three times a week, and loses every game he plays, for he has no skill at it, and pretends a great desire to be instructed by Mr. O'Neil, who prides himself on being an adept in whatever was fashionable in his younger days; and thinks the present age degenerated in every thing, even their amusements; a common notion amongst old people, who mistake their own incapacity to enjoy amusement, for some defect in the entertainment itself.

It was, however, no bad policy in your cousin to ingratiate himself there; for if he can gain her father's approbation, it will go a great way in recommending him to Emily, who is a perfect pattern of obedience; but I fancy it will take time to bring that matter about.

Gertrude answered all the letters from the family of Rousillon, in REALLY a very pretty manner; I am sure I could not have wrote half so well on the subject, but you young ladies, who are so conversant in Love matters, are never at a loss on your favourite theme.

I doubt not if Louis will get her letter, as she had one from him yesterday, dated on board the fleet, which was only waiting for sailing orders; so she has had a most rueful countenance ever since, and we are all employed in diverting, or rather laughing her out of her dismals: to do her justice, though she bears it very well, for she does not torment herself with far-fetched terrors, but as he is going into very imminent dangers, one cannot be surprised that she is affected by it.

I rejoice that Mrs. Fitzgerald is on the recovery, and hope soon to see her and her fair daughter in Dublin.

Emily and Gertrude present their best affections.

Ever your's,

LOUISA MORTIMER.

LETTER XXV.

THE SAME TO THE SAME.

Jan. 8 —

ONLY think, Eliza, how unexpectedly things come about, and learn to depend on the wise Disposer of events. What Gertrude could not have hoped for in less than a year, is now come to pass in a moment, as one may call it, and that by the very means which she thought such a formidable bar to her wishes; I mean the young Count being ordered abroad. But to be a little methodical, (a thing I am not much addicted to) as I sat reading this morning in my dressing room, where we usually breakfast, waiting for the two ladies who had not yet appeared, Jenny announced the arrival of a strange gentleman, who, she said, seemed to be a foreigner, and enquired for me; she had shewn him into the parlour, and I chose to go to him rather than ask him up, it was such an early hour; his back was to me as I went in, but when he turned his strong resemblance to the picture I saw with Gertrude, at once informed me who he was, before he had time to speak; and I asked him had I not the pleasure of addressing the Count de Rousillon? he answered he was the person, but could not guess by what means I came to know him, which I soon explained; and he proceeded to inform me that the fleet had been but three days from France, when a violent storm arose which separated them, and the vessel he was in having suffered greatly during the gale, was endeavouring to make the port they had so lately quitted, when they were attacked by an English frigate, to which they were obliged to strike,* not being in a condition to fight, and were brought into Cork; from whence he had come on parole, to pay his devoirs* to my lovely kinswoman, but not wishing to surprise her, had taken the liberty of first introducing himself to me. He concluded with saying, though he was disappointed of the glory he promised himself in the campaign, his love would not suffer him to call the accident a misfortune, since it would be the means of procuring him the happiness he had long sighed for.

As I know the happiness he meant was Gertrude's presence, I was not so unfeeling to deprive him of that pleasure long, and thinking it necessary to prepare her a little, as his delicate caution had hinted, I went up and met her just quitting her chamber; we came to my dressing room together, and by degrees I let her know who was in the house: her agitation was so great I thought she would have fainted, and calling for help, in ran her maid in as bad a state as her mistress, having got a glimpse of the Count, and supposing it was his ghost; the foolish girl ran about the room like one frantic, crying out, O! madam, the Count! the Count! Her exclamations helped to rouse Gertrude, and brought Emily into the room, who stood staring at us all, totally unable to account for such a scene of confusion, till the Count himself hearing the hurry, no longer able to check his impatience, and following the sound of our voices, flew into the room, and clasping Gertrude in his arms, said a thousand tender things which explained the mystery to Emily, and relieved Sally from her terrors, who had on his first appearance covered her face with her apron, to avoid seeing what she firmly believed to be a spirit.

When the first transports of such an unexpected interview had subsided, the Count gracefully apologized for the freedom he had taken; and Gertrude who was blushing to death at having so quietly permitted it, would, I believe, have remained silent till now, if I had not relieved her by saying I would venture to engage for his pardon, as I saw in her eyes she was not mortally offended; therefore I hoped he would be able to partake of our breakfast, and I seated myself at the table; they all followed my example, and Sally being restored to her senses, paid her tribute of joy on the happy occasion, (for she knew the whole affair) and withdrew, leaving us to enjoy a little rational conversation, and compose ourselves after the hurry of spirits some of us had undergone.

I can easily excuse Gertrude for any little imprudence she committed in attaching herself to this young man, without knowing how either of their friends would relish it, for he is so perfectly amiable in his person, and his sentiments so uncommonly refined, as I could observe from the little conversation I have had with him, that it would require a large share of stoicism to listen to his soft tale with indifference, provided one was free from any other prepossession.

He is of the finest stile of manly beauty, both as to face and person; much superior to his picture, which is very handsome too; but he was quite a stripling when that was drawn; and Gertrude says, he is amazingly improved in his form.

He has all the agreeable vivacity of his country, tempered by an excellent understanding; in short, I am a little in love with him myself, and quite entertained with his chat, for he speaks broken English divinely, and gives it such a softness as makes it wonderfully pleasing; it is what the language much wants; its native accent is so very tart, it always gives me an idea of scolding, so that in my mind a soft Munster brogue* is an improvement to it, provided it be not a vulgar one.

As he did not like continuing at a Hotel, I sent Jenny to take a lodging for him near this, and she got a handsome apartment in the next street, with which he is greatly pleased; Harry Maunsell to whose care I have recommended him, attended him home just now, for he was easily prevailed on to stay all day with his adorable.

Harry will introduce him to all the men of genteel rank, and takes him to all the places worth seeing; it was lucky enough that he happened to be in town.

I dare say the Count will not think of leaving this till he takes Gertrude with him; so if you wish to be at the wedding you must not make much delay in the country; for I expect we shall be put all into a hurry when he gets letters from home. As he has wrote from Cork, it is not to be doubted but he has asked permission to conclude an affair so interesting to him while he is here.

Gertrude has been so prettily fluttered all day, that if it was not for a little of my assistance, she would not have been able to stammer out a single sentence of common sense; but when I saw her likely to make a very silly figure, I stopt her short with some very ridiculous observation, that drew the laugh upon me, and gave her some time to recollect herself, by which means I saved her from a good deal of raillery, which I saw Harry and your cousin James was much inclined to; as they presently discovered how matters stood between her and the Count: indeed her own confusion would have betrayed the secret, if his particular attention to her had not done it.

Surely this letter will dispel your melancholy ideas, and teach you to think every thing will turn out for the best, if our own perverseness does not prevent it.

Mr. Skeffington's sudden departure, and your consequent low spirits, having given me a subject for my two last epistles, I forgot to tell you, I was quite pleased with your account of the method by which you encourage your tenants children, to industry as well as to the learning that is necessary for them; and I agree with you, in regard to the advantage of their knowing how to read, though I have heard people argue against it;* but I never heard them say any thing convincing on the subject.

I am not surprised that your mother should be mortified at not being able to go amongst them, as was her custom during so many years; and to a mind like hers it must give singular satisfaction to see so many people chearful and happy, whom she knows she contributes to make so; it is well for them, and I am sure, a great pleasure to her, that you are disposed to follow her example.

Good night, dear Eliza, it is now past twelve, and I grow drowsy.

Your's affectionally,

LOUISA MORTIMER.

LETTER XXVI.

Miss FITZGERALD, to Miss MORTIMER.

Jan. 11. —

HOW kind is my dear Louisa to take so much pains to amuse me, as well as to reason me out of my melancholy; it would be ungrateful if I would not let her endeavours succeed, by seconding them with my own efforts, especially when I must assent to the force of your arguments; they had such an effect that I was growing quite chearful, when, (I am almost ashamed to tell you) an unlucky dream, made such an impression on my mind, as rendered me totally unfit to write to you for two days, which was the cause of my not answering your's of the 6th sooner. Do not however be very angry with me, since I acknowledge my own folly, and have got the better of it, at least for the present: besides you know my mother, who is in other respects a sensible woman, has great faith in dreams which is some little apology for me.

I never heard Charles say any thing, that gave me room to think he was of the same opinion which you say Mr. Maunsell, and many other men are; but if we ever meet again I will try to discover his sentiments, and be that as it will, I will certainly try to correct what is amiss in my own disposition.

I did not think James had so much art, and though it is a talent I do not much approve in the present case, I cannot help wishing him success; for since Emily does not dislike him, it is no harm to use a little artifice to obtain her father's good graces.—Your's of the 8th is just brought me, I mean I have just read it, and heartily congratulate Gertrude on the agreeable accident that has put an end to all her fears. It is indeed a proof that we should never despond,* let our prospect be ever so dark, since the scene may be changed in a moment when we least expect it; though striking the instance, it is probable I should have passed it over unnoticed, if your judicious observations had not pointed it out to me, with intention, I know, that I should profit by it, which I hope I shall.

I read part of your letter to my mother, who was highly pleased both with your serious reflexions, and your sprightly description of the confusion the Count's arrival occasioned in your family. Sally's terror diverted us much; I cannot but say it was natural enough in the girl, who thought he was on his way to America, to be frightened at his sudden appearance, and concluded it was something supernatural; for I dare say, she is quite convinced that Ghosts are continually stalking about the world.

Your picture of the Count is very captivating, and does great credit to Gertrude's choice; I shall be horridly disappointed if he leaves Dublin before I get there, at present I cannot judge when that will be, my mother's health is so uncertain, sometimes better, sometimes worse; though on the whole, she is not near so bad as she was, because she is not so bad for a constancy; therefore I am in hopes she will recover time enough for me to be at the wedding, as there must be letters from France, and several preliminaries settled before it comes to that.

I am not surprized that Gertrude was so much fluttered; had I been in her place it would have half killed me, but she is not such a weak creature as I am, though her form is very delicate.

I like as well as you to hear foreigners speak English; they give something I cannot describe to the language, which improves it prodigiously. I suppose you are partial to the Munster brogue, because Harry Maunsell is of that Province; not that I think he has more of the accent than just what is agreeable; no doubt you think so too, and therefore give it the preference.

My mother's good wishes with mine, wait on you, and your friends at your house.

Your's, as usual,
ELIZA FITZGERALD.

LETTER XXVII.

Miss MORTIMER, to Miss FITZGERALD.

Jan. 14. —

YOU never, I believe, had a more punctual correspondent than I am; and sure I deserve credit for it now, if I never did before, since I withdraw myself from most agreeable conversation, to enjoy the pleasure of writing to my dear Eliza, and, if possible, keep her from dwelling on unpleasing ideas, which I am sorry to find possesses your sleeping as well as your waking imagination. You bid me not be very angry with you, yet how can I be otherwise, when you give way to such a debility of mind, as to let your peace be disturbed by a dream, at a time too when you might naturally suppose it proceeded from that lowness of spirits, which I fear you but too much encourage.

I am aware you will tell me there are examples in scripture, for putting faith in the fleeting forms of the night,* and I grant there are several; but you must also grant, that when Heaven thought proper to give mankind notice of its intentions by dreams, it gave them skilful interpreters;* at present such notices would be useless, since we have no prophets, and must depend on old nurses, who always explain them according to their own fears or fancies, not having the spirit of divination to direct them. You must give me leave to say, it is being rather unthankful for the blessings you enjoy, to torment yourself with imaginary ills. If you must weep, Eliza, seek out the sons and daughters of affliction,* (with which every neighbourhood abounds) and weep over their sorrows; it will make you ashamed to brood over imaginary evils, when you see so many suffering real calamities: it will beside have this good effect, you will relieve them as far as you are able. Let me entreat you to let your understanding operate as it ought, and it is impossible you can fall into such superstitious follies.

I am really ashamed of appearing so conceited, as I am sure I must do, in taking upon me to be your instructor, but you force me to it, by laying aside the use of your own reason, for it is not that I think myself by any means qualified for the office, of which I am the more convinced, since all I have said has so little effect upon you, whose partiality would allow my arguments perhaps more weight than they deserved; yet it seems they do not carry conviction; so all I can do is to wish for Mr. Skeffington's speedy return, who I hope will at least convince you of the truth of my assertion, that the pleasures of meeting those we love, far out-ballances the pain of parting, which I acknowledge I know from experience, and I have no apprehension that your meeting will be productive of any thing but satisfaction to you both, though you are so industrious in seeking occasion to fear the contrary.

I hope both for your mother's sake, and yours, that she will be able to come to town before our affairs here are brought to a conclusion; and you have a good chance, as all the necessaries cannot be done without time.

Young Rousillon is a pleasing addition to our society: and I assure you Gertrude is much improved in chearfulness since his arrival. He puts our less lively swains quite out of their way, for he gallants us all, and I sometimes make Harry Maunsell look grave, by giving my hand to the Count, and leaving him to attend Gertrude, who I tell him is much fitter for him, because she is so sedate; he takes the first convenient opportunity of expostulating on what he calls my cruelty, in denying him the only pleasure he has to hope for, that of enjoying as much of my company as circumstances will admit.

I do but laugh at his rueful face, and tell him, situated as we are, it is absolutely ridiculous to see him always at my elbow; besides it is not in nature to resist the temptation of flirting with a French man, they do it so agreeably. He sighs, and looks sad, and is so very sorry he has not talents to make himself as pleasing as the Count, that if I did not revive his spirits by a sweet smile, which he interprets to his own liking, I should be a little afraid he would be found hanging in his garters: it is mighty silly however in him, to indulge himself in such a hopeless passion; these sort of early entanglements sometimes prevent the happiness of our future lives, we should be therefore very cautious of a first attachment; but the mischief is, we are ensnared before we think of the consequence.

Perhaps I may be a little partial to the Munster accent; nothing extraordinary that, since it has been made pleasing to my ear, by my first hearing the soft language of love in that tone, to which I think it is exceedingly well adapted; no doubt the northern accent* is music to you.

I expect to hear in your next Charles is safe arrived in London, for you may have had a letter from him by this time.——This unmerciful Frenchman thinks we should never be weary of public amusements, and is continually hurrying us from one to another, till I am half dead with fatigue, for you know I am not fond of a life of dissipation, but as it is not to last long, I submit, and he is now calling me to the play.* I must therefore subscribe myself

My dear Eliza's,

Affectionate,

LOUISA MORTIMER.

LETTER XXVIII.

Miss FITZGERALD, to Miss MORTIMER.

Jan. 17. ——

I ACKNOWLEGE my dear Louisa is not only the most punctual, but the most agreeable correspondent I could possibly have, and I might add, the most instructive, without being accused of flattery; for any one who saw your letters must allow, more persuasive arguments cannot be advanced, than what you set forth to engage me to conquer the little weaknesses of my disposition. I am thankful for your kind intentions, and determined to follow your advice and example, and become a rational creature as fast as I can, or I find I am likely to be very unhappy, since one should in this life meet perpetual cause for uneasiness, if, as I have done, they always look at the worst side of every event, and give themselves up to fruitless repinings: I will therefore try to fortify my mind against disagreeable circumstances, as I think it very probable I shall have some such to encounter, from that unfortunate defect in Charles's temper, which he seems himself to have such doubts of conquering.

I have had a letter from him since I wrote to you; he was in London, but meant to leave it next day and set out for Sussex,* to settle the business he went on. He took over young McNeil, and will settle him there as his agent, since he is of tried integrity; and the person that hitherto managed his English estate, has certainly not been honest.

When Charles has concluded his business he will return to London, and see every thing that is worth seeing there, before his return: but a month, he says, will be more than sufficient for that; and he hopes to find me in Dublin, as he will not go to the castle till summer, unless my mother's illness should detain me there longer than we expected. He says the English women are handsome, and in general, fairer than the Irish; yet he gives the preference to his country-women, for the modest sweetness of their looks.

I cannot but join with Mr. Maunsell, in thinking it rather cruel of you to give another the pleasure of attending you, when you know it would make him happy, especially since (as he observes) it is the only happiness he is likely to enjoy with you; and besides, he seldom has opportunity for that; being the greatest part of his time separated from you; that I think he deserves some little consideration: but I believe, my dear Louisa has now and then a small propensity towards flirting.

But pray how does Gertrude approve of your engaging the Count? I should suppose she would not be much obliged to you for the exchange, as it is likely Mr. Maunsell is not at such times a very chearful companion, though he is usually extremely pleasing. I allow his constancy to you, who have crushed all his hopes, is no great proof of his wisdom, but I would be glad to know, who that loved was ever wise except yourself, and we cannot expect to meet with prodigies often. You advise me to what most people would think a bad remedy for low spirits; to visit the afflicted: I always thought so myself, and therefore avoided it, though my purse was always open to those who applied to me: however I have such an opinion of your judgement, that I am resolved to try what effect it will have. On consideration, I believe you are quite right, for they must have very little humanity that would not forget their own afflictions, when they saw others suffering much greater; and very little religion, that would not be thankful to Heaven for exempting them from such calamities.

The obvious consequence is, one will be ashamed to complain of trifling ills.—Why could not I think of that before? but you see by it how much I need your instructions, and that they do carry conviction, though they did not take effect all at once: so I hope you will not give up an office, you are so capable of; for without your advice, I feel that I should often act very foolishly.

Your arguments against believing in dreams, is so conclusive, I could not help reading it to my mother, who used to be a great advocate for them; she seemed struck with what you said, and, after a short silence, indeed Eliza, says she, I never considered the matter in that light, and do not know that it can be confuted: but this I know, I never met with any young lady who has so just a way of thinking on every subject as Miss Mortimer; I am sure, my dear, you will not be jealous that I do not except you, which with all my partiality I cannot; but your friend is four years, at least, older than you, and has made so good use of her time, that many women old enough to be her mother, might be improved by her conversation.

I will not tell you all she said of you, because I know it distresses you to hear your own praises; but you may believe, it gratified me very much.

My mother intends going into the drawing-room to-day, for the first time; I wish she may not take cold: She joins me in sincere affection to you.

Your's, in tenderest friendship,
ELIZA FITZGERALD.

LETTER XXIX.

Miss MORTIMER, to Miss FITZGERALD.

Jan. 25. —

A RE not you surprised at my long silence? to be sure you are, as it is very unusual with me to neglect writing to my dear Eliza for so many days; but your wonder will cease when I tell you, I am absolutely out of breath with the hurry this wicked Count has put us all into. You have not the least chance of being at the wedding, for the preparations are going on with unreasonable speed, and the settlements are actually very near finished, he has so effectually quickened the clerks.*

He got letters from France soon after I wrote to you last, I believe the day or two after; he says himself, it was as soon as an answer could possibly arrive; and immediately he communicated them to Gertrude and me, requesting if we disapproved of any part, I might say so, and it should be altered. There was, however, no objection to be made, every thing was done so genteely by his father. When I signified my approbation, (for you must know I am her guardian on this occasion) he told me, he should immediately give proper orders to an Attorney, and hoped I would use my influence with Miss St. George, to prevail on her not to make unnecessary delays, but fix an early day for his happiness.

I undertook the embassy, and gave it as my opinion, that she should not take an unreasonable time, as he is appointed to a place at Court,* and will return home as soon as he conveniently can; for I believe he will be permitted to go on parole. She mentioned four or five weeks, and then said six or seven, upon which I left her, lest she should increase it to so many months; and telling him what she had said, he began to exclaim most vehemently in French, against her determination; and begged me to remember what a tedious time that would be to him, who had already suffered such a long probation, by losing her just at the time he had hoped to be united to her for ever.

I then told him, if he would leave it to me, I would endeavour to get her consent for the 10th of next month, which will be her birth-day, and sooner than that, he could not expect. He said he would abide by my decision, and after much persuasion, she agreed to it, but insisted it looked like being in too great a hurry.

This weighty point being settled, there is a thousand little matters to be done, as we do not know how soon after the marriage they will set out for France. The sight of those preparations recalls to poor Harry's memory the time when he returned to Ireland, in full hope of being in that situation, and the idea, that all his prospects of happiness in that way, are now shut in, makes him sigh; and at times raises a momentary sadness in my heart; not that I cannot marry him, believe me, I have no regrets on that account, but because I see the disappointment continues to sit too heavily on him. The Count, whom I find, he has let into the secret, said to me to-day, "Ah! Miss Mortimer, my happiness reminds poor Mr. Maunsell of his disappointment; can you give him no hope?" I laid my hand upon his mouth; "that is a prohibited subject, Count; the thing is impossible; Mr. Maunsell knows it is." He shook his head, and with the softest expression of compassion in his eyes, (you know how expressive French eyes are) said, "'tis pity, 'tis great pity!" I am sure he makes Harry much worse than he would be, by pitying him, and indulging him in talking over the affair; for he was chearful and easy before.

You say it is cruel in me to let any one else attend me; you do not, however, consider, that though there may be no impropriety in his making a public shew of his attachment to me, it would not be quite so proper for me to do so; which I should in effect, if I refused the little offices of politeness from any other man: and notwithstanding you say, I have a propensity to flirting, you know me too well to think I could find any pleasure in giving pain to a heart that doats on me: but you must confess, we are in a very peculiar situation, and it requires some degree of circumspection to avoid the tongue of slander.

Gertrude was not a bit displeased with me for leaving Harry to be her Gentleman-Usher; for besides that, he is a great favourite with her, she was well pleased not to be the object of the Count's attention in public. So you see the exchange served two good purposes, it kept people from making particular observations, either on her or me.

I rejoice to hear your mother can leave her room, and am not a little proud of her good opinion.

Adieu, dear girl;
Your's ever,
LOUISA MORTIMER.

LETTER XXX.

Miss FITZGERALD, to Miss MORTIMER.

Jan. 28. —

ITHINK this last jaunt of mine to the country has produced nothing but disagreeable events. In the first place, it separated me from my Louisa; then it
deprived me of meeting Emily; of seeing the Volunteers; gave occasion for
Charles's jealousy to break out; and to sum up all, the coldness of the place
brought on my mother's illness, which will now detain me from Gertrude's
wedding; and that, I acknowlege, is a very great mortification to me; and what
is still worse, I have no one pleasing reflection to make me amends for all my
disappointments, except that my mother continues tolerably, and I have hopes
we shall get to town in less than a month.

I never liked the Country in winter, and from this time, I believe I shall hate
the sight of it.

My acquaintance with the Miss Boyle's is the only agreeable circumstance
that has occurred since I left Dublin: I fancy they will be in town before me, as
the servants they left in the house, tell our's, they expect their master soon; and
I know he was to come home when his daughters set out for town. When I
come, I will introduce them to you.

I have been trying the experiment you recommended to me, Louisa, and it
has succeeded to the utmost of your wishes. I am ashamed of having ever been
so unthankful for the many blessings I enjoy; as to overlook them all, and make
myself unhappy with the apprehension of evils, that, perhaps, may never come
to pass; and if they did, would not be equal to half the miseries which I have
seen one family patiently suffering; but people bred up in ease and affluence,
have no idea of what real misfortune is; and therefore lament as such, trifles that
ought not to give a reasonable creature a moment's pain.

The day after I wrote to you last, I took Kitty with me in the chaise, and
went about three miles off, where she told me there were several poor Cottagers
on the estate of a young gentleman now on his travels; for thank Heaven, the
lower class of tenants on Charles's estate, or mine, are none of them in want.*
We had turned into a bye-road that led to a few scattered cabbins, and were
driving towards the nearest, when I saw a pretty girl, about nine years old, run
out, and clapping her hands together, in an agony of grief, cried out, "Oh! my
mammy! my mammy!" and without seeming to hear the carriage, in a manner
flew across the road to a cottage at the other side, into which she went. The
child's exclamation raised both my pity and curiosity, as I guessed it must be
occasioned by some distress she had left her mother in; and calling John to stop,
I stepped out, followed by Kitty, and went directly into the house: but what a

scene of woe presented itself! at one side of the room lay the corpse of a man, on a bed; at the other, near the dying embers of a turf fire, lay the woman on a bed of straw, in a fainting fit; an infant about three days old, sleeping at her side. With Kitty's assistance I raised her, and applied my Eau de Luce* to her nose, which soon revived her, and she looked wildly round; when casting her eyes on her dead husband, she clapped her hands over them, as if unable to bear the sight, and cried out, who was so cruel as to bring me back to a life of misery! I bid her be comforted, as I hoped she and her children would yet be happy. The strange voice struck her ear, (for I believe she never observed my appearance) and she took down her hand to view me, just as the little girl came in, followed by an old woman.

They all looked astonished, and seemed at a loss to account for what they saw; when I, who was supporting the poor woman, and apprehensive she would faint again, asked if they had any thing fit to give her? The old woman with tears in her eyes, answered, she feared there was nothing but a little butter-milk, and a few potatoes, which the poor neighbours brought in. I then called for some water, and gave her a little, with Eau de Luce in it, which recovered her from the faintishness; and tears flowing plentifully, she was much relieved, and we laid her down again.

I sent John to an Inn about half a mile off, for a bottle of Wine, and some other refreshments; and while he was away, enquired of the old woman, how the people came into such distress. She told me the man had been a Linen-Weaver, near Armagh;* and lived very comfortably, till he fell into a lingering illness; which disabled him from working, and having nothing to support him but what his wife earned by spinning, they were forced to sell most of their furniture, to pay their rent, and brought the small remainder to the place they were now in, where they had been but a few months; they made a shift to maintain themselves by the woman's industry, and what little the child could do, till the man grew so bad, his wife could do nothing but attend him, and they were reduced to the greatest distress, when to add to it, she was brought to bed a few days ago; that she staid with them as much as she could, and had not left them half an hour, when the child ran to tell her, her father was dead, and her mother dying; she concluded with saying, she hoped Heaven had sent me that way for their relief.

John returned sooner than I could have expected, and I gave the woman some warm Wine and Water, and gave directions for a Chicken he had brought to be made into broth for her, and the old woman undertook to stay and do every thing that was proper, to whom I gave some money to provide firing, and whatever was necessary for that night: promising to send a supply from our house next day.

You may be sure I rewarded her for her trouble, in a manner that will secure her attendance while it is wanted; and as soon as the woman is well enough, I intend to bring her to a neat little house that is now unoccupied on my lands, where she shall be rent-free, till she can, by her industry (for I do not wish to encourage idleness) get a few guineas to lay by, and then I will let her have it at a very easy rent: the garden is now well cropped, so that she will have nothing to do but attend her spinning for some time.

I am now convinced that the wise man's saying, It is better to go to the house of mourning,* provided one makes a proper use of the lesson it teaches; for those poor people's distress has engrossed all my thoughts; and relieving them, given me more pleasing reflections than ever I enjoyed before on doing a charitable action: because till now, I never saw the wretchedness from which I relieved the objects of my compassion.

While I stay in the country, I shall often step into the little huts, and see what way the poor inhabitants are in, and in Dublin the news-papers frequently furnish us with notice where to find the distressed:* for the future I shall always visit them myself; it will teach me to set a proper value on the blessings that are extended to me, and to bear light evils without repining.

I will not again pretend to blame you in regard to Mr. Maunsell, for I acknowlege you are uncommonly circumstanced; nor do I know a woman, except yourself, that would act with such propriety in the same situation: but I cannot help pitying him. No doubt, the Count, who has so much sensibility, is quite affected with his melancholy tale.

I hope soon to hear from Charles in London, for then his stay in England will not be very much longer; perhaps we may reach Dublin nearly at the same time. Do you think James has made any declaration to Emily yet? I find all our family look on it as a match very likely to take place: I hope it may.

Tell Gertrude how mortified I am that I cannot fill the office of Bride-Maid at her nuptials, which I had promised myself I should. Who is she to have beside you. Believe me, dear Louisa,

Your affectionate,
ELIZA FITZGERALD.

LETTER XXXI.

Miss MORTIMER, to Miss FITZGERALD.

Feb. 1. —

I HAVE got such a habit of answering my dear Eliza's letters immediately, that it is a distress to me to miss a post; but in the present posture of affairs here, I am obliged to do it; and until the hurry is a little over, I think you will not hear from me again.

What a bustle a wedding makes in a family; even the servants are anxious to have their finery ready on the occasion; and I assure you, our maidens will make no small figure, as Gertrude insisted on bedizening* them all at her own expence, not excepting Emily's damsel, who by the way, is quite a Belle amongst her own class, and I believe is much delighted at being permitted to throw off her mourning for that night, when I dare say, she will appear in all her airs, for I see she lays herself out for admiration.

There are to be three Bride-Maids, besides your humble servant, all Gertrude's near relations; and she could not ask one without offending the rest; so she might as well let them all have the name of it. There is Miss Ponsonby; and the two Miss Fortescue's; you know they are very young ladies, and I find they had set their hearts on the matter, for they all came together, to pay her a visit, and when she asked them to be her Bride-Maids, their eyes sparkled with joy, and it was impossible not to smile at the eagerness with which they accepted the invitation, and the hurry they were in to be gone, that they might buy new gowns, and a million of other things, which they repeated with amazing volubility, all talking at once; and I dare say, have talked and thought of little else since: though we do not mean to make any great parade of it, there must be a good many people, as it is a compliment she cannot avoid paying some uncles, aunts, and cousins, that are now in town; I think it best so, for I always observe, the more company there is, the less notice is taken of the Bride, their attention being engaged by each other.

I wish the affair was over for Gertrude's sake, who begins to look serious as the day draws near; I am not surprised she should, as it will make such a material difference in every circumstance of her life; it is not only the change from a single state, in which she is intirely mistress of her own actions, to one wherein she must accommodate herself to the temper and disposition of another, but it will also remove her from her country, and all her connexions, and place her amongst people who can have no other attachment to her, than what her own merit may entitle her to. No wonder her reflections should be rather melancholy; I must confess, I think she stands in need of all her affection for the Count, and a large share of philosophy besides, to enable her to support her spirits. One thing is much in her favour, that is, she is so little alone, that she has scarce any time for thinking. Was I in her place, it is my opinion I should have declared off, when I came to consider the consequence.

Harry expects to hear from Charles when he has seen a little of London; I am not sure that I did not tell you that before.

I was a good deal affected for your poor family, and should have been quite distressed but that I knew, now you had met with them, they would be effectually relieved: I must beg of you to give them five guineas, to make some little addition to their furniture and cloaths, and set it down to my account, it would be too much for you to take it all upon yourself, when you will meet with so many others that want your assistance.

I knew your visiting the afflicted would have the desired effect, because you are alive to the distresses of your fellow-creatures. You are not one of those who fancy they are possessed of superfine feelings, yet never feel for any one but themselves, and are so apprehensive of hurting their spirits, that their dearest friends, if in sickness or affliction, must find some one of less feeling, and more humanity, to perform the tender offices of friendship; for in this age of delicate nerves, the terms are by no means synonimous. I am sure we know one or two ladies who are always talking of their fine feelings, and were never yet known to do a good-natured or charitable action.

I am obliged to you for your approbation, though at the expence of the rest of the Sex; it is no reflection on them, however, for I believe a peculiarity of sentiment is necessary to enable one to conduct themselves in such a particular situation as mine; and that cannot be expected from many, nor do such circumstances often occur. Indeed there is very few to whom my example should be recommended; for it would be a most dangerous state to those who have great sensibility, and very little command of their passions, to keep up an intimate friendship with a young man they like, and are effectually restrained from marrying: the tryal would be too great for female fortitude to support, if not assisted by such a singularity of disposition as I happen to possess. If Harry's was similar, there would be no more debating on Platonic Love, as we should be proof positive of its existence. As it is, I think the point must remain undecided.

Yes, the Count deplores Harry's misfortune in the most pathetic terms, and Harry, in consequence, is mighty sad, and mighty silly: I should be obliged to alter my conduct towards him, if I did not conclude that his friends departure, which is not far off, will restore him to his understanding.

What a detail you have given of the disagreeable events produced by your going to the country; they were not very pleasing to be sure, however, I look upon the accident which occasioned Charles's jealousy to break out, as rather fortunate than otherwise: had it been smothered till after you were married, the consequence would have been much worse, since you would have no remedy but parting, which will be much better done before marriage, if you should find him incurable, but I hope you will not.

No, I do not believe Mr. Fitzgerald and Emily have come to any explanation; but his behaviour cannot be mistaken, she is forced to acknowlege it cannot, and is grown more reserved to him upon it, probably that deters him from speaking; he fears to give her offence by entering on such a subject so early in her widowhood, as he must see she studiously avoids giving him any opportunity. I am, however, of opinion, it will come to something in due time, for she does not dislike him, and can have no other objection to him, unless her father forbid the banns, on account of his fortune not being equal to her's; but I am in hopes he will allow his birth to make up for the deficiency, as I know he sets some value on ancient gentility; a new title would not have half the weight with him.

I should not have thought of the objection, only Mr. O'Neil is so fond of money; otherwise I would suppose he might think his fortune and her's together, quite sufficient for happiness, as his is not inconsiderable, and her's very large, exclusive of what is settled on the child. James is exceeding fond of the little thing, and I can tell you, that is no bad way of paying his court to its grandfather, who is mighty foolish about the baby: it is a pretty creature too, and one cannot help taking notice of it.

My next will give you an account of the wedding; Gertrude wishes you could be with her. Tea waits, while I tell you, I am, most affectionately,

Your's,

LOUISA MORTIMER.

END OF THE FIRST VOLUME.

THE

TRIUMPH

O F

PRUDENCE over PASSION:

OR, THE

HISTORY

O F

MISS MORTIMER

A N D

MISS FITZGERALD.

By the AUTHORESS of EMELINE.

IN TWO VOLUMES.

VOL. II.

D U B L I N:

Printed (for the Author) by S. COLBERT, No. 136,
Capel-street, opposite Abbey-street.
M,DCC,XXXI.

THE

RECONCILIATION;

OR

HISTORY

OF

Miss *MORTIMER,*

AND

Miss *FITZGERALD.*

An Hibernian Novel.

IN TWO VOLUMES.

By an IRISH LADY.

VOL. II.

LONDON:

Printed for W. LANE, *Leadenhall-Street.*

M D CC LXXXIII.

THE

HISTORY

OF

Miss MORTIMER,

AND

Miss FITZGERALD.

VOLUME THE SECOND

LETTER XXXII.

Miss FITZGERALD, to Miss MORTIMER.

Feb. 6.—

ICOULD not get time till this day, to answer my Louisa's very agreeable favour, of the 1st instant, as some old friends of my mother's have been with us these ten days, and I could not leave them long enough to compose an epistle, for we were always engaged either in conversation or cards, as I happened to please the old ladies; and besides that, they played whist, and could not make a party without me.

I had a letter from Charles yesterday; he had settled his affairs to his satisfaction, and was returned to London, where, he says, his stay will be but short, though he has made some agreeable acquaintances, and is engaged in a perpetual round of amusements; but adds, he has so little relish for them when I am absent, that he shall quit them very soon without the least regret, and hasten to Dublin, where he hopes to meet me. Though I have not the least doubt of his affection, I do not think myself bound to give credit to all he says on the subject; especially as the liveliness of his stile contradicts what he says of not having a relish for amusement; I dare say, he enjoys them with a very good goût,* nor am I so weak as to expect he should not have any satisfaction but when I am present.

Poor Gertrude! Indeed I think she must have a good deal of resolution, if she can keep up her spirits tolerably on the approaching change in her condition; for there is something very melancholy in the idea, of leaving ones friends and country for ever: I shall be extremely sorry if they go before I get to town; though to be sure she will come over now and then to see us all, and no doubt you will sometimes pay her a visit; if I can prevail on my mother to undertake it, we will make a party to spend two or three months at Montpellier; and I think she would be the better of it.

Gertrude's cousins are fine girls, I hope she will provide agreeable young men for their partners: Harry Maunsell, without doubt, will be a bride's-man,* but we all know who will be the object of his attention. You say there is very few to whom your example should be recommended; and I will venture to assert, there is very few indeed who would chuse to follow it; for notwithstanding the many pretenders to sentiment in both sexes, there is not one in a thousand that has really such refined notions, as to be capable of considering love in any other light than as a passion; so you need not be the least apprehensive that any of the Misses will bring themselves into danger, by attempting to adopt your ideas on the subject: for I must confess you have a singularity in your opinions, that is perfectly adapted to your situation; or, I believe, it will be rather more proper to say, you have adapted your situation to your sentiments; for it is certainly of your own chusing. You are a character, my dear Louisa, an amiable one, every body acknowledges, but at the same time, very uncommon for so young a person. I wish I was just such another, for I do not know any body so happy.

You are very severe on fine feelings, and I cannot but say, the ladies you hint at have left you great room to be so; however, I think it can be only an affectation of sensibility, when one feels only for themselves; but weak nerves are so fashionable, there is no being a fine lady without them.

I have got my poor woman removed to her new habitation, and presented her with your generous donation; part of which she will apply to the purposes you mention, when she is able to attend to those matters; as yet she is very weak, though surprizingly recovered since she has had proper care and nourishment; where she is now all her neighbours will assist her, till she is well enough to do her own work; and I am sure they will always be kind to her, for they know it will oblige me; and besides that, the natural disposition of our country people, is compassionate in a high degree: even the poor creatures she lived near, when I met with her, shared their scanty provision with her; I gave them all some little matter, and will do more for them hereafter. I need hardly tell you what prayers were put up for your happiness, when I gave her your present; one may easily see the woman has known better days, she has such decent notions.

I shall be dull on the 10th, with the recollection of all the amusement I lose by being here. I shall expect you will write to me next day, and will long for the arrival of the post.

I think it is quite right in Emily to discourage any declaration from James till she has changed her mourning,* at least; there is something very indelicate in a woman listening to a lover, while in her weeds; even though she had no reason to lament her husband: but in a proper time I hope she will lay aside her reserve, and that her father will not object, though James has but a thousand a year, and she has four,* besides all the money he can give her; yet the qualities of his mind ought to be considered. I shall be much concerned if he is disappointed.

My mother joins me in wishing Gertrude all the happiness she can expect or desire; as well as in affectionate regards to you.

I am,

> Dear Louisa,
> Unalterably your's,
> ELIZA FITZGERALD.

LETTER XXXIII.

Miss MORTIMER, to Miss FITZGERALD.

Feb. 11.—

IT was a most unconscionable task you imposed on me, Eliza, to write the day after a wedding, when all the folks are crouding* to pay their compliments, and I as mistress of the house ought to be ready to receive them; however as I feared the disappointment might be too much for you, I have left the bride to do the honours to her own company, with Mrs. Rochfort to assist her: and I assure you, Gertrude looks very matronly to-day, and becomes her title extremely. I have quite provoked her, by saying, her ladyship when I spoke of her, or to her; you may think it was to make her laugh I did it, as you know I am not much dazzled by titles:* but I must tell you about yesterday; for to hear of a wedding is the delight of all females, from fifteen to fifty. Gertrude, by my advice, was dressed early, and in the drawing-room before the company came, as I thought it would distress her less than coming in where they were all assembled; she had only a white sattin night-gown and petticoat, trimmed with ermine, gauze apron, and blond cap, and robbins, with a very fine net tippet, no jewels, except three brilliant pins in her cap, which there was no being without, but she wore as few as possible, because she did not wish to be glittering. My gown was off the same piece, trimmed also like hers, but I had a lay-lock sattin petticoat,* elegantly quilted; the rest of my dress quite in her stile, except I had a beautiful painted gauze shawl, instead of a tippet: her cousins were as fine as hands could make them, in white and silver, and a profusion of diamonds in their hair.

Captain St. George, and Mr. Fitzmaurice were bride's-men, as were Mr. Fitzgerald, and Harry Maunsell.

The Count had a suit of pearl colour tabbinet,* with a slight pattern of silver, and he really looked very handsome; but I have seen Gertrude look better than she did; she was rather pale, and kept up her spirits very indifferently: a woman cannot appear to advantage at her own wedding, unless she is very thoughtless indeed.*

The company were all assembled at seven o'clock, and the instant the tea-table was removed, the bride-groom stept forward, and leading out the bride, the ceremony was immediately performed, and she went through it much better than I expected, but was very near fainting when it was over; she soon recovered herself, and when cake and wine was handed about, we all sat down to cards, till supper, except Mr. O'Neil, and your cousin James, who retired into another room, and played back-gammon till ten o'clock, when the old gentleman went home, but as a very particular compliment to Gertrude and me, permitted his wife to stay as long as she pleased; and I assure you, that was a very great favour to us, and a remarkable indulgence to her; had I been his wife, it is an indulgence I would take without his leave, for I should not submit to be treated like a child.

Supper passed over chearfully, and about twelve, Mrs. Ponsonby, (being the oldest matron in company) rose to withdraw, and was followed by all the ladies: Gertrude, indeed, would have encreased her own confusion, by being the last to move, only I perceived her slowness, and pretending her chair was on my gown, obliged her to rise, and putting her forward amongst the bride-maids, hurried her off, before the gentlemen had time to observe her; when the young ladies had got garter and pins to dream on,* all the women went home, and the Count quitting his company soon after, they were all gone by one o'clock. To-day we had several morning visitors, and the young folks that were at the marriage, are to spend the evening with us. This week will be intirely taken up in receiving compliments, and the next in returning them; for as Gertrude's stay here will be very short, it is necessary for her to get that piece of ceremony over as soon as possible: I shall be heartily glad when it is over, for I am fatigued with the bustle we have had this while past; you know I am no friend to a continual round of dissipation. I have not time now to take notice of your last, nor does it require any particular answer. I give you joy of hearing from Charles, and hope I shall soon see you both in Dublin.

Farewell, dear Eliza,
Affectionately your's,
LOUISA MORTIMER.

LETTER XXXIV.

Mr. SKEFFINGTON, to Mr. MAUNSELL.

London, Feb. 12. —

DEAR MAUNSELL,

I HAVE been about three weeks in this centre of Amusements, and so borne down by the torrent of dissipation with which people here are overwhelmed, that I could not find time to perform my promise of writing to you, till this day, that a violent cold has obliged me to stay at home and nurse myself; I got it by walking home late from a Tavern.

To confess the truth, raking* does not agree with me, but it is scarce possible to withstand the temptations that are continually thrown in one's way, in a place where vice puts on the most alluring form, and covers her deformity with the specious appearance of pleasure, which one must be almost insensible to resist; at least, till experience has taught us wisdom.

You cautioned me against Sharpers, and I was on my guard; but you did not tell me, I might be in as much danger from those whose birth intitled them to be called Gentlemen; but perhaps you never met with such, I would hardly believe it myself, if I had not purchased my knowledge at the extravagant rate of two thousand pounds. I did not at first suspect, but latterly I perceived the cheat, and rising, gave the gentleman a draft on my Banker for the money, informing him at the same time, I did not chuse to play any longer with one who understood all the game; and instantly quit the room, expecting he would follow to demand an explanation, as there was a deal of company present, who all heard what I said.

It happened as I thought, for I had not gone ten yards when he came up with me, and asking what my words meant, I answered, the meaning was so very obvious it could scarcely be mistaken; on which he drew his sword, and bid me defend myself: I did it so effectually, that in less than a minute I wounded him in the sword arm, and the weapon dropped from his hand; as he bled fast, I advised him to return to the house we had just left, and send for a Surgeon; then bidding him good night, stepped into a Chair* I met, and went home very much dissatisfied with myself.

I had no apology for playing so deep, because my fortune is already too large to receive any advantage from winning that sum, and though the loss is no way material to me, yet since I had it to spare, I might have disposed of it in a way that would have made several happy: the event too, might have been fatal, and duelling,* you know, I greatly disapprove; but when his unfair practices were so plain, that I must see it, I should have been looked on either as a fool or a coward, if I had not taken notice of it.

I took great care, however, not to wound him in a dangerous place, for I soon perceived he had very little skill: he is recovering fast, but I shall always chuse to avoid his company, as I must dislike the man; besides, I am determined never to play again, but for a few guineas, which will not be worth any one's while to cheat for.

My intercourse with the other Sex has been more agreeable; for affairs of Gallantry have offered every day without my seeking. I should be sorry my lovely Eliza knew how I have been led astray, though they were only venial transgressions, in which the heart was no way concerned, and indeed, the man must be void of all passion that could withstand such temptations.

The women have such a fund of vivacity, that they are the most agreeable mistresses in the world; but for a wife, I would prefer the more reserved chear-fulness of my pretty country-women. That, perhaps, may be prejudice; for it is likely an English-man would think them insipid.

I have paid pretty high for my amusements in this way, though I assure you, it was not with those who set their charms to sale; but presents must be made, and of value according to the rank of the fair one.

In all my dealings here, I find money is the Idol of the place,* and the whole force of the people's genius is turned towards the different methods of obtaining it.

I often think if a medium could be struck between the English and the Irish, it would just produce a proper standard whereby to regulate our œconomy;* for one loves Gold too much for their eternal welfare, the other too little for their temporal peace; as their total disregard of it keeps their domestic affairs in continual embarrassment: I speak of the general character of the two nations; for I know there are many exceptions in each.

I made an acquaintance in Sussex, with a Miss Freeman,* who was in a visit with a family where I was intimate; she lives in London, and when she was coming to town, a few days before me, gave me an invitation to her aunt's house in Jermyn-street,* where she lives. I availed myself of it, and have passed several agreeable evenings there.

They are genteel people, and very pleasing. Miss Freeman is a pretty lively girl, about nineteen; her aunt's daughter something younger, and handsomer, but more serious than her cousin. I find the former has a large fortune at her own disposal: I believe the aunt gave me that hint with some view, but my heart is already fixed, and if Eliza's sentiments remain unaltered at my return, I have nothing more to wish for, except being at age, as I cannot marry till then; but I have a very short time to wait for that.

I shall not expect to hear from you, since I mean to set out for Ireland in less than a week, and hope to find you and all those I most wish to see, in Dublin.

My best compliments to Miss Mortimer, but do not tell her I am indisposed, for I shall write to Eliza this post, and will not mention it, lest she should be uneasy.

Tell Fitzgerald, I have just received his letter, and will answer it if I have time, before I quit London.

Adieu, dear Maunsell:

Your's,

C. SKEFFINGTON.

LETTER XXXV.

Miss FITZGERALD, to Miss MORTIMER.

Feb. 14. —

I HAD the pleasure of my dear Louisa's letter, with an account of the wedding, and beg you will make my mother's compliments of congratulation, with mine, acceptable to Madame La Comtesse. Seriously, no one can wish her happier than we do; and I hope to have an opportunity of telling her so in person, before she leaves Ireland, as we are to set out for Dublin in ten days, which has raised my spirits more effectually, than a large dose of ASSA-FÆTIDA.* Indeed there is no one inducement here, to make me wish to stay; for though the place is beautiful in Summer, at this season I can find nothing pleasing in the country, especially when every one is gone to town, except a few old ladies and gentlemen, that are kept prisoners by the Gout, or else are past all inclination for amusement; and them you may think cannot be very agreeable companions for me.

Mr. Boyle, who returned a few days ago, is the only one that keeps us alive; he left his daughters in Dublin, and brought me a letter from the eldest, requesting, if I was not to be in town very soon, I would give her some excuse to make you a visit; for she longs of all things to be acquainted with you: and though she could be easily introduced, by some who visit you, yet, as an intimacy is what she wishes for, she says, that would be sooner accomplished if she brought her credentials from me; these are her own words.

I have wrote, to inform her, I shall soon be in town, when I shall perform the part of Sir Clement Cottrel,* and introduce her to your presence. Mean time, if you should meet her in company, as probably you may, I flatter myself, you will, on my recommendation, make some advances towards an acquaintance; and I am very sure you will like her, and her sister too, though not so well, for the reasons I mentioned. She is equally desirous of being acquainted with you.

Their father will be in town again shortly.

I have not heard from Charles since. Little as he says he relishes amusements, I find they engage a good deal of his attention, else he might have wrote to me more than once, since he has been in London.

I expect you will answer this, as I have still ten days to stay here; and my next will be just to tell you, what day I set out for Dublin.

I am going with my mother to take an airing; must, therefore, conclude abruptly.

Your's, affectionately,
ELIZA FITZGERALD.

———

I hope Gertrude has recovered her spirits, now the awful* day is over.

LETTER XXXVI.

Miss MORTIMER, to Miss FITZGERALD.

Feb. 17. —

MY dear Eliza's letter has given me infinite pleasure, by informing me I may soon hope to see her. Gertrude too, is quite joyful, for she began to fear she should be gone before you arrived.

Yes, she begins to lay aside her melancholy, except at times, when she thinks of leaving us; and I assure you, it is well you have had a letter from your Swain, who he supposes has left London ere this; but you will hear from him by this post, for he says, at the conclusion of his, to Harry, he was going to write to you.

He mentions a Miss Freeman he is acquainted with there, and her cousin, as pretty agreeable girls; and says, he passes some of his hours very pleasingly with them; you need not, however, be alarmed, for he, in the same paragraph, speaks of you as the mistress of his heart.

Mr. Maunsell read all those extracts to me, but did not offer to shew me the letter, from which I guess he gives some account of his Adventures;* and I believe the adventures of young men in London are not always fit for females to hear; so I would not ask to see it.

I hope this is the last I shall write to you for this season, as I expect the return of the post will inform me that you set out in a day or two. What delightful news that will be!

Adieu, dear girl. Commend me to Mrs. Fitzgerald, who I hope will get well through her journey; and be assured, I am,

my dear Eliza,

Affectionately your's,

LOUISA MORTIMER.

LETTER XXXVII.

Miss FITZGERALD, to Miss MORTIMER.

Feb. 22. ——

I HAVE the pleasure to acquaint my dear Louisa, we shall begin our journey the 24th; but as my mother is still weak, and cannot bear fatigue, we shall be four days on the road, so the 28th in the evening I expect to find you waiting for me, that we may lose no time, in once more enjoying each other's society.

The same post brought me your letter, and one from Charles; as you supposed he will not leave London till the 27th; and as he does not mean to travel post,* I shall be in Dublin some days before him. He does not mention Miss Freeman to me, but I assure you, I am not a bit inclined to be jealous of her, or any other person; I am rather apt to fear my uneasiness will arise from Mr. Skeffington's having too much affection for me, than too little; but I hope his going more into the gay world than he used to do, will cure him of any little defect in his temper, for people who have confined themselves much to their study, are apt to fall into some particularity, which they grow ashamed of when they see more of life.

I wish Mr. Maunsell had shewn you his letter, for his not doing it, makes me think there was something about me in it, that he was unwilling you should see: though upon consideration, I believe it is more likely to be as you imagine; for as Harry knows how much you interest yourself in my happiness, he would hardly conceal any thing that was material to it from you.

I am obliged to you for your intention of taking notice of the Miss Boyles, if you meet them before I arrive, I would not request it of you, but I am sure you will find them agreeable, and I expect we shall be very happy together, while they stay in town, which I dare say will be till the Parliament is up, for their aunt stays till then.

I have no doubt but you will cure Harriet of her affectation, for I never met with any one that had the art of making one ashamed of their own foibles, without giving offence, equal to you; your raillery is so void of satire, that it both pleases and instructs.

I do think it is best for Mr. Maunsell to be absent from you; for though I have no idea he can ever cease to love you, since his attachment is of so long a standing, yet I dare say, variety of objects will amuse his mind, and keep it from dwelling so incessantly on a subject that must distress him, as he has not the most distant hope to support his spirits with; and I agree with you, that some variation of place and company, is absolutely necessary to make life pleasing: a love of society* is natural to us, and without enjoying it in a moderate degree, every one must sink into gloominess, and, like your friends, will grow peevish and dissatisfied, for it is impossible that three or four people, living constantly together, retired from the rest of the world, can always find a fund of conversation or entertainment in each other. I know it by experience, when I am in the country with my mother and Charles, who I need not tell you, are two of those I love best; yet when we are any time without company, or going abroad, I find myself grow stupid, and tired of every thing about me; to tell truth, I am at this instant in the very state I am describing, as I think my letter will convince you.

I am very glad I do not belong to the comfortable family you mention; what a treat your company must be to the young people, for I suppose they are not much delighted with the comforts of being shut up from society, though their parents may have out-lived all taste for earthly enjoyments; very thankful am I that my mother is not of that disposition.

Farewell till the 28th, when I shall have the happiness of telling you in person, how affectionately I am

Your own,
ELIZA FITZGERALD.

LETTER XXXVIII.

Miss MORTIMER, TO THE COUNTESS ROUSILLON.

May 6. —

THE receipt of my dear Gertrude's letter, relieved me from great uneasiness, which I suffered by not getting an account of your arrival in France; but the round you took, and all the visits you made to the Count's relations, on your journey, is sufficient reason for my not hearing from you sooner. I am happy to find they all received you so kindly; for politeness alone would be only what you had a right to expect; one wishes to meet with something more from the family they go into; and it gives me much satisfaction, that you have met with that tenderness and affection, which I am sure you will merit from them.

Your departure made us all melancholy; and each morning when Emily and I met at breakfast, we renewed each other's concern, by observing how lonely we were without poor Gertrude; and indeed, if I was inclined to forget you, Wilson would not let me, for she laments you daily, when she comes to take my orders, and brings her accounts for my inspection, always observing how good you were, to spare me that trouble; and I must acknowlege I have a loss of you in that respect, though she is so careful and exact, that I find it less disagreeable than it would be, if I had a different sort of person in her place; but she is faithful and honest, and I esteem such a servant to be invaluable.

I have had several letters from Harry, since you left him in London, and think he is recovering his usual chearfulness; the first to be sure was filled with lamentations and regrets, and all the etcetera's of soft nonsense; but I have absolutely prohibited that subject, on pain of returning his letters unanswered: he murmured a little at my cruelty, but was obliged to comply with the restriction; and now he writes like a rational creature, and is a very pleasing correspondent. Your CARO-SPOSO* did him no good, for he encouraged him in all his romance and folly, and only for this fortunate call to England, I should have had him sighing, and dying at my feet, till both for his sake, and my own, I would have been under a necessity of quarrelling with him; when he goes to France, I beg you will not indulge him in talking of certain circumstances, that had better be forgot.

Mr. Hamilton has been in town this month; Charles and he are on the most friendly terms, without any appearance of the suspicions his presence formerly raised; so you may judge how happy Eliza is: I suppose matters will soon be brought to a conclusion there, as Mr. Skeffington will be at age* early in June, and then I think there will be nothing to prevent it.

Miss Freeman, that you heard him mention, has been in Dublin some weeks, and I have a strong idea, that it is an attachment to Charles has brought her over. She says, she was ordered sea-sickness* for a disorder in her stomach; and as she had a desire to see Dublin, she thought she might as well come here as any where; the story is plausible, and I fancy is believed by every one but me: however, if she was ill, the remedy has been very effectual, for she has not the least remains of any complaint whatever; besides, I think it very extraordinary, that her friends would let her come to a strange country, in such ill health, without any companion but her waiting-maid.

She has brought letters of introduction to some genteel families here, who of course pay great attention to her; but I observe she takes great pains to cultivate an intimacy with Eliza, who went to visit her, on account of the civility she and her aunt had shewn Mr. Skeffington, for she sent to him the day after she arrived, and had first fixed herself in a lodging next street to him.

Eliza gave her a general invitation, to come to them whenever she was disengaged, and she avails herself of it in a manner that shews she means to be quite on free terms with her; all these things make me very observant of her, as I fear she has some scheme of supplanting Eliza in Charles's affections; I do not, however, think that would be easily done, unless she should discover that tincture of jealousy in his temper, by which he might he wrought upon.

She is rather pretty, and uncommonly lively. In my opinion, if her vivacity was a little tempered with discretion, she would be much more agreeable, for at present it borders upon levity.

I know the English women are of a more sprightly disposition than the Irish; but I never met any of them that could not set some bounds to it, but this young lady, who quite over-powers me with her amazing volubility, and you know I have a downright horror of being talked to death. One happiness to her hearers is, she does not talk nonsense, and though I am not much delighted with her, she is generally thought agreeable.

I can perceive I am no great favourite with her, notwithstanding she effects an esteem for me to Eliza; but I am sure she would not wish I was so often at that house, for she has said (more than once) she believed I had a deal of penetration.

I have said perhaps too much on surmise, (for I acknowlege it is nothing more) except so far as relates to her liking Charles, which I have no doubt about; but my suspicions arose from observations I have made on her behaviour.

I shall, however, be well pleased to lose my character for penetration in this particular.—Mr. Fitzgerald has declared himself in form to Mrs. Rochfort; and she has positively refused to listen to him again on that subject, during the first year of her widow-hood;* a pretty hint that, for him to renew it at the expiration of that time. When she told me what passed between them, I said, very seriously, (but with a significant look) it was really kind of her to limit his time of probation. She had not been aware of the inference I would draw, and it threw her into the utmost confusion; when she could speak, she said, no one would think of such a thing but myself: if, said I, Mr. Fitzgerald does not think of it, he is more dull of apprehension than any lover I ever heard of; but do not be uneasy, for you know widows are privileged to give a modest hint of their intentions. She blushed so excessively, and seemed so distressed, that I pitied her, though I could not help laughing at her being so affected; but she has an uncommon degree of bashfulness: I relieved her, by saying, I owed her that teizing for her reserve to me on that affair; for she constantly denied her partiality for James, though it was very visible, and I was determined to mortify her for it.

I allow it is not delicate to make open declaration of our favourable opinion of a man, however worthy he may be; but to deny it so positively to a particular friend, that one was living in the house with, looks, I think, either like prudery, or distrust.

When she found I had taken it amiss, she apologized, by assuring me, it proceeded only from a wish to conceal her sentiments from every body, (even herself if possible) till she knew if her father would approve of Mr. Fitzgerald, as she meant to be guided by him. I could not help saying, I thought it would be carrying her obedience too far; though I have as high a notion of the duty we owe our parents as most people; but as she had once made herself unhappy to oblige him, I did not think it necessary to consult his caprice in a second choice, when we knew his love of money, and that inequality of fortune, was the only objection could be made in the present case. She certainly ought to inform her father of the affair, but if he objected merely on the grounds I mention, I did not think she was under any obligation to comply with an unreasonable humour, considering she was now her own mistress: if she was still under her parents authority, I should think her right extended no farther than to refuse a person she could not be happy with, but not to marry any one against their consent.*

She seemed to join in my opinion, but said she had been used to obey so implicitly, and besides was of such a timid disposition, she doubted if she would have resolution to follow her own inclinations.

I hope she will not be put to the trial, as Mr. O'Neil professes a most violent friendship for James, and sets him up as a pattern for all young men that he knows.

I shall continue to write to you an account of all our proceedings here, without the formality of waiting for an answer, since the war* prevents a regular intercourse between the two countries.

The Miss Boyles and I are become intimate; you were prejudiced in their favour by the little you had seen of them before you left us, and if you had known more of them, you would like them still better, as they improve on an acquaintance; particularly Harriet, whose good sense is a little obscured by affectation, which however she is throwing off very fast; you cannot think how much I made her ashamed of it, so much, that it is only long habit makes her ever practise it, and the least look from me corrects her.

I think Mr. Hamilton begins to attach himself to Miss Boyle, but I do not find it is observed by any one else, nor am I quite sure of it, but I wish it may be so, since it would remove all causes of uneasiness from Charles, as he is the only one he ever seemed to fear would rival him.

Mr. Boyle is my CE CISBEO,* and flirts most delightfully, considering he is old enough to be my father. I am a prodigious favourite of his, and indeed I return the compliment, for I think him the most chearful, pleasing man, I ever met with; of an elderly one, I mean.

You must suppose a million of compliments and good wishes, from all your friends and acquaintances here, for it would fill a sheet of paper to enumerate them.—Do not be jealous that I desire my love to your husband. Are not you shocked at such an obsolete epithet?

Believe me,
Affectionately your's,
LOUISA MORTIMER.

LETTER XXXIX.

Miss FREEMAN, to Miss VERNON.

Dublin, May 8. —

SINCE my arrival in this metropolis, I have wrote three letters to my dear Charlotte, and have received but one from her; but as the packets* are kept out by contrary winds, I take it for granted, your answers to my other two are detained by that means, and shall proceed to give you an account of my Irish acquaintances.

I have already informed you of the polite, or, I may rather say, kind reception I met with, from every family to whom I brought letters; and I have now to tell you, their civility rather increases every day; indeed I think there is no end to the attention a stranger meets with in this land of hospitality,* which has in spite of all my prejudices, reconciled me to a people of whom we are taught to entertain the most unjust ideas; for I assure you, I find them the very reverse of every thing our country folks usually imagine them to be: and I begin to see, it is very illiberal to suppose merit is confined to any one particular clime or kingdom.

I told you Miss Fitzgerald, (Skeffington's intended) had paid me a visit, and given me a genteel invitation to go to their house, whenever I was not other-wise engaged, as they live in the next street, for I took care to fix myself near them. She has since shewed, she meant more than mere compliment, for she came herself several times and took me with her, after taking me airing, or to such places in the town, as she thought worth my seeing; so we were now as free as if we had been acquainted this twelve month.

She is a pretty gentle soul, entirely composed of the tender passions, and has too much sensibility for her own peace of mind, which I am very sorry for, since there is a great deal of uneasiness in store for her; I wish it was otherwise, but I never was used to put any person's happiness in competition with my own; a stranger cannot therefore expect that compliment from me; besides I really think I shall do them a service in separating them, for were two such quiet mortals as Skeffington and she, to go together, they would inevitably fall into a lethargy, by the perfect sameness of each other's temper: now if I take him, I believe I may engage to keep him from that disorder, by the continual variety of my disposition; not to say any thing of my spirit, which I flatter myself is sufficient to keep any man awake, for though I love him to distraction, and will go any lengths to obtain him, I do not mean to be the same turtle,* when married, that his Eliza would be: it is necessary to rouse them sometimes, that they may set the higher value on your good temper, when you chuse to treat them with it.

There is a Miss Mortimer that stands very much in my way, for she is Eliza's bosom friend, and chief adviser, she is very civil to me, and asks me to her parties; but she has quick discernment, and, I think, observes me with a penetrating eye; for which reason I am in awe of her, and of course do not like her; but that I keep to myself, for I find she is a general favourite, even amongst the women, though very much the taste of the men.—Is not this odd? She is not handsome, but has great expression in her countenance, and is by no means ugly; her disposition is exceedingly lively, and a vein of humour runs through her conversation, that makes it vastly pleasing; however, her vivacity never leads her into an impropriety, for her understanding is in the superior degree, and she conducts herself with the same prudence you might expect from her grandmother. I have been particular in my description of her, because I think her rather an extraordinary character for a woman, not above four and twenty: but do you know, I hate those pieces of infallibility; their manners are a tacit reproach on us, who are too volatile to be restrained by dull rules of decorum.

The women here, would, in general suit your taste better than mine; for though very chearful, they have a sedateness in them, that would be just the thing for you, who are a good deal in that stile yourself.

I have this instant got a piece of intelligence, that is of the utmost importance to me: Skeffington has a spark of jealousy in his bosom, which if I do not blow into a flame, I deserve to lose him. It never broke out till within these few months; the person who raised it is a Mr. Hamilton, a most accomplished young man; he is at present in town; is very intimate at Mrs. Fitzgerald's, and seems to be on the most friendly terms with Charles; however since he once looked on him as a rival, there can be no great difficulty in placing him in the same light again, for suspicions of that nature may be revived with very little address.

Letty, whom I ordered to make an acquaintance with Miss Fitzgerald's maid, got this information from her; but as she is not in her mistress's secrets, she could not tell how he was convinced there was no cause for his fears; it was from some unguarded expressions of his own, she discovered his foible; she said she told her lady of it at the time, who bid her not mention it, and she never heard more of it after, though she perceived her very low-spirited at times, till of late she seems quite easy: be that as it may, I think I cannot fail of succeeding, now I know his weak side, as I shall direct all my attack against that; but how I shall proceed, I cannot at present inform you, since my operations must be determined by the circumstance of the moment.

I never gave you a more convincing proof of the confidence I place in you, than by letting you into my intention of going such lengths to accomplish my wishes, since I know you will not approve of it; but I also know, your affection for me, will prevent your taking any steps to frustrate my designs, as your knowlege of my disposition must tell you, such a measure would inevitably be attended with fatal consequences.

Whatever I do, must be done soon, for he will be at age in a few weeks, and they are to be married as soon after, as he can go through some necessary forms of law, to enable him to make proper settlements; for notwithstanding they have loved, and been intended for each other from their infancy, she has patiently waited till all these matters could be done regularly.

So important do the ladies here esteem the security of their fortunes, that a girl who would marry without that precaution, would be looked on as a prodigy of imprudence, while we give away thousands, without asking any return but love. Surely the Irish women must have very cold constitutions, or very great command of their passions, else their reason could not act so powerfully.

What has reason and love to do with each other! The association is unnatural, and never entered into a breast truly occupied by that tender passion, as I can vouch from experience.

I would not venture to speak so openly, but that I know your mother cannot be returned to town yet; if you should find she means to come sooner than we expected, let me know, as I would not for the world one of my letters should fall into her hands: no doubt she was greatly astonished when you informed her I was gone to Ireland.

You must not expect I shall write frequently now as I have done, because my mind will be otherwise employed.

Adieu,
Dear Charlotte,
Your's,
CAROLINE FREEMAN.

LETTER XL.

Miss FREEMAN, to Miss VERNON.

Dublin, May 21. —

I HAVE a whole packet of my dear Charlotte's letters now before me; and as Skeffington and the Fitzgeralds are gone to dine a few miles from town, I take the opportunity of answering them, for when they are at home, I am generally with, or expect them to call on me.

Chance has been favourable to my design, and put it in a train, that perhaps my own ingenuity could not have so easily brought about: Miss Fitzgerald, and Mr. Hamilton have accidentally met at my lodgings, on morning visits, two or three different times, when by the greatest good fortune that could happen, Charles luckily called in, and found them there; the first time, he did not seem to mind it; but the second I saw, made an impression on him; and the last, which was yesterday, they all looked embarrassed. Hamilton soon took leave; (you must know I encouraged an intimacy with him, in hopes it would some way answer my purpose) Charles and Eliza sat a while, and then I went home with them, being engaged to pass the day there.

He continued very serious, and she very badly affected chearfulness: in the evening, however, we were set a little to rights; two Miss Boyles, who are frequently there, came into tea, which roused them from their thoughtfulness, and when tea was over, we all went to the Rotunda,* where we were joined by Mr. Hamilton; but as he attached himself to the eldest Miss Boyle, whom I think he admires, Charles's good humour rather encreased; the music too, of which he is very fond, seemed to compose his spirits, and he went home much easier in mind than he had been all day; but as this meeting by chance affects him so much, I shall take the hint, and improve upon it: I cannot now be more explicit as my plan is not thoroughly digested.

You ask how I can be so barbarous as to make an amiable girl wretched, who has shewed me such friendship? I answer, because my own happiness is dearer to me than that of any other person; and as to the civility she has shewn me, she would do the same to any other stranger that was introduced to her; it is the natural disposition of the people here, therefore I do not esteem it any particular compliment to me; so my conscience is easy on that head, and I beg I may have no more of your preaching; it comes mighty ill from a girl of eighteen.

My aunt, you tell me, is much displeased at my expedition; I guessed she would, which was the reason I took the opportunity to come off while she was in the country; I was determined, and there was no use in having an argument upon it. If she knew my purpose, I suppose she would come over express to prevent it; and if she was not two hundred miles from London, and likely to be detained there, till as I hope my business will be accomplished, I would not have given you the smallest item of it; but I caution you to dread the consequence of betraying me.

If I can but succeed, in making a quarrel between Skeffington and his fair cousin, I have no doubt but I shall easily obtain her place in his heart, and then you shall see how good, how religious, and all that, I will be the rest of my life.

I wish I was rid of this Miss Mortimer for a while; I think she perfectly keeps guard over Eliza, and there is no having her to one's self, long enough to get into her confidence, which I am sure I would have done long since, if her friend was out of my way; and that would be of great use to forward my scheme, for I am sure I could draw her into things that would confirm his suspicions, if she was without the advice of one who is so well acquainted with her disposition, and so interested in her happiness; besides that, I have reason to think she suspects my attachment to Skeffington, and is therefore more anxious, to prevent Eliza from being too open in her communications to me; for neither of them has ever dropped the least hint of his jealousy: however, I believe all her wisdom and precaution, will be insufficient to obstruct the success of my plan, which I look upon as certain, now that the knowledge of his temper gives me such a sure foundation to work upon.

You ask me of Miss Mortimer's family, and situation, and seem wonderfully taken with her character; she is descended from one of the oldest families in England, and I think values herself on her pedigree, though she is at the same time exceedingly complaisant and affable to every one. Her father and mother are dead; but I suppose her fortune must be quite easy, since she has a house elegantly furnished; visits, and is visited by all the fine folks here, and is treated with all that respect and attention that is usually paid to those who are totally independant: in short, she ranks in the upper class of life, but will not be a slave to particular forms, and empty ceremonies, which, she says, is the very reverse of true politeness; how she manages, I do not know, but every thing she does pleases, and she is set up as a pattern to all young ladies, as soon as they are brought into company; and as I told you, much admired by the men. To all that I have ever seen with her, she behaves with such perfect equality, that I cannot guess which of them she prefers; yet it is scarcely probable that she has not some attachment: besides I have heard hints among them that convinces me she has, but I believe there is some mystery in it, that I cannot fathom; and the ladies here are very reserved on those subjects: I am dying to find it out too, for I should have great satisfaction in knowing she had an imprudent intanglement; but no matter, I shall triumph over her sagacity yet, notwithstanding all her endeavours to watch me, for I see plainly her suspicions of me encrease.

When, you hear from me next, probably something decisive will be done, for the time advances fast.—Till then farewell.

Believe me,

Ever your's,

CAROLINE FREEMAN.

LETTER XLI.

FROM THE SAME TO THE SAME.

Dublin, June 6. —

Dear Charlotte,

I HAVE separated them I hope, for ever; but it has produced a consequence I was not prepared for; he went off to England in the first transports of his jealousy, and I fear he may take the fancy of going abroad to amuse his mind; but I am hastening after him, and if I can but keep him in England, his going there will be much to my advantage, because it will effectually prevent their coming to any explanation, and baffle all Miss Mortimer's cleverness.

I write while Letty is packing my things, and you may expect me in a day or two after you receive this, when I will tell you how I brought the matter about.

Your's, in a violent hurry,

CAROLINE FREEMAN.

LETTER XLII.

Miss MORTIMER, to HENRY MAUNSELL, Esq.

June 7. —

WHAT poor weak mortals you men are! borne away by every gust of passion, and with all your boasted wisdom, incapable of conducting yourselves with propriety, in the common occurrences of life!*—Any girl just escaped from the nursery, can, if she sets her wits to work, make you believe improbabilities.

Excuse me Harry; I have no reason to accuse you of those follies, but I am angry with the whole sex, and vexed to death, that it should be in the power of any of you to make my poor Eliza unhappy.

Your friend Mr. Skeffington, is flown off to England in a fit of jealousy; and upon the credit of an anonymous scrawl he received, has accused the sweet girl (whose heart he has possessed from her infancy) of inconstancy, and I know not what nonsense. Mr. Hamilton is still the object of his suspicions, though he is actually paying his addresses to Miss Boyle, and that any body might see, that did not chuse to shut their eyes against conviction. He will certainly avoid you, and I do not wish you to seek him out; it could be of no use at present, besides our pride forbids it.

I am certain that Miss Freeman he mentioned to you, is at the bottom of it all; I told you she was here, and that I thought she liked Charles; every day convinced me I was right, and I have now no doubt of it, for she set off for England this morning, which was as soon as she could go, after she heard of his departure, and she had never mentioned her intentions before. She lives with her aunt, a Mrs. Vernon, in Jermyn-street, and I should be glad you would keep a watch on the house, to see if he goes or sends there; he has taken Will Lacky* with him; the fellow you know is his foster-brother,* and I am sure has his master's happiness at heart; so if your James could meet with him, I dare say he would give some intelligence how he means to dispose of himself.

I do not suppose he will continue in England, unless that little witch contrives some stratagem to detain him; and I would wish to know where he is, or is likely to be, because Mrs. Fitzgerald, who loves him nearly as well as she loves Eliza, is quite miserable about him; besides one would chuse to know his motions, as something may yet happen to set matters right again, and make him ashamed of a weakness that causes so much unhappiness to those, whose felicity I know he would wish to promote.

I make no apology for the employment I give you, as I know your regard for the parties concerned, exclusive of the pleasure you will have in obeying my commands.——You see I have said that for you, just to save you the trouble of repeating what you have so often told me.

Adieu,

Your's,

LOUISA MORTIMER.

LETTER XLIII.

MISS MORTIMER, TO THE COUNTESS DE ROUSILLON.

June 8. —

IPROMISED to give my dear Gertrude, an account of all the occurrences among us that were worth relating, and I have now to inform you of one that I believe will give you much concern; Charles Skeffington departed abruptly for England, four days ago, in a paroxism of jealousy, which I am certain has been roused by the machinations of that Miss Freeman, of whom I hinted my suspicions in my last; they are confirmed by her setting out for England as soon as she found he was gone, on a pretence of being wrote for on material business, though there had not a packet arrived in the time; for as I suspected her, I sent to enquire.

Eliza bears it surprisingly; she is hurt by his behaviour, and her pride supports her for the present, but I fear that will not continue long; she is too gentle, and loved him too well, not to regret her disappointment. I do my best to keep up her resentment, but I know it will not do; tender recollections will obtrude themselves on her mind, and interrupt, if not totally destroy her happiness.

Her mother too is greatly to be pitied, for she loved Charles as if he had been her own son, and you cannot imagine how much his present conduct affects her: add to that, she has terrible apprehensions for Eliza's health, which indeed, I think, likely to suffer from the shock she has received.

I shall advise them to go to Montpellier; changing the scene may be of use to her, and as you mean to leave Paris this month, you will be at Rousillon before they could reach it, and I am sure would contribute all in your power to amuse the dear girl; if I possibly can, I will accompany them, but that is at present uncertain.

It is time for me to tell you how the affair happened, at least as much as I know of it: I told you in my last, I was sure Miss Freeman liked Charles; as I observed her closely, I was every day more convinced of it, as well as that she must have some scheme in coming over; for which reason, I gave her as few opportunities of being alone with Eliza as possible; for being extremely artless herself, I feared she would be too unreserved, and lay herself open to the other's cunning to take advantage of.

I was constantly uneasy for her, though I did not know precisely what to fear; and was much more so when I found Mr. Hamilton and Eliza had met by accident, at Miss Freeman's lodgings several times; Charles had found them there, and shewed strong symptoms of returning jealousy; when Eliza told me what had happened, I mentioned my suspicions of Miss Freeman, and cautioned her to guard against her artifices, and not to go to her without Charles. She promised she would not, but seemed to think I wronged the girl very much, who she said, was too volatile to manage any deep laid plot. She however took my advice, and seldom went to her, but invited her to their house as usual. Matters were in this way when Mrs. Rochfort got a violent cold which confined her, and you may think I would not leave her.

Mrs. Fitzgerald was also indisposed; so that I had not seen Eliza for three days, when I was much surprised at receiving a note from her at twelve o'clock, Monday night, requesting I would go to her immediately, and prepare for staying till morning, as an accident had happened which greatly affected her; to prevent delay she sent the carriage for me.

I shewed the note to Emily, in whose chamber I was sitting, begging she would excuse me, if I should not be at home at breakfast, and ordering Jenny to put my night cloaths into the chariot, went off, very much alarmed, as both Emily and I had concluded it to be something relative to Charles.

When I stepped into the hall, the servants all looked sad and silent, Kitty met me, with her eyes quite red from crying, as she was lighting me up stairs, Kitty, said I, what ails your mistress? Oh! ma'am, Mr. Skeffington; and bursting into tears, was unable to say more, but conducted me in silence to Mrs. Fitzgerald's bed-chamber, who sat in her easy chair weeping. When she saw me, you are very good, Miss Mortimer, says she; my poor girl wanted such a friend to comfort her, looking towards Eliza, who sat leaning her elbow on the dressing table, her hand supporting her head, in the other she had two letters open, which she held out to me, saying, read them Louisa; they will explain our present situation better than I am able to do, and be my excuse for bringing you out at this late hour. I took them, and read as follows:

Madam,

When you receive this, I shall for ever have quitted a house, where once my chief happiness was centered. I will not endeavour to raise your compassion, by describing what I feel at parting; for since I have lost your affection, I will try to set myself above your pity, and will, at least, convince you, your felicity is infinitely dearer to me than my own, by relieving you from that restraint, which my presence must have laid you under, and leaving you at liberty to give your hand to him, whose shining qualities, I am not all surprised, should rob me of your heart. It is not in woman, to withstand such perfections, and I have no right to expect a miracle should be wrought in my favour.

To shew you I am not actuated by mere suspicion, I inclose a letter that was put into my hand this morning, as I was stepping into my carriage; I followed the writer's directions, went to the Rotunda, and was convinced of your inconstancy.

As you wished to deceive me, you should have been cautious who you trusted with your secret; no doubt you will know the hand, and remove that person from your family.

I know, and grieve for what my aunt will feel on this occasion; but I hope Mr. Hamilton, will, by his attention, reconcile her to the event, and make you as happy as I would have rejoiced in doing, had the pleasing task fallen to the lot of your still

> Very sincere friend,
> C. SKEFFINGTON.

———————

The letter alluded to, was badly wrote, and worse spelt, it contained the following lines:

Sir,

Knowing how long, and tenderly you have loved Miss Fitzgerald, and that you are now flattering yourself, with the pleasing hope of being soon united to her; I could not bear to see you any longer deceived; and therefore (from a perfect knowlege of her intentions) assure you, she only wishes to stand fair with you, during her mother's life, which from her ill health, she thinks cannot be long.

You soon perceived the growing attachments between her and Mr. Hamilton; but so high was your opinion of her, you persuaded yourself to discredit the evidence of your own senses, rather than think she could be guilty of so much baseness.

If you chuse to be convinced of the truth of this information, go to the Rotunda, about nine o'clock to-night, where (though you fancy she is confined to her mother's apartment) you will find her in company with the present object of her affection. She thinks herself secure, as you were to stay at Lucan* till to-morrow, but I presume, this will be sufficient to bring you back.

> I remain, Sir,
> Your humble servant,
> An unknown FRIEND.

———————

You will observe, this was calculated to make him suppose it wrote by some one in his own family; accordingly his suspicions fell on Kitty, for she says, when he was quitting the house, he called for her, and giving her the letter for Eliza, put five guineas into her hand, saying, he believed he was under an obligation to her; though if her mistress confided in her, she did wrong to betray her secrets. He forgot he had once endeavoured to tempt her to do the very same thing, he now disapproved. The girl did not know what he meant; she must be innocent of it, for she could not possibly tell her mistress would go to the Rotunda, before she knew it herself: that could only be told by the person who was determined to take her there.

Having read the letters, I asked Eliza, had she been at the Rotunda that evening? she answered yes; but begged I would not condemn her, till I heard her story. She then proceeded to tell me, that in the morning Miss Freeman had come to breakfast, as she often did, but would not stay the day, though much pressed, alledging, she was geting a beautiful fancy trimming on a gown, and must go home to shew her maid how to put it on, for she would not let the mantua-maker* do it, lest it should not be to her taste; but said if it was done, she would come in the evening, as she knew Charles would be out of town.

She left us soon after, and we heard no more of her till six in the after-noon, Letty came seemingly in a great hurry, with a request from her mistress, that I should go drink tea with her; I answered, she knew I could not leave my mother. Ah, ma'am! she bid me tell you, she is in the utmost distress, for Mr. Harman is come to tea, and she does not think it prudent to entertain gentle-men at her lodgings, without having some other lady with her, and she cannot make so free with any one but you, as to expect they would come on such short notice.

As Mr. Harman is reputed to be an admirer of Miss Freeman's, my mother was charmed with her discretion, and insisted I should go, saying, she was now well enough to amuse herself by reading. I therefore told the girl, I would follow her as soon as the horses could be put to, which I did. Miss Freeman met me on the stairs, and in her own rattling way, said I was the best girl in the world; if I had not come she would have been ruined, for there was two of them with her now; but bid me not say any thing of being just sent for. We had by this time reached the drawing-room, where I found the gentleman already mentioned, and Mr. Hamilton; I would rather he had not been there, but as Charles was not likely to know of it, I was the less concerned; be it as it would, I would not go away again. We had tea immediately; and a great deal of wit and repartee passed between Miss Freeman and her admirer, who seemed to think it incumbent on him to follow her lead, and she was remarkable lively, even for her that you know is always so.

All of a sudden, she proposed going to the Rotunda, which I readily assented to, thinking it more eligible than staying at home; the evening was so fine, we agreed to walk, and I ordered the carriage there at ten. It was very full, and rather warm, so between the acts we walked in the garden;* when we returned to the room, Miss Freeman complained of fatigue and thirst; the forms were all filled; but the gentlemen proposed going into a recess, and having coffee; which she accepted, saying, she was choaked with dust, and we went into one that a set of company had just quitted. Coffee and several other refreshments were soon brought, and we were sitting making our observations on the variety of figures that were moving in a circle before us, when Miss Freeman cried in a tone of astonishment, there is Mr. Skeffington; instantly he turned his head, and when he saw it was us, stepped in; I said, I was surprised to meet him there, as I did not expect him to town; he answered, I am sure you did not, and seemed to lay a particular emphasis on his words; I hope, says I, nothing extraordinary has happened; yes, madam, said he, something very extraordinary.

I was silent, perceiving at once what he meant, though I could not conceive how he got intelligence of my being there: the gentlemen pressed him to take coffee, but he declined, saying, he had some material business to transact, and had only called in to look for a person he had heard was there.

He cast a look full of indignation at me, and bowing to the company, withdrew, leaving us all looking at each other, as if we did not know whether we should take notice of his behaviour or not; till Miss Freeman said, laughing, she thought we looked as if we had got anger, and were afraid to speak.

To be sure Mr. Skeffington's temper was much ruffled at something, or he would not have behaved so odd: then turning to me, he will make an agreeable husband, my dear, if he has frequent returns of those humours.—I was confused at her directing the speech to me, but answered, the woman would deserve to be unhappy, that knowingly subjected herself to such caprice.

Mr. Hamilton, whom I saw, guessed he was the cause of what had passed, looked concerned and serious; but as for me, I was so full of resentment, that it kept up my spirits, and I was determined to speak to him when I came home, and put a final end to the affair; for since he has no confidence in my affection, it is impossible we could be happy.

It seems he was of the same sentiments, for he was gone before I came in. Kitty gave me a letter, saying, Mr. Skeffington left it for me, when he was going away.— Away where? she answered to England, ma'am. I asked no more questions, but came to my mother's chamber, who I found so chearful, that I knew she had not heard of it; so I went to my dressing-room, (as if to undress) and there I read the letters. I immediately ordered the carriage to go for you, and then returned to my mother, and broke the matter to her as gently as I could, by telling her of the first commencement of Charles's jealousy, which I never mentioned before, wishing to save her from uneasiness, and still hoping a little reflection would cure him of that weakness; the hope I find was vain, added she, sighing, but my greatest concern at present is, to see my mother so much afflicted by his ingratitude. She wanted me to send after him, as he could not have got down to the packet when I came home; but I begged her not to insist on it, as I never would condescend so far, to a man, who upon such slight foundation could suspect my sincerity; I said, I thought her right, for it would probably be to no purpose, since he did not now seem capable of using his reason; it was therefore better to let him alone, till time and circumstances might open his eyes to conviction.

Mrs. Fitzgerald agreed with me, saying, she had not considered the matter properly at first. I asked them had they no suspicion of the author of that letter? Eliza said, she had no doubt it was Miss Freeman had it wrote; perhaps by her maid, but the words she was sure were her own, as the stile did not suit the writing and spelling, which were both of the vulgar kind. She said, she had not asked any particulars about his going, but would call Kitty now, for she had heard the chariot return since I came in.

When Kitty came, she was asked where John had left his master? she answered, he had staid to see him in the wherry,* and the sailors said, the wind was so fair, he would be at the Head to breakfast. I then asked her, what had passed before he left the house; she said, the servants told her, for she was not below, that he came in soon after nine, which surprised them, as they did not expect him that night; he went to his study, and called for Will, who found him walking back and forward in great discomposure; he took no notice of him for some minutes, then bid him pack up all his things, with what haste he cou'd, for he was setting off immediately for England; and Will, if you chuse to come, you may pack up your own things too; but probably I shall not return these two or three years, therefore take your choice. Will said, to be sure he would attend his honour, as long as he would give him leave, and went to do as he was ordered, but first stepped into the hall to tell the servants the news.

Mr. Skeffington came down in about half an hour; desired one of the men to call me, and when I came, bid me deliver that letter to my mistress; she then repeated what he had said to her; adding, he charged her not to mention his departure to his aunt; her young lady would tell it when she returned. He left directions for Will to follow with the trunks, as soon as possible, and drove off, leaving them all in great consternation; and for her, she said, she had been crying almost ever since, for though she did not know directly what the words meant, she guessed some mischief was between him and her mistress, and that he suspected her to be the cause of it; Eliza bid her not be uneasy, for she was convinced of her innocence, and then dismissed her.

We all retired to bed soon after, but I cannot say to rest, for Eliza and I talked over the affair the remainder of the night, which was already far advanced; and I took care to place his treatment of her, in such a light, as should raise her resentment, for I found her several times inclined to melt into tears. We determined if Miss Freeman came next day, to say Charles was gone to England on business of importance, and watch her looks and behaviour, to see if they would confirm our suspicions, which in my opinion did not want confirmation, since it is impossible any one but her could know Eliza, and Mr. Hamilton would be at the Rotunda together, as it was by her means the thing happened.

She came as we expected, in the forenoon, just as sprightly, and to all appearance as thoughtless as usual; but she is not what she seems to be in that respect: she had not sat long before she asked for Charles; and Eliza made the answer we agreed on; she looked astonished; and exclaimed, to England! you quite surprise me. Why should it surprise you, says I, that Mr. Skeffington, who has a large estate in England, should have business there? she was disconcerted at first, but recovered quick enough, and replied, because ma'am, I thought a certain event, (looking towards Eliza) was to take place so soon, that he would defer every other business till that was over. Eliza blushed, and was silent; but I made answer, Miss Fitzgerald was in no hurry about that affair. Here the subject dropped, and we talked of indifferent things till she left us, which she did very shortly, saying, she had a hundred visits to pay.

I went home to see Emily, and tell her what had happened, but returned again to stay the day with them; it passed over very well, as several friends had called in to see Mrs. Fitzgerald, and the Miss Boyle's came to tea; they always come early, so we had a good deal of time for chat; and I thought it best to tell them the real truth in regard to Charles's sudden departure, for it will be certainly talked of, and reserve to them was unnecessary. They immediately fixed on Miss Freeman as the cause; and I found Mr. Hamilton had told them what passed at the gardens. We were still talking it over, and had sat down to tea, when Miss Freeman arrived; she told us, she was come to take leave, for since she saw us in the morning, she had received a letter with some news, which made it necessary for her to go home directly, and she meant to sail in the next packet; we all cast a look at each other; and I said, it was a sudden call indeed, that put her in such a hurry; she made no reply to that, but chatted away in her usual stile about two hours, and then took leave, making a profusion of acknowlegements to Mrs. Fitzgerald, and Eliza, for the many civilities she had received from them; which provoked me so much, I could scarce forbear giving her a hint of my suspicions; but I considered it best, to say nothing, as it could not answer any purpose, since she certainly would not own it.

After she was gone, we agreed there could be no doubt of what was taking her back; and I mentioned to the Boyle's what had been my opinion of her all along, and my reasons for it.

Eliza said, she would never dispute my penetration again; but she had thought her too giddy to be so designing. I have wrote to Harry Maunsell an account of Mr. Skeffington's behaviour, and begged him to have a watch on Miss Freeman, perhaps something will come out that will be of use to us, for I think, if his eyes were effectually opened, by a discovery of her artifice, it would cure him of his foible, and they might yet be happy.

Mr. Hamilton's marriage with Miss Boyle, when that takes place, must go a good way towards undeceiving him.

Mr. Fitzgerald does not abate the least bit in his attention to our lovely widow, and she receives them very graciously.

When I freed my heart from its fond prepossession, I thought I had done with love, and all its attendant perplexities, but I find I was mistaken, for I am now as much affected with the soft distresses of my friends, as I could possibly be with my own; I think rather more so, because if any of the fellows took such airs with me, I should discard them at once, without a moment's pain. I wish I could inspire Eliza with a little of my spirit, for it is such tender souls as you and she are, that make the men so saucy.

Do not call this a letter, it is quite a volume; by the time you have got through it, perhaps you may hear from me again.

The best wishes of your friends here, waits on the Compte,* and your lady-ship.——None more sincerely, than those of my

Dear Gertrude's,

Very Affectionate,

LOUISA MORTIMER.

LETTER XLIV.

Mr. MAUNSELL, to Miss MORTIMER.

London, June 21. —

I DEFERED acknowleging the receipt of my dear Miss Mortimer's favour, till I could give some satisfactory account of my unhappy friend; unhappy I call him, though I think him blameable, but I must feel for him, since I too well know what he suffers, who loses all hopes of being united to the object of his fondest wishes. But I forget myself, and am transgressing against your cruel commands, not to mention that subject, which is, and will ever be nearest my heart; yet surely Louisa, you will pardon me, as you must at least allow there is some merit in my endeavours to obey you, when I find the task is so difficult.

I was under the necessity of letting James into the whole secret, as I should want his assistance, and have no doubt of his fidelity, I then gave him proper instructions, and sent him to Jermyn-street, where he took a lodging, nearly opposite Mrs. Vernon's, so that he must see who went in and out there: it was in the evening, and as his landlady keeps a shop, he bought some tea, and begged leave to try it in her apartment, and sent for cakes to treat her and the children; she was much pleased with his civility, which made her very communicative, and in the course of conversation she gave him the history of every family in the street, and told him all the genteel female servants frequented her shop, and often made parties to drink tea there, and be merry, just to help her, because she was a poor widow. James requested she would introduce him to some of them, as opportunity offered, which she promised; telling him, Miss Vernon's maid was the prettiest girl in the street, and she would invite her next evening: it was the very thing he wanted; so giving her to understand, he would provide the entertainment; he took his leave, telling her he should sleep there next night, and came to inform me of his proceedings.

I was well pleased at such a beginning, not doubting but he would so manage matters with the pretty damsel, as to get into the secrets of the young ladies, so far as would be useful to us. I sent him next day, that he might watch if Mr. Skeffington went there, and told him I should not expect to see him that night again.

Accordingly, he did not return till morning, when he informed me, he had the greatest hopes of succeeding to my wishes; for the girl he had been introduced to, was sister to Miss Freeman's maid; that she told him, that young lady had met with an accident by the overturning of the carriage, on her road from Ireland, which rendered her unable to travel, and her young lady was to go to her in a day or two, to stay with her till she recovered.

Finding he was an Irishman, she enquired if he knew Mrs. Fitzgerald's family; being answered in the affirmative, she asked several questions about them and Charles in a manner that convinces him she knows the whole affair.

I have therefore laid a plan by which I think we shall come at the truth.

James is a well-looking lad, and the girl seemed pleased with his company; by treating her with a little gallantry, it is more than probable he will learn all she can tell him. He is already become a favourite, and is frequently with her, for her mistress is gone to attend her cousin, who still remains too ill to be moved; and Mrs. Vernon has been out of town some time, by which means he'll have great opportunities of getting into her confidence.

As you guessed, Charles did not come near me, but I made private enquiries, and found he was at his house in Sussex; however, I could get no knowlege of his intentions till yesterday, James luckily met Will Lacky, who had been sent to town on business; they were rejoiced to see each other, and stepped into a public house to take a glass; where William told him his master had some unfortunate misunderstanding with Miss Fitzgerald, and had left Dublin in a huff, was determined not to return this long time, and was now preparing to go abroad, he believed to Germany, and from thence to Italy.

He lamented greatly what had happened, saying, he was sure the young mistress was not to blame, but his master would not hear reason.

James expressed his sorrow on the occasion, and having obtained a promise from Will to keep up a constant correspondence, they parted, and James came to tell what he had heard; and that he proposed corresponding, that I might have always intelligence of Mr. Skeffington's movements, which it seems he did not intend to make any of his friends acquainted with.

I approved what he had done, and commended him highly for his attention to the business.

I hope my proceedings will meet the approbation of my lovely Louisa, and obtain her good opinion of one, at least, of that sex, against which she is so justly incensed by the folly and ingratitude of another.

I sincerely wish your fair friend had some share of that fortitude of which you exhibit such an example on all trying occasions: indeed, I should do well to wish for it myself too, since I have even more need of it than Miss Fitzgerald; because it is most likely resentment will keep her from repining; but I have not that to support me, and am, I think, more unhappy than if I had been ill used by the woman I adore.

Why will these ideas perpetually recur? I shall not fail to inform you of every thing material that passes, and have no doubt but matters will yet take a happy turn, if Mr. Hamilton marries Miss Boyle. Sure that alone will be sufficient to convince Charles of his error.

I will not now give you room to laugh at me by repeating what you have already anticipated; so shall only say, I wish you may ever retain that charming vivacity which so exceedingly becomes you.

Adieu, my dear Miss Mortimer. Assure yourself I shall always be,

Unalterably your's,

HENRY MAUNSELL.

LETTER XLV.

FROM THE SAME TO THE SAME.

London, July 1. —

Two days after I wrote to my dear Miss Mortimer, I received a short letter from Mr. Skeffington, apologizing for not calling on me, as his mind was in too distracted a state since he came to England, to make him a pleasing companion to any one; before that would reach me, he said, he should have set off with an intention of quitting these kingdoms, till the memory of some late events, which no doubt I had heard of, were so far worn out, as to enable him to return to his own country with some degree of satisfaction, when he hoped we should renew that friendship which had ever afforded him so much pleasure.

James same time received a note from William, informing him, they were just setting out for Harwick, there to embark for Helvoetsluys;* and promising to write to him from the first place, where he should find they were likely to make any stay: if he keeps his word, we shall not be at a loss where to find him; and as I am to go to France, I shall certainly make whatever place he is in my way, if he is not lost to reason.

I have now such a proof as must convince him the whole plan was laid by Miss Freeman; but I think it best he should suffer a-while; as the torments he feels from jealousy, will, when he finds how groundless it has been, be the most probable means of effecting his cure: and if Mr. Hamilton is married before I leave England, it will be a strong testimony in our favour.——But to the most material point; James continued his visits to Mrs. Betty, but quit his lodging, informing her, his master was returned from Ireland, where he had said I went on business; and that he found I had heard something very particular about Mr. Skeffington, who she had been speaking of, and who was his master's very particular friend.

This raised the girl's curiosity, and she made it a point that he should find out what it was; her young ladies were expected in a few days, and I suppose she was desirous of having what intelligence she could against they came.

James told me what had passed, and we agreed he should not go to her for two or three days; he then paid his visit with a face of great concern, and when she questioned him in regard to what he had heard from me, he evaded answering, and seemed unwilling to enter on the subject, which made her more anxious to know, till at length he suffered himself with great difficulty to be prevailed on to tell her, I had by some means discovered that there was mischief made between Mr. Skeffington and the lady he was going to marry, by a scheme of Miss Freeman's; that Mr. Skeffington was gone abroad in consequence of it, but he found I was determined to lay the whole matter before Mrs. Vernon, and insist on her using her authority with her daughter, (who he knew was privy to the affair) to produce all her cousin's letters from Dublin, by which means he said, I hoped to effect a reconciliation* between the parties concerned; and concluded by saying, he flattered himself she had nothing to do in it, for if she had, she would certainly lose her place, besides being greatly exposed, as they all would, who had entered into such a wicked plot,

The girl was terrified, and said it would be the ruin of both her and her young lady, if his master should acquaint Mrs. Vernon of the affair; though she declared, neither of them had any farther to do with it, than by knowing there was such a plan, and how it was carried on; of which her sister constantly informed her by letter, as Miss Freeman, she was sure, did her mistress; for she had often heard her wish, her cousin had never gone to Ireland, as she feared it would have bad consequences.

She then asked him, could he think of any way to prevent his master telling Mrs. Vernon; for if it was done, she did not see how either her mistress or she could stand the anger they would get for not discovering it at first; for her part, she was determined to run away, though she did not know where to go, since she had neither father nor mother living, and must earn her own bread; here she cried bitterly, and James affected much uneasiness for her, she pressing him all the time to think of some expedient that would save them from being exposed to the old lady's wrath.

After much pretended consideration, he told her he had just thought of one, which if she consented to, he believed would not fail of satisfying me, as all I wanted was to lay open to Mr. Skeffington and Miss Fitzgerald, the art that had been used to separate them, and if that could be done without applying to Mrs. Vernon, he was sure I would at once give that up.

She was earnest to know what she could to do; and he said, if her sister's letters to her contained sufficient information, and that she would part with them, he was certain he could prevent all farther enquiries, and perhaps obtain a reward for her besides; as he could put her behaviour in the best light to his master.

Betty who was most hearty, readily complied with his proposal, making no other terms than those, that he should get my promise never to make the affair known to Mrs. Vernon; for she was sure them letters contained every thing I wished to know, and she believed more than Miss Freeman's.

She delivered a parcel of letters to him, which he brought in triumph to me, mightily elated with his success. I immediately sat down to examine them, and found a long account of her mistress's attachment to Mr. Skeffington, and her intention to seize the first opportunity of creating a quarrel between him and his intended bride; and says in one of them, she had discovered by Miss Fitzgerald's maid, that he had been jealous of a Mr. Hamilton; and her mistress had given her a silk gown for the information: she observes, the girl that told her meant no harm; but she was a simple innocent body, and was not aware of the consequence.

The last letter is however the most material, as it contains the whole plan, which was to be put in execution the day after it was dated, and mentions her having wrote that note, dictated by her mistress, that was to be delivered to Mr. Skeffington just when he was going out of town.

The whole collection is wretchedly spelt and wrote, so that I could scarce decypher some of them; however as it was the same hand wrote the anonymous note which Charles gave such credit to, I think he must believe his own eyes when he compares them together, for I hope that is not destroyed.

I sent the girl a few guineas by James, and my promise not to mention the transaction except to those it concerned; for I find by her sister's letters, she advised her not to have any thing to do with such a wicked scheme, and had great scruples of conscience about it.

The young ladies are come to Town, but Miss Freeman is confined to her chamber after the journey: the hurt she got was in her head, and the effect will not, (as the surgeons say) be speedily removed.

She ought to have remained where she was, at least a fortnight longer; but her impatience to get home in hopes of finding Charles, was so great, she could not listen to advice; and she now makes herself worse with fretting, lest he should go from England before she is able to see him.

At present she supposes he is in Sussex, as Betty tells James, and she on her own account does not pretend to know any thing about him.

I am exceedingly happy in being able to dive so far into this contrivance, as will I think bring matters to a pleasing conclusion between our friends, at least, my endeavours shall not be wanting for such a desirable purpose.

I hope to be favoured with a line on the receipt of this; and am,

My dear Louisa's,

Most devoted servant,

HENRY MAUNSELL.

LETTER XLIV.

Miss MORTIMER to HENRY MAUNSELL, esq.

July, 5 —

I Cannot express how much you have obliged me by interesting yourself so heartily in the affair I mentioned to you; and Eliza to whom I communicated your success, is quite ashamed at the trouble you have had, attended with some expence; she is however a good deal pleased that the truth will be brought to light; for though she has not now a thought of marrying Mr. Skeffington, she wishes to be cleared of the imputation of jilting him; which she looks on, (and so to be sure does every one of common delicacy) as a most scandalous blot in a female character;* indeed I who know every secret of her heart, can venture to affirm she never had the smallest tendency to any kind of levity.

The anonymous epistle is safe in my possession; and you will shortly have the happiness of receiving it from my fair hand—now I know you are overwhelmed with joy and surprise, and can scarce believe you have read it right; but you may, for so it is.

I have promised to accompany Mrs. Fitzgerald and Eliza to Montpellier; the late shock they received, has had a bad effect on their spirits, and I advised them to this jaunt, but they would not go without me; so I have consented to be of the party; for beside the pleasure I shall have in being with them, I long to see Gertrude, and I know she and her agreeable Count are now at Roussillon; I shall write by this post to inform her of our intention, and get her to secure accommodations for us in the town.

Now I mention that, will you be so good to take a lodging for us for a week, against we reach London, where we stop merely to rest, for this is not a season for making any stay there: two floors will do us.

We mean to set out in two days, and will go to you when we arrive, to know where you have fixed us.

But pray now moderate your transports when we meet; for positively those raptures, which were pretty enough when we were eighteen, are mighty silly at four-and-twenty.

Mr. Hamilton and Miss Boyle are certainly to be married.—Farewell till I see you,

LOUISA MORTIMER.

LETTER XLVII.

—July 6 .—

MISS MORTIMER TO THE COMPTESSE ROUSSILLON.*

I Believe my dear Gertrude will hear with pleasure that I shall set out in two days from this date on my way to Montpellier, in company with Mrs. Fitzgerald and Eliza, whom I have prevailed on to take the journey, which I hope will recruit both their health and spirits, at present very much affected by Mr. Skeffington's behaviour.

I must trouble you to secure apartments for us in the most agreeable part of the town; our family will consist of ourselves, Eliza's waiting damsel, and mine, one man servant we take with us, and we must certainly get a French valet de chambre* for the time we stay, so you will provide accommodations accordingly.

Mrs. Fitzgerald does not take her woman, because she has her town housekeeper, and being a trusty body, can be depended on to take charge of every thing in the house, and the furniture you know is very valuable; therefore Eliza's maid is to supply her place.

I know you would wish to have us at the Chateau; but it will be more agreeable to Mrs. Fitzgerald to have a lodging in the town; besides there is too many of us to go to you, who are not in a house of your own; however, as we shall be so near you, we can be every day together.

Miss Freeman was, as I suspected, the author of all the disturbances I mentioned to you in my last: Harry Maunsell has letters in his possession that prove it past contradiction; how he came by them is (in the language of auction bills) too tedious to insert, as I have still several little things to do preparatory to my journey; but the story will serve us for conversation when we are traversing the shady walks of Roussillon together, which I hope we soon shall.

We mean to go through Holland, and make as little delay on the road as possible.

The first of August is fixed for the marriage of Mr. Hamilton and Miss Boyle; they are to set off for Belle Park next day, where they make a short stay, and then go to Hamilton Hall for the remainder of the summer, but will be in town every winter: he has taken an elegant house in Merrion-square:* they will be an amiable couple, and I am pleased on every account they are to be so soon married.

Mrs. Herbert informs me her sister-in-law is just on the eve of matrimony with a young man of large fortune in that country; Patty is very happy on the occasion, as she feared her brother would absent himself a good deal from her house while Miss Herbert remained single; for as he knew her prepossession in his favor, and could not return it, it certainly would not be agreeable to him to be much in her company, and she was frequently at her brother's.

Patty tells me Mr. Herbert is determined to come to Dublin in about a year, their eldest girl will by that time want proper masters, and he is so fond of her, he cannot bear sending her to a boarding-school,* nor does she much like that mode of education if it can be avoided; she chuses to have her daughters under her own eye; but Mr. Herbert is so fond of the country, she feared he would never consent to living for any time in town; but to her great joy he made the proposal himself.

They have got a large addition to their fortune by the death of a distant relation.

How happy shall I be to have this dear companion of my childhood settled near me once more; for to be sure, on the child's account, they'll stay in town at least six or eight months in the year.

Emily left me yesterday; she is gone with her father and mother to the country, but they will all return early in the winter: Mr. O'Neil has taken a house, so Mrs. Rochfort must be there when next she comes to Dublin; but I fancy it won't be for any long time, as matters between her and Mr. Fitzgerald are, I find, most likely to be concluded to the satisfaction of all parties, her father being quite content.

I have told you a deal of news, and reserved as much more for our meeting.—Till then adieu,

Believe me

Sincerely your's,

LOUISA MORTIMER.

LETTER XLVIII.

Miss MORTIMER To Mrs. ROCHFORT.

Montpellier, Aug. 14 —

AS I am persuaded my dear Emily is anxious to hear of our safe arrival, I seize the first leisure moment that has offered to inform you we performed our journey surprisingly well, and Mrs. Fitzgerald bore it to a miracle, scarce complaining of fatigue till the last day or two: We made but three days stay in London, for as she found herself quite able to proceed, there was no occasion for delay, nor did we stop longer than was necessary amongst the high and mighty Lords,* so could make no material observations on the people, except those obvious ones of their cleanliness and industry, which are thread-bare themes, they have been so often expatiated on already.

I think indeed they excel their English neighbours in both those qualities; as for the former, they are downright slaves to it, since they debar themselves the use of their rooms for fear of dirtying them; which is carrying the point to excess, and excesses even in virtue border on vice.

We have been here some days, and are settled very agreeably in the midst too of acquaintances, for here are several of our country people that we had some knowledge of, who paid us their compliments as soon as we were known to be here, and we are now quite sociable.

Gertrude, though prepared by my letter to expect us, was very near fainting when we met, her joy so far overcame her. She is somewhat increased in size since you saw her, and is nearly as much ashamed of it as if she was not married; it is surprising that she has not conquered her bashfulness in this country, where I believe she is herself the only example of it; but she seems not one bit altered in that respect.

The Count's affection is, I think, rather warmer than before she was his wife, and she says all his family treat her with the greatest tenderness, so that I have the satisfaction of seeing her happy; only she now and then wishes to be in Ireland amongst her own friends, but as she will come over some times to see us all, and will also see many of them here at times, she will by degrees be reconciled to the necessity of living in France.

Next to my own country it is the place I would chuse; the disposition of the people here being very like the Irish in kindness and attention to strangers; and if their present Monarch* goes on as he has begun, they bid fair to be restored to their natural rights, liberty I mean; for he is daily loosening the bands of oppression and slavery;* while our Rulers are only studying how to rivet the chains* with which they have been loading the people as long as I can remember.

Poor Eliza tries to be chearful, but her heart revolts against the attempt, and it does but make the settled languor that has overspread her countenance more visible; her forced smiles make my heart ach,* and bring the tears into her mother's eyes, who anxiously watches every turn of her features.

I grieve that the dear girl cannot combat her tenderness for one who, I fear, would never make her happy, but I am not surprized at it, for in a temper so gentle as hers, that cannot long harbour resentment, one might expect ill usage would have just the effect it appears to have on her; you know it was what I feared, and was the reason I wished she would change the scene; as every object at home would revive some idea it was necessary she should forget.

I am in hopes that time, and the agreeable variety she meets with here, will in some degree restore her peace.

The letters Mr. Maunsell has are exactly in the same hand as the anonymous one sent to Charles; therefore he must be convinced, when he sees them; but unless it could make an absolute change in his disposition, I would never advise her to marry him; for a jealous husband would be misery indeed.

Well, and how goes on your affair? Do you still keep up that matronly gravity with which you used to receive Mr. Fitzgerald's attentions? for I dare say he has paid you a visit in the country before now; do tell me all about it, that I may amuse Eliza with the recital.—You shall hear soon from me again; mean time, believe me,

Affectionately
Your's,
LOUISA MORTIMER.

LETTER XLIX.

THE SAME TO THE SAME.

Montpellier, August 30.——

Dear Emily,

I HAD the pleasure of yours within these few days; and am much obliged to you for writing, without waiting to hear from me; there is however a letter of mine on its way to you, which I suppose you will soon receive, and which contains an account of our health, and so forth, I am sorry I cannot tell you that Eliza is better, but indeed I cannot as yet perceive the least amendment, tho' I do not think she is any thing worse.

Mrs. Fitzgerald has received great benefit from the air and exercise she takes here, if Eliza was well I believe her mother wou'd have no complaint.

I hope little Emily is quite recovered from the small-pox,* and congratulate you on her having it so favourably, and while she is so young; it is best early, let the event be what it will: for if they recover, there is a deal of anxiety over; but if it pleases Heaven to take them, the affliction cannot be so heavy for an infant, as if they were taken from us at a later period of their lives.

I had yesterday a letter from Henry Maunsell; he tells me Miss Freeman's health is in a most dangerous state; she was pretty well, and sent down to Sussex to enquire about Charles, but when she received for answer that he was gone abroad, disappointment and vexation, threw her into violent hysteric fits, which continued, with short intermissions, for two days, and have left her so weak and low that the phisicians apprehended a galloping consumption* will be the consequence, as medicine seems to have little or no effect; to be sure it cannot have much, as the cause of her disorder lies in her mind, and not likely to be removed.

What a dreadful thing it is to be governed so absolutely by our passions; for it brings on the worst kind of bodily complaints, which one would think sufficient to deter people from giving the reins to their headstrong inclinations, supposing they have no regard to religious precepts, which however ought to be the first motive with a christian to correct the wild sallies of an impetuous disposition.

Nature had been liberal of her endowments to Miss Freeman, both as to person and understanding, which had she made a proper use of, would have enabled her to make a pleasing, if not a shining figure, in life; but by forsaking the path of moral rectitude, she has lost both her health and her peace; the gentle heart of Eliza is grieved for her, tho' she is herself suffering from the unhappy girl's misconduct.

You cannot form an idea of any thing more beautiful than the situation and improvements of Roussillon;* I think the very air that blows there inspires one with the softest, most pleasing serenity imaginable, and I am not at all surprised that Gertrude should learn to love, and even be prevailed on to acknowledge it, in these delightful bowers; for doubtless external objects operate powerfully on the disposition of the mind;* especially of Women.

Place a pair of lovers on a barren rock, the wind and sea roaring round them, and I think the dreary prospect would extinguish every wish but that of finding shelter from the jarring elements; at least I will venture to answer for the damsel, that the tenderest eloquence would be lost on her in such a place; but change the scene, and place them in a blooming arbour, a gentle rivulet murmuring by, and all nature smiling round them, there let him tell his soft tale, and I think he need not doubt a kind reception; for me, I am so convinced of it, that I am arming my heart with all its insensibility against Harry Maunsell comes; for I think it will require no small degree of stoicism, to remain unmoved by the soft language of his speaking eyes, joined to the love-inspiring scene around me.

I fear if I was not fully prepared for the danger, I should, forgetful of my promise, and even of my own disinclination to matrimony, step to the next church and present him with my fair hand.

I think I hear you say, this girl's pen runs faster than her wit; but consider child, tho' I rattle a great deal, there is many a true word*— pardon me, I had like to write a whole proverb, in defiance of Lord Chesterfield.

The old Compte and Comptese and their daughters arrived at the Chatteau four days since; their son-in-law is to follow soon; they are most agreeable people; as for Madame St. Variolle I am quite charmed with her; and delighted to see the tender friendship that subsists between her and Gertrude; she is exceeding sprightly, but does not give into the gallantry that is usually practised here; I mean, she does not encourage any particular gentleman to attend her; as to the men in general, the custom of the country permits a degree of familiarity with them, that appears odd to us, whose manners are more reserved; it would throw us into the utmost confusion to have our male visitors ushered into our bedchambers before we were up, or to our toilet, while we were dressing: yet so powerful is custom; it is done here without the least idea of indelicacy by women who, I am convinced, are as perfectly virtuous as any woman in Ireland; and that I think is saying every thing for them: even amongst those married ladies who fall in with the fashion of having a particular admirer, (which most of them do) I am satisfied the greater number of them are as chaste as Lucretia.*

I know several of them, who from the justness of their sentiments, and the whole tenor of their conduct, I am persuaded, would not deviate from the right path, in so material a point; be it as it may, they are more refined in their gallantry than the English ladies, who are gross enough to stoop so low as their footmen and grooms, of which we have had several instances within these few years.*

Gertrude cannot be brought to comply with any of the customs I have mentioned, and is a good deal rallied for her bashfulness, even by the Compte: I dare say, she will in a while admit gentlemen to her toilet; it is almost impossible to avoid it, without being impolite and singular.

We have thoughts of taking a trip to Paris, that is Eliza and I, accompanied by Gertrude and her Lord, and Madame St. Veriolle, who has invited us to her house, and was indeed the first proposer of the jaunt; I had it in contemplation before, as a thing that would amuse Eliza, but had not mentioned it: she seemed pleased when it was spoke of, and Mrs. Fitzgerald consented at once; saying, she could never want company, there were so many of our acquaintances in town.

I fancy we shall set out in day or two; our stay will not be very long; so you need not expect to hear from me again, till after we return; by that time, perhaps, I shall have some interesting intelligence from Henry, who I imagine is ere now on his way to Geneva,* where he was informed Charles meant to make some stay.

We are going to dine at Roussillon, and I am yet to dress; I shall therefore bid you farewell, for I must take a little more time than usual, to make myself very lovely, as there are to be three or four young Dukes, and as many Marquisses* (nothing under to be met with here) who are all candidates for my favour.

Do you know that I am the admiration of the French Men! I quite eclipse Eliza, who is acknowledged to be infinitely handsomer; they say, if she had Miss Mortimer's vivacity, she would be but too charming; indeed I wish I could give her a little chearfulness; I would willingly share my conquests with her, if that would blot Charles from her memory—but it will not be.

Compliments to Mr. and Mrs. O'Neil:—believe me,

Affectionately

Your's,

LOUISA MORTIMER.

LETTER L.

Montpelier, Sept. 15. —

Dear Emily,

A Sudden illness which attacked Mrs. Fizgerald put a stop to our intended jaunt to Paris; for though she was well again in two days, we would not venture to leave her, as from the symptoms we feared it was the gout* in her stomach, which might return, and we could not have enjoyed ourselves under that apprehension, if we were three hundred and fifty miles from her: we therefore contented ourselves with making short excursions of two or three leagues, and have visited several of the nobility and gentry, who are relations or friends of the Roussillon family, and were every where received with that pleasing attention and politeness, for which this nation is distinguished, and which makes it such an agreeable residence for strangers.

The adjacent country is very delightful; but not near so populous as England or Ireland;* it is impossible it should, if we consider the thousands of both sexes that are buried in Convents;* besides their clergy being condemned to perpetual celibacy.

I will not dispute about the piety of shutting up their youth from the world, though, in my opinion, our duty to God does not consist in secluding ourselves from society; but putting religion out of the question, it is certainly the most impolitic custom, that was ever allowed by any government, since it must depopulate, and consequently impoverish the country.*

Spain and Portugal,* where this religious phrenzy* is carried to the highest excess, are melancholy proofs of it, for at least half of each kingdom lies uncultivated and uninhabited, while their convents and monasteries are crammed with people, who, were they exercising their different talents in the world, might be useful members of the community.

France is not so bad in this respect, as there are some bounds set here to superstition, and I think some limitation to the number of those houses; they begin to see how destructive these institutions are to the prosperity of the kingdom in general.

I have given you a dissertation upon Convents, as it is a subject England or Ireland does not afford us, and I thought you would expect something new from France.

I have had a letter from Harry Maunsell; he is yet at Geneva, and lodged at the same house with Mr. Skeffington.

The first night he arrived he stayed at the house where he set up; but you shall have it in his own words as follows:

"I went next day to a Coffee-house, where I thought it likely I should meet him: He was not there when first I went, but there were several Gentlemen of the town, with whom I had been acquainted when on my travels, who all came up to compliment me, and I had been conversing with them about half an hour, when Charles came in; his countenance shewed his mind was not at ease, for he appeared pale and languid, and much altered for the worse since last I saw him. He spoke to some Gentlemen near him, and then took a seat, without once perceiving me, and seemed so lost in thought, that when I went up to him, the sound of my voice made him start.

He however expressed great pleasure at seeing me, and asked was I going to Montpellier, as he knew I intended? Having answered him in the affirmative, he said he should be glad to accompany me, if I would wait till he got letters from England.

You may guess this proposal was instantly complied with on my part, as he could not have made a more agreeable offer.

At his request I then walked to his lodgings, and as we went he apologized for leaving England without seeing me, saying, he was at that time in a situation of mind not to be described; he was now better, and hoped time and proper reflexion would restore his peace; but added, sighing, it is hard to break the cord of affection that has been for years twining itself round the heart; I believe, Harry, that is a truth your own feelings will make you acknowledge. He touched a tender string; I too sighed assent to his observation, and the ideas it raised kept us both silent till we were seated in his apartments.

He then insisted I should dine with him; and said if I was not already fixed, I could be accommodated in that house, and it would make him very happy.

I soon agreed about it, and sending James with my Trunks, took immediate possession of my chambers.

In the evening we went out to pay some visits, and did not return until late, so that nothing farther passed that night on the material subject; but I determined to introduce it the first convenient offer he gave me, as I thought it necessary the affair should be thoroughly discussed before he and Miss Fitzgerald met.

But I do not mean to tell him she is at Montpellier; shame would certainly prevent his going there, for he has declared he never can bear to see her, after the unpardonable folly he has been guilty of, as he cannot expect forgiveness.

I had soon an opportunity of entering on the subject, by his mentioning Miss Freeman.

You are possessed of a happy insensibility, Charles, said I, that can speak with so much indifference of a woman that is dying for you.

He looked very serious, and said, he was not now in a disposition for joking: I assured him I did not mean it as a joke, then replied he, excuse me Mr. Maunsell, if I disapprove of your seriously affirming such an indelicate story of a young lady I highly esteem; though I am not coxcomb enough to suppose she loves me.——If, answered I, you really did not see her partiality to you, which I find other people did, I am not surprised you should be displeased at my mentioning it, as a woman's delicacy ought to be sacred; but when she herself departs from it, and goes such unwarrantable lengths to gratify her passion, surely she has no right to expect others will speak of her with much tenderness.

He looked astonished, and saying, he did by no means comprehend me, begged I would explain myself.

I immediately went for a small box, in which I kept the letters, and laying it on the table, told him, he would find in that a full explanation of the matter, and also of some disagreeable circumstances, which I believed would appear to him in a quite different light, after he had read those papers, from what they had done.

Being engaged for the evening, I left him to peruse them at his leisure, and make his own reflections on them.

I did not return until late, so went directly to my chamber, though James told me, Mr. Skeffington was not in bed, but had been walking about his room for some time, as if under an agitation; but as that was not an hour to enter on the topic, I retired to rest, and did not see him until we met at breakfast.

He looked embarrassed, and continued silent, seemingly at a loss how to begin the subject, until I led the way, by asking, had he looked over the letters? he replied, I have, and am ashamed of my own folly and ingratitude in affronting, by my unjust suspicions, the sweet girl who was incapable of giving me any real cause for them, though I have been so industrious in seeking out imaginary ones; but, said he, I have suffered severely for it, and shall continue to suffer even more from reflecting on the happiness I have wantonly flung from me.

I expressed a hope that matters might still be made up between him and Miss Fitzgerald; but he declared he could never bring himself to appear before her; or if he did, to what purpose would it be, for though the gentleness of her disposition might prevent her harbouring any violent resentment against him, yet he could not expect she would hazard her peace by uniting herself to a man who had given such proofs of a jealous temper; for notwithstanding I feel myself perfectly cured of that foible, how shall I convince her that it would not break out again: No, Maunsell, she never can so far forget the unkind treatment she has met with from me; and I must bid adieu to all the felicity I once promised myself.

He ceased speaking, and was so much affected, that I was moved at his affliction, especially as I thought his fears were well founded, and that it is very probable, though Miss Fitzgerald may pity and forgive, she will not marry him; unless she can be brought to believe, (as I really do) that he will never again yield to a passion which caused him so much uneasiness.

It was not for some time that he thought of asking how I came possessed of those letters? I told him James had some how got acquainted with Miss Vernon's Maid, who let him into the secret, and he knowing how much I was interested for your happiness, persuaded her to give him these papers, which would lay the whole scheme open; but I must tell you, Charles, your friends saw at first there was a plot in it, and as Miss Freeman immediately followed you to England, concluded it was concerted between you; till your going abroad, and the intelligence James gave me of the effect it had on the lady's health, convinced us, it was all her own contrivance.

He said he had no right to complain of our suspicions, since he must own appearances were much against him, especially to Eliza, who was conscious of her own innocence.

I took occasion from thence to preach to him on the folly of trusting to appearances, and not giving our own reason fair play; it was that hastiness in judging had caused all this misunderstanding, and interrupted his own peace as well as that of his dearest friends.

He acknowledged the justice of my observation, and said, he was so perfectly sensible of his error, that he hoped he was quite secure from falling into it again.

Indeed I hope and believe so too; if my Louisa should be of that opinion, will she not become his advocate with her fair friend? I have since told him all I had heard of the accident Miss Freeman met with on the road, and the very precarious state she is now in; for when I left England there was very little hopes of her: but I did not think it necessary to tell him it was I employed James to dive into the affair, since he did not seem to suspect it.

He made some pertinent remarks on the impropriety of the young lady's conduct, as well as her ingratitude to his Eliza, who had shewn her so much friendship.

We are now only waiting for the letters he expects from England, which I hope will not detain us much longer; as I have the utmost impatience till I again view that enchanting face, and hear the music of those accents, which vibrate to my heart, and cause such pleasing sensations, as none but those who love as I do can feel."

So far Harry Maunsell; you see I have given you the conclusion of his epistle, least you should imagine he was so stupid as not to be affected by our approaching meeting, or so impolite as not to tell me so:—Besides, I know young widows like to hear soft nonsense, whether said to themselves or others; not but I suppose you have sufficient entertainment of that sort from your own swain, now that all impediments are removed.

I charge you do not think of marrying till I return, for I intend the same day shall serve for you and Eliza, and then I can perform the part of bride-maid to you both; as I foresee my mediation will not be necessary to bring about a reconciliation* in that quarter.

Harry knows little of the matter, if he thinks his friend has need of an advocate; but I do not mean to tell him so; for it gives these men such consequence in their own eyes, when they find their influence is so powerful over our fond hearts.

Instead of pleading for the offender, I am endeavouring to fortify Eliza with resolution to keep up some degree of dignity on their meeting, and to take at least a few days before she suffers herself to be persuaded to sign his absolute pardon.

But I fear all my good lessons will be forgot, when the loved youth appears; unless the sense of his own demerits may make him too humble to ask a compleat restoration to her favour.

Harry's letter threw her into the prettiest agitation imaginable, when she found they were coming to Montpellier; but the idea of Charles's sufferings melted her to tears; in short, she was quite fluttered, and affected a hundred different ways; but that I am not surprized at, for her mother was not much better, though the affection she bears him is only that of a parent, while her daughter's are of a much tenderer kind.

Her health mends apace, and her countenance begins to wear its usual serenity; even the country seems to have new beauties for her; at least she had hitherto passed them over unnoticed; so true is that line of the song,

"We only can taste when the heart is ease."*

Well, these sensitive plants may boast of their exquisite feelings, but for me, I am content to be only moderately happy, on condition of never being supremely miserable; and for that purpose took pains to suppress those violent sensibilities that would not be controuled by reason, and are therefore always dangerous, and frequently fatal, to the person who possesses them.

A letter from Harriet Boyle to Eliza, informs her of her sister's nuptials with Mr. Hamilton; I wonder how Charles will look when he hears of it; for Harry does not say he had mentioned any thing of that to him.

Mrs. Fitzgerald begins to long for home; however we shall not leave this for some time yet; it would be foolish to make so short a stay, after so long a journey.

I shall not write to you again till I can inform you how matters are accommodated between Charles and Eliza.

Your's,

LOUISA MORTIMER.

LETTER LI.

MISS MORTIMER TO MRS. ROCHFORT.

Montpellier, Sept. 28. —

I AM sure my dear Emily will be full of impatience to know how our lovers quarrel has ended; why, as all love quarrels do end; in an encreased affection for each other.

As I foretold, she signed an act of oblivion,* as soon as he could assume resolution enough to ask it, which was not for two days, such a just sense had he of his high crimes and misdemeanors.*

I am provoked that she could think more lightly of them than he did; I would have taken one little week's beseeching, at least, before I would have suffered myself to be prevailed on; a pardon so easily obtained may encourage him to farther transgressions; but Eliza has no art, and as her heart forgave, she could not keep her tongue from acknowledging it: to tell truth, I believe she will have no cause to repent; for he seems so perfectly convinced of his fault, that I think it impossible he can ever fall into it again—But I must tell you how matters were conducted to bring them together.

Harry never gave the smallest hint of our being here, and contrived not to come in till night, least they should by any accident meet us or our servants; he then made some excuse for going out, and came himself to inform me of their arrival.

Fortunately Eliza was in her mother's chamber; and it was agreed between him and me he should bring Charles in the morning, as if to visit a friend of his; and I was to prepare the ladies for the interview.

When he left me, which was not till I positively insisted on his going, I went to Mrs. Fitzgerald's room to communicate the matter to them, having first bid Kitty withdraw; but I was soon obliged to recal her; for I had but just said Mr. Maunsell was with me, when Eliza dropt on the floor in a fainting fit, which put us all into a hurry and confusion for some minutes, when she began to revive, and soon after, by proper applications, was perfectly recovered.

Her spirits, which were always weak, have been still weaker this while past, and sunk under the sudden mention of Harry's arrival, knowing who accompanied him.

When we were once more left to ourselves, I told her, if she had not resolution to support the idea of seeing Mr. Skeffington, I feared she would never stand a meeting next morning, so I had better write a note to forbid his coming, as such another fit might have a bad effect on her health.

She begged I would not teaze her, but tell her was he really to come, since she found some preparation would be necessary to enable her to receive him with any degree of composure.

I then informed her how we had settled it, and advised her to retire to rest, and try to conquer the flutter she had thrown herself into, else Charles must have a physician for his gentleman-usher; as I supposed his palpitations would be as great as her's, some of the faculty* should certainly be at hand to apply proper restoratives.

I was obliged to talk nonsense, to prevent her making such a serious matter of it, and when I had set her and her mother laughing, at the ridiculous description of what I suppose their meeting would be, I bid them good night, and went to my bed, where I slept very comfortably, till disturbed by Eliza, who, I dare say, had not closed her eyes.

I arose, and was but just dressed, when our French Valet informed me two gentlemen enquired for me.——I instantly went to them, and soon as I entered the room, Mr. Skeffington approached with a rueful countenance, and with great humility kissing my hand, said, will Miss Mortimer receive a penitent, and deign to intercede with her lovely friend for a man who has so high a sense of his faults, that he is incapable of pleading his own cause!

I told him, smiling, his sex were seldom so humble; therefore, as I loved to encourage good dispositions, and had beside a proper state of the case laid before me by Mr. Maunsell, I had ventured to become his advocate, and had so far succeeded, that his aunt and cousin had promised to receive him as a friend that had been absent, without any retrospect to former disagreeable occurrences, which I believed it would be best not to mention as yet.

He was full of acknowledgments for my kindness; and I conducted him to his audience.

His colour went and came as he approached, and his voice faultered so, he could not articulate a word, which Mrs. Fitzgerald observing, stept forward to meet him, and kindly taking his hand, said, my dear child, I rejoice to see you, (indeed she loves him as if he was her own) then turning to Eliza, will not you welcome your cousin my love? The dear girl, who was little less agitated than he, held out her hand, which he pressed to his lips, and then ventured to salute her; while she was utterly unable to speak, as a tear stood trembling in her eye, which would have overflowed its bounds on the least attempt at speech: their silence however was sufficiently eloquent, since it plainly discovered how their hearts stood affected to each other.

I thought it high time to put an end to the pantomime, which was likely to become too distressing, so hurried them into the breakfast room where Harry was; who, advancing to pay his compliments, relieved them all from a very aukward situation.

The conversation then became general, till the gentlemen left us, to pay a visit at Roussillon; being first invited to dinner by Mrs. Fitzgerald.

Harry told me after, he had informed Mr. Skeffington, when he got him near our hotel, who he was to meet, and it was with the greatest difficulty he could prevail on him to proceed; not till he assured him, I would interest myself in his favor, and knowing my influence over Eliza he had no doubt of my success.

They continued on these terms for two days, not a hint of past transactions dropping from either party; when being all engaged to pass the day at the Chateau, every one, as is usual there, disposed of themselves as they found most agreeable.

Eliza, it seems, had retired to that arbour, where the Compte first declared his passion to Gertrude, and was followed by Charles, who had observed where she went.

I also was straying in the garden, and passing in sight of the place; she came out and joined me, not thinking I saw him there: but if I had not, the blush still mantling* on her cheek would have betrayed her: I just patted it saying, well Eliza, that blush is not for nothing; Charles has pleaded his cause more effectually than the ablest advocate could do; is it not so, she said, I was a provoking girl, and she would not tell me; she knew I would blame her, and she could not help it now.

Indeed, Eliza, you wrong me; I never blame any one for consulting their own happiness; and I suppose, my dear, you are the best judge of what will constitute your's.

Fie Louisa, said she; there is no standing your looks, no more than your expressions, when you chuse to be teizing.——Just then, to her great relief, we were joined by Madame de St. Veriolle, which prevented our pursuing the subject.

I am sure she was heartily glad of the interruption, for I dare say, she could not have brought herself to tell me, she had consented to give her hand to Charles as soon after our return to Ireland, as matters could be settled for the purpose; which I was informed of by Henry, the first opportunity he had of speaking to me alone.

He was full of joy at his friend's success; and asked if Eliza had told me; no, I replied; but I knew something of the kind had been the consequence, when I saw she had been with him in the arbour, for arbours are of all other places the most dangerous to female resolution; he laughed at the idea; and clasping me to his bosom, wished, if that was the case, he could find me in one.—When we get home, you will be all marrying and giving in marriage;* I only shall remain in the singular case.

I don't however find myself a bit uneasy at the reflection: the epithet of old maid, is not at all formidable to me; for as I at present meet as much respect as most of the matrons I know, I suppose that will not be lessened, when encrease of years makes me wiser and better than I am now.——I tell you, Emily, I shall retain my good humour, when you and Eliza are fretting over your squalling Infants.

Charles means to set off in a few days, as he had a good deal of business to do, preparatory to making settlements, and so forth; and wishes to be in Dublin before November.

We shall remain here till the latter end of October, and Mr. Maunsell stays to be Eliza's Cecisbo: as for me, I have about a dozen lively Frenchmen at command, amongst whom I dispense my smiles so equally, that one cannot be jealous of another, and I reign sole Empress of them all.

Eliza's ideas are so totally engrossed by one object that she can find no amusement in the agreeable gallantry she would receive here, without their having the least design on her heart; but she would not take it on her conscience to encourage it, fearing least any of them should think her serious, and be hurt when he found she was engaged.

I cannot perswade her that those things are mere matters of course here, and meant only as politeness; it is impossible to argue her out of romantic notions.

Harry takes up his abode at Roussillon as soon as Charles goes, according to invitation, the old Compte and Comptesse return soon to Paris, and their son-in-law accompanies them: their daughter stays till Gertrude and her lord goes, which will be immediately after we leave this; as she would shortly be unfit for travelling.

You need not expect to hear from me again; for I do not intend writing any more while I am here: and I hope to find you, and most of my friends, in Dublin, by the time I get there.

You are very idle, or rather you have more agreeable amusement *pour passer le tempts*,* than writing to me; I have had but one letter from you yet: Had I thought of that sooner, I would not have said a word about Charles and Eliza, and that would mortify you.

Perhaps you will say, it would be no loss since I have so bad a hand at describing love scenes; true, but I have given you the outlines, and as I dare say you are now pretty conversant in them, you may supply the deficiency by the power of your own imagination. —And so, in the true royal stile, we bid you

    Heartily farewell,

LOUISA MORTIMER.

P. S. I forgot to tell you the news of Mr. Hamilton's marriage, which I took an opportunity to mention, seemed to strike Charles with great surprise; and when I observed to him, it was a thing guessed at by most of their acquaintance, before he left Ireland; he looked in some confusion, and said, indeed, Miss Mortimer, I think I was under infatuation, for many circumstances now come into my mind, that might have convinced me it was so, if I had not been blinded by that unhappy passion.——But I hope it is for the best; as the misery I have endured, has most effectually cured me, and since my gentle Eliza pardons me, I am once more happy.

LETTER LII.

Dublin, Dec. 12. —

MISS MORTIMER TO THE COMPTESSE DE ROUSILLON.

HERE we are, my dear Gertrude, after four months ramble, enjoying our-selves under our own vines, and under our own fig-trees: No, that will never do in a city.—But what is far more comfortable at this season, and in our climate, we are snug at our fire-sides, talking over the pleasing hours we spent with our kind friends at Roussillon.

As I wrote to you on our arrival at Harwick; I have taken a little time to rest since I came home, before I would take up the pen again; for I assure you, our journey from London was very fatiguing and disagreeable; the weather being extremely severe; at least we found it so, we had been so long used to the mild air of Montpellier, where none but gentle breezes fan the rosy bowers.

While we were in London, James brought us the account of Miss Freeman's death—she had languished in a wretched state, from the time she heard that Charles was gone abroad, mostly delirious, in which way she died, a martyr to her own ungovernable passions.

There is something shocking in a woman's so far departing from the delicacy of her sex, and all the rules of decorum, as this unhappy girl did, I think her friends may rejoice that she is no more; for had she lived, with so little regard to religion, or rectitude, as appeared in her conduct, it is more than probable, she would have brought a reproach on herself and them.

I found Mr. and Mrs. Herbert in town, and all their little ones; they have five lovely children; and the best behaved babies I ever saw.

Their mother, without any harshness, has let them see they must obey her, therefore it is a point they never dispute, and a grave look from her, is more effectual, than correction from one who only indulges or chides her children rather according to her own caprice than their deserts.

Mr. Herbert is very partial to his eldest girl, though Patty frequently remon-strates against it as unjust; and in her own behaviour, takes care to shew equal affection to them all, when they equally deserve it, which prevents their little hearts from being filled with jealousy and animosity against each other.

You may guess how happy it makes me, to have Patty once more in the same street with me, as she now is we call to remembrance a thousand pleasing circum-stances that occurred in our childish days, and enjoy over again our early friendship.

Harry, who tenderly loves his sister, and has, as you know, some small regard for your humble servant, is quite delighted to get us together, and joins in rec-ollecting past pleasures: but then he is too apt to dwell on those incidents that made the deepest impression on his heart; however, his tranquillity seems restored, which adds much to my satisfaction.

It is quite distressing to see our friends repining at disappointments that cannot be remedied; and refusing the happiness within their reach, because some one thing they wish for is with-held; perhaps if it was granted, the acquisition might make them miserable, a thing we have frequent examples of: yet we are not to be convinced that Providence is wiser than we are.

Mrs. Rochfort is come to town with her father and mother; her marriage is fixed for the 16th; Eliza's the day after.

She insisted on Emily taking the lead, as she was determined to be bride-maid; I would not say any thing against it, because I was glad to see her in such good spirits; but I have a notion she will repent placing herself in such a conspicuous light, the day before her own wedding. She must probably stand many jokes on the occasion, but that to be sure has never occurred to her.

She looks, and is as well as ever I saw her; the cause of her illness, which was uneasiness of mind, being removed, the effect has ceased.

Mr. Skeffington has given James Grady fifty guineas as a reward for the part he took in bringing those letters to light; and I find this encrease of fortune has encouraged him to offer his hand to my Jenny; (his heart has long been her's) and Jenny has condescended to accept it, with my approbation.—You may be sure I shall make some addition to her portion; and I assure you, she has saved a good deal in my service.

They mean to go into business, linen and haberdashery* they have fixed on.

I shall certainly countenance them; for I think it but right to promote the interest of servants who have been honest and faithful; though I totally disapprove of making them confidants, or allowing them any influence over us: their education renders them unfit for advisers, and we often see the bad effects of young ladies placing confidence in their waiting-maids, who always encourage them in whatever they know to be their inclination, as they are sure of being rewarded for any assistance they lend; or even where they mean well, ignorance often leads them into errors; they do not foresee the bad consequences that may attend their repeating what they hear, as was the case with Eliza's Kitty; for I am sure the girl loves her mistress; yet Charles incautiously betraying his temper to her, was near proving fatal to the peace of the whole family.

Eliza has talked to her a great deal on the subject, and intimated an intention of parting with her, lest her indiscretion might hereafter create disturbance; for as she exposed the only defect she had discovered in Mr. Skeffington's disposition to a stranger, she was no longer to be trusted.

Poor Kitty came in great woe, to request my interest with her mistress not to discharge her, promising never to commit such a fault again; and she is accordingly reinstated in Eliza's favour.

You shall hear from me when the weddings are over. I am anxiously expecting an account of your being safe and well; *faite me baisemens a Monsieur La Compte:** and pray present my best respects to all his agreeable family, particularly his amiable sister.

Your friends here join in the most affectionate wishes for your health and happiness, none more sincerely than

Your

LOUISA MORTIMER.

LETTER LIII.

FROM THE SAME TO THE SAME.

— Dec. 18. —

At length, my dear Gertrude, Eliza's novel is concluded, like most other novels, with the serious catastrophe, matrimony.*

The ceremony was performed yesterday evening, in what we call a private manner; that is, quite in the family way; but in such a family as theirs, you know what a croud they make when gathered together on these occasions.

Eliza did not behave quite as well as your ladyship in the same circumstances; for it was with the utmost difficulty she could say, "I will" loud enough to be heard by the Clergyman, and as to the rest, we could only perceive her lips moved to the words; the good man, however, who saw her heart was consenting, took the will for the deed, else I think she would still have remained a maiden; indeed he espoused the cause of his sex so far, as to insist on her pronouncing the word obey,* pretty audibly: now had I been in her place, that of all words never should have passed my lips; I whispered that to Harry first opportunity; he replied, smiling, he would venture to take me even on them terms, if I would say I loved: No, said I, for if you would dispense with my promising obedience, I should fear you meant to enforce the doctrine by some more powerful argument: he called me some fond name, saying, he must be a brute indeed that would desire me to comply with any thing that was disagreeable to me.

How mild and gentle those men talk before marriage, and how soon they change their tone after; yet you can produce one that continues the same stile, and I have some little idea that Harry would have been like him.

I wish he could conquer an attachment that promises so little satisfaction; for I want to make up a match between him and Harriet Boyle, whose heart seems perfectly disengaged, and she has wholly laid aside her affectation—but it is in vain to think of it, for he is quite determined.

How I wander from my subject: to return to it then—Charles's behaviour was tender and attentive, but delicately so, endeavouring all he could to keep up her spirits, in which Harry and I assisted him; for the rest of the young folks were more inclined to amuse themselves at her expence.

Cards however relieved her from their raillery, beside some share of it was directed to Emily and her bride-groom, who, as I told you, were married the night before, and a good many of the same company had been at their wedding.

She too was much affected; though she had gone through all the ceremony before; but her heart was now concerned, and she was agitated by all the hopes and fears, so natural to those who love.

Doubtless the unhappiness she had already experienced in the state, must have caused some disagreeable sensations, when she reflected on the possibility of being again subject to the same, though there is all the reason in the world to believe she has nothing of that kind to fear from her present choice, as there does not appear to be the least defect in his temper, and she, you know, is all sweetness.

They are to accompany Charles and his bride to Castle Skeffington; as will all the bride men and maids; of which number are Mr. Maunsell, and your Louisa.

We spend the christmas there; then pay a visit, by invitation, to Mr. and Mrs. Hamilton, and return from thence to Dublin.

I forgot to tell you Mr. Fitzgerald looked a little cool on Charles when first they met, after our return from France, and not very cordial on Eliza; he was displeased with him for his behaviour, and with her for not resenting it; till I laid the true state of the affair before him, which reconciled him to them both, else it might have had unpleasing consequences, as he would have certainly told Mr. Skeffington his mind, who would probably have been too high spirited to enter into any explanation of the matter.

The prevalence of that most horrid custom, duelling,* makes one tremble at the prospect of warm words between men.

Eliza, who observed her cousin's coolness, was very apprehensive, till I undertook to remove it: I was happy in succeeding; and they are now just as usual.

We shall leave town, the 20th, do not expect another epistle till I come back; for I know we shall live in a perpetual hurry of company while we remain in the country; as all the people will croud to pay their compliments to the two new married couple.

Mrs. Fitzgerald is, I suppose, the happiest creature now in the kingdom, in seeing her two darlings united, after the great danger there was of their being separated for ever.

She has forgot all her complaints, and is as young as any of us: I hope she will long continue to enjoy her present satisfaction, which nothing can add to, except living to see half a dozen grand-children playing about her.

I expect my next will be a congratulation on the birth of a little Monsieur or Madamoiselle; be it which it will I beseech you, Gertrude, do not dress it in the French stile* till it's childish years are somewhat passed.

I think the children in France, so be-powdered, and curled, have just the appearance of a race of dwarfs; do let yours look like infants while they are so; for you cannot make them like any thing half so pleasing.

The time employed in writing this, I have stolen from the hours of rest; finding it impossible to obtain a moment for the purpose during the day, I am so entirely engaged with the wedding folks, who will not excuse my absence.

They all desire me to assure you and the Compte of their kindest regards.

I kiss your hands:*

And am,

My dear Gertrude's

Very affectionate

LOUISA MORTIMER.

FINIS.

NEW BOOKS,

Printed and sold by

S. COLBERT,

No. 136, *Capel-street, opposite Abbey-street.*

I. E M E L I N E : a Moral Tale:*

By an I R I S H   L A D Y ,

Price 1s. 7dh. sewed, 2s. 2d. bound.

This Tale is written in a pleasing manner, and displays much merit and literary talents, distinguished by many just and pertinent remarks.

II. The Tutor,*

OR

History of GEORGE WILSON

AND

LADY FRANCES MELFONT,

In a Series of Letters,

Price sewed 2s. 2d. bound 2s. 8dh.

By the Author of LOUISA
MILDMAY, &c.

"These Letters describe several characters and relate many interesting events in a new and agreeable manner. Throughout them are interspersed many generous sentiments and noble observations that do honour to the heart and head of the Writer."

REVIEWERS.

Notes

t/p *Authoress of* Emeline: The author of *The Triumph of Prudence over Passion* had earlier written *Emeline: A Moral Tale* (1780), described as being by '*An Irish Lady*', and also printed and sold in Dublin by Stephen Colbert (see following note); see also n. to t/p 2 below.

t/p *S. Colbert*: Stephen Colbert (d. 1786), Dublin bookseller and printer, in business at 69 St Stephen's Green before moving to 136 Capel Street. Although fiction was an important part of his output, he also ran a circulating library, and published *Sketches of the history of Poyning's law* (1780), at a time when this law, which subordinated the Irish parliament to the parliament at Westminster, was a cause of the widespread public discontent that animates the novel's opening pages. See Mary Pollard, *A Dictionary of Members of the Dublin Book Trade, 1500–1800* (London: Bibliographical Society, 2000), p. 110.

t/p *M,DCC,XXXI*: The given publication date of 1731 is an obvious error; the correct date should read MDCCLXXXI: i.e., 1781; *The Triumph of Prudence over Passion, or the History of Miss Mortimer and Miss Fitzgerald* was first advertised on 8 December 1781 in the *Dublin Evening Post*.

t/p 2 *The Triumph of Prudence over Passion* was republished in London by William Lane two years after its appearance in Dublin, using the same sheets, but with a new title-page, and different title. Lane also published a London edition of the earlier novel by the same author, again with a different title: *The Fairy Ring; or, Emeline: A Moral Tale. By a Lady* (London, 1783); see n. to t/p, 'Authoress of *Emeline*' above. Lane appears to have had some more general business connection with Stephen Colbert, since in 1783 he produced a London edition of another novel first printed by Colbert in Dublin: *The School for Majesty; or, The Sufferings of Zomelli* (1780). After 1790, Lane became celebrated as owner of the Minerva Press, the most famous publisher of Gothic and sentimental fiction of the late-eighteenth and early-nineteenth century.

p. 31 *Nov. 4 1779*: Louisa's letter is written on a signally important date in late-eighteenth-century Irish history, when the Dublin corps of the Volunteers paraded on College Green, before John Michael Rysbrack's equestrian statue of King William III, the anniversary of whose birthday was marked by public celebration throughout the eighteenth century. On this occasion, the statue, situated outside the Irish parliament building, was decorated with slogans in capital letters, including 'A FREE TRADE: OR ELSE', so that the parade, ostensibly a mark of loyalty to the monarchy, was in fact a challenge to the British government and its supporters in parliament to allow Irish merchants the right to trade with Great Britain and the colonies on equal terms with British merchants. See also n. to p. 31, 'Volunteers' below.

p. 31 *diverted*: Louisa Mortimer's declaration that she intends to do no more than 'amuse' or 'divert' her correspondent Eliza Fitzgerald is not to be taken literally for many of her letters offer decisive social or political opinions, making them, in the much-quoted phrase of the Roman poet Horace, both 'dulce et utile': i.e., 'entertaining and useful' (Horace, *Ars Poetica*, ll. 343–4).

p. 31 *town*: i.e., Dublin. Like other characters of genteel background in the novel, the Fitzgeralds have both a country residence and a town house.

p. 31 *ponds and lakes*: This topography, taken with evidence in the novel that the implied location is three days' travel from Dublin, and in the north, and using a standard calculation for late-eighteenth-century travel of four British miles per hour, suggests that the Fitzgeralds and the neighbouring Skeffingtons live in north Co. Cavan, close to the Sheridan family home of Quilca; Arthur Young described the county as having 'a great deal of bog and mountain, which with lakes, amount to half the county', *A Tour in Ireland ... made in the years 1776, 1777, and 1778*, 2 vols (Dublin, 1780), I, p. 290.

p. 31 *laudable custom*: Agrarian unrest had increased in Ireland during the 1770s but a paternalism in which relationships between conscientious landowners and their tenants were characterized by mutual obligation still obtained to some degree.

p. 31 *Mr. Skeffington*: Originally from Leicestershire in the English midlands, the Skeffingtons were a politically active family in eighteenth-century Ireland, especially in counties Antrim and Derry.

p. 31 *sett*: i.e., let, leased.

p. 31 *Volunteers*: The Irish Volunteer Corps was a voluntary association of protestants initially dedicated to preserving law and order in Ireland following the departure of regular troops for north America, in the wake of the American Revolution of 1776. In 1779, their numbers more than trebled to around 40,000, giving the administration in Dublin Castle cause for serious concern, since the Volunteers were becoming increasingly politicized, particularly in support of the 'Free Trade' movement, a political challenge that led to the British government's concession of equal trading rights for Irish merchants in the following year. The parade of 900 Volunteers on 4 November 1779 is the subject of the celebrated large group painting, *The Dublin Volunteers on College Green, 4th November 1779* (1779–80), by the English artist, Francis Wheatley (1747–1801).

Francis Wheatley, *The Dublin Volunteers on College Green, 4th November 1779* (NGI 125), reproduced courtesy of the National Gallery of Ireland.

p. 31 *memory of King William*: Protestants held annual public celebrations in Ireland on both 4 and 5 November, the former date being the monarch's birthday, the latter the date of the arrival of the-then Prince William of Orange at Torbay, en route from Holland to London, to take the throne, along with his wife, Mary, daughter of the deposed Roman Catholic king, James II.

p. 31 *Regulars*: i.e., the troops of the regular army, whose regiments had been transferred to north America; see p. 31 note, above, 'Volunteers'.

p. 32 *friends to Government*: Louisa extols the virtues of the so-called 'Patriot' members of the Irish parliament in contrast to the 'friends' of the British administration, opposed to the granting of equal trade rights.

p. 32 *Liberty and my country*: Louisa's version of the Latin phrase 'Libertas et Natale solum', here denoting Protestant Irish freedom from both Roman Catholic and British arbitrary power.

p. 32 *first rank and property ... most eminent citizens*: Eighteenth-century political rights were founded on landed property and the principal characters of the novel are members of the gentry, with the extensive landed estates understood to give them a fixed, inalienable interest in their country, unlike those citizens who, without landed estates, were nonetheless enfranchised.

p. 32 *November the 5th*: See n. to p. 31 above, 'Memory of King William'.

p. 32 *post-chaise*: A four-wheeled enclosed carriage.

p. 32 *up to their bellies in the mud*: The detail alerts Louisa to the fact that the post-chaise has just arrived in the Irish capital from the countryside.

p. 32 *Gertrude ... mother of this family*: Louisa, whose own mother is dead, has ceded management of the domestic economy of the household to Gertrude because she makes a 'much better figure in the office' (p. 32).

p. 32 *jointure*: An estate limited to a wife, designed to support her in the event of her husband's death.

p. 33 *a child has a natural right to a negative voice*: That both parents and child had a right to exercise a veto over the latter's prospective wedding partner was a commonplace in eighteenth-century conduct literature, regularly invoked in late-seventeenth and eighteenth-century fiction; for an articulation of this in a work that continued to be reprinted into the 1780s, see Richard Allestree, *The Ladies Calling* (Oxford, 1673): 'a negative voice in the case is sure as much the Child's right, as the Parent's', p. 162.

p. 33 *All for Love ... deep tragedy to them*: *All For Love; or, The World Well Lost* (1678) was the version by John Dryden (1631–1700) of the story told in Shakespeare's *Antony and Cleopatra*; the play, Dryden's finest, was much more often performed on the eighteenth-century stage than Shakespeare's.

p. 33 *competency*: An income sufficient for the necessities of life, 'necessities' being variously understood, as Louisa acknowledges, according to one's 'rank in life'.

p. 33 *fierce flaming love ... passion ... sentiment*: Passion is understood in the novel as a manifestation not of love but excessive desire, allied variously to lust and madness; sentiment, by contrast, suggests a rational emotion.

p. 33 *Louisa Mortimer*: The name, Mortimer, is of Anglo-Norman origin; see also n. to p. 68 below, 'from the oldest families in England'.

p. 34 *Castle Skeffington*: See n. to p. 31 above, 'ponds and lakes'.

p. 34 *warm*: i.e., angry.

p. 34 *Mr. Hamilton ... county of Derry*: The name Hamilton is Scottish in origin, and was common in the north of Ireland following the seventeenth-century plantation of the province by mainly Scottish settlers.

p. 34 *travels*: Mr. Hamilton has just returned from making the Grand Tour, the completion of a wealthy eighteenth-century gentleman's education, taking him to France, Italy, and perhaps Germany, the Low Countries and Switzerland; the study of the laws, customs and manners of the different nations he visited were supposed to fit him to play an appropriate role in his own country on his return, not least as a prospective member of parliament.

p. 35 *adventure*: The use of the term 'adventure' to describe the chance encounter with Mr. Hamilton suggests the limited scope for experience appropriate to young women of Eliza Fitzgerald's social background; though 'The Adventures of ...' was a familiar formulation for eighteenth-century fiction the inappropriateness of young women of virtue and social rank experiencing 'adventures' is considered at length in Charlotte Lennox's *The Female Quixote; or, The Adventures of Arabella* (1752), esp. volume II, chapter 6.

p. 35 *penetration*: insight.

p. 35 *mal-a-propos*: i.e., *mal à propos* (Fr.), inopportune.

p. 35 *Rochfort*: A surname present in Ireland from the time of the Anglo-Norman invasion and relatively widespread, especially in Munster; here, indifferently, Rochfort and Rochford.

p. 35 *a time of slavery*: Eliza's comparison of marriage to slavery draws on a long tradition of early feminist thought epitomized by Mary Astell's *Some Reflections upon Marriage* (1700), in which the author asks 'If *Men are born free*, how is it that all Women are born Slaves? as they must be if the being subjected to the *inconstant, uncertain, unknown, arbitrary* Will of Men, be the *perfect Condition of Slavery?*', *Some Reflections upon Marriage ... To which is added a preface* (London, 1706), 'The Preface', p. [xiii].

p. 36 *Roman Matron ... commonwealth*: Eliza's reference is not only to the Roman republic (*res publica*=commonwealth) which lasted from the overthrow of the monarchy at the beginning of the sixth century BC until Gaius Julius Caesar became the first Roman emperor in 27 BC, adding Augustus to his name, but more specifically to Thomas Sheridan's adaptation of *Coriolanus*, made after Shakespeare, and including passages from James Thomson's 1745 version of the play, acted under the title, *Coriolanus; or, The Roman Matron* (1755), in which Veturia, mother of Coriolanus, declares: 'A Roman Matron knows, in such extremes, what part to take', as she persuades her son to desist in his alliance with the Volscians, leading him to exclaim: 'Ah, Veturia!/Rome by thy aid is sav'd' (Act V).

p. 36 *luxury and corruption*: That Roman virtues were lost to 'luxury and corruption' was a commonplace view at the end of the eighteenth century; see, for example, Oliver Goldsmith, *The Roman History* (1769) which reached its fourth edition in 1781, besides abridgements for use in schools.

p. 36 *public virtue*: Eliza prides herself on the possession of the quality – a desire to act *pro bono publico* (for the public good) – deemed necessary for the existence of the republic or commonwealth.

p. 36 *patriots*: Here, the phrase suggests both those activated by disinterested love of their country and the 'Patriots' in the Irish House of Commons; see n. to p. 32 above, 'friends to Government' and n. to p. 52 below, 'staunch patriot'.

p. 36 *glorious times of Greece and Rome*: i.e., during their republican government; see also n. to p. 36 above, '*Roman Matron ... commonwealth*' and n. to p. 39 below, '*Spartan wives or mothers*'.

p. 36 *present mode of education*: Eliza's reflection on the limitations of female education anticipates the criticisms of such later educational reformers as Catharine Macaulay (1731–91) and Maria Edgeworth (1768–1849).

p. 36 *pen runs on of itself*: Eliza seems to recall Laurence Sterne's *The Life and Opinions of Tristram Shandy, Gentleman* (1759–67): 'But this is neither here nor there—why do I mention it?——Ask my pen,—it governs me.—I govern not it' (VI, vi).

p. 36 *Eliza Fitzgerald*: Anglo-Norman in origin, the Fitzgeralds had been earls of Kildare since 1316; the 21st earl, and second duke of Leinster, William Robert Fitzgerald (1749–1804) was closely involved in the Patriot movement, and he was commander-in-chief of the Volunteers at the time of the demonstration in Dublin of 4 November 1779, though succeeded by Lord Charlemont in 1780.

p. 37 *Parliament*: The 1779–80 session of the Irish Parliament opened in October, when there was a demand for free trade; the crisis came to a head at the end of November 1779.

p. 37 *a good head, and a good heart*: i.e., possessed of both reason and feeling.

p. 37 *sensibility*: Here, in an unusual usage, emotional consciousness or awareness.

p. 37 *Mr. Boyle*: Boyle was the family name of the one of the most important political dynasties in seventeenth- and eighteenth-century Ireland, with extensive land-holdings in Munster.

p. 37 *Bell-Park*: The name recalls two particularly notable contemporary estates in Co. Cavan: Bellamont Forest, the home of Charles Coote, earl of Bellamont, at Cootehill, and Belleville, the home of Thomas Fleming, just outside Cavan town.

p. 38 *handsome widow, of eighteen*: In the eighteenth century, and with parental consent, the legal marriage age for men was 14 and for women 12.

p. 38 *women are rational creatures ... themselves*: Eliza's sentiments perhaps echo her praise of Roman society, since the late-eighteenth century gave the Romans credit for promoting female education, in order to fit women 'for society, and for becoming rational companions'; William Alexander, *The History of Women* (1779; repr. Dublin, 1779), I, p. 151, though in *A Vindication of the Rights of Woman*, Mary Wollstonecraft still felt the need to assert that women were indeed 'rational creatures', arguing for instance 'that not only the virtue, but the *knowledge* of the two sexes should be the same in nature, if not in degree, and that women, considered not only as moral, but rational creatures, ought to endeavour to acquire human virtues ... by the *same* means as men' (London, 1792), p. 77.

p. 38 *ENTRE NOUS*: (French) between ourselves.

p. 38 *I who hate monopolies*: Louisa has particularly in mind Great Britain's monopoly of trade in relation to Ireland; see William Eden, Baron Auckland, *Considerations Submitted to the People of Ireland on their Present Condition with Regard to Trade and Constitution* (2nd ed.; Dublin, 1781), p. 71: 'They [the Irish] now see that their constitution had been shackled only for the purpose of securing to Great Britain a monopoly in their trade; and that the cause being removed the effect must cease'. Auckland was Chief-Secretary in Ireland 1780–2.

p. 38 *trading style*: It was Daniel Defoe (1660–1731) who first gave instructions for 'writing to Correspondents in a Trading Stile', *The Complete English Tradesman, in Familiar Letters*, 2 vols (2nd ed.; London, 1727), I, title-page.

p. 39 *tyranny and oppression*: Louisa again echoes sentiments most notably expressed in the eighteenth century by Mary Astell; see also n. to p. 35 above, 'a time of slavery'.

p. 39 *Spartan wives or mothers*: Louisa has perhaps been reading Oliver Goldsmith's *The Grecian History, from the earliest state to the death of Alexander the Great*, 2 vols (London and Dublin, 1774), which reports Spartan women to have been 'bold, frugal, and patriotic, filled with a sense of honour, and a love of military glory', and that the wife of Leonidas declared that 'the Spartan women alone bring forth men' (Dublin, 1774), p. 23; see also n. to p. 36 above, '*glorious times of Greece and Rome*'.

p. 39 *lords of the creation*: Louisa alludes scathingly to the account of the creation of woman from Adam's rib, Genesis 2:19–23.

p. 40 *supper*: In the late-eighteenth century supper was usually taken between ten and eleven in the evening.

p. 40 *true born Irish-man*: Though the phrase perhaps most immediately brings to mind Charles Macklin's successful farce, *The True-born Irishman* (1762), Eliza praises Mr. Boyle in more positive terms such as Richard Lewis used in his dedication of *A Defence of Ireland* (Dublin, 1776) to Sir Edward Newenham, MP for Co. Dublin, whom he describes as 'A true-born Irishman, who has made the most costly sacrifices to the liberties of his country, when violated by arbitrary and wicked English ministers' (p. [iii]).

p. 40 *prudent œconomy*: Eliza's account of Mr. Boyle suggests an idealized contrast with the popular image of the spendthrift Irish gentry most famously represented in fiction by Maria Edgeworth in *Castle Rackrent: an Hibernian Tale* (1800).

p. 40 *rational being … garden*: See n. to p. 38 above, 'women are rational creatures … themselves'.

p. 41 *staid*: i.e., stayed.

p. 41 *Harpsicord*: Although the harpsichord was slowly giving way to different models of the fortepiano or pianoforte in the second half of the eighteenth century, Dublin had as many as seventeen known harpsichord makers in the eighteenth century, and the instrument remained popular for domestic use; see Edward L. Kottick, *A History of the Harpsichord* (Bloomington, IN: Indiana University Press, 2003), pp 380–3.

p. 41 *flute*: The flute was one of the instruments considered appropriate for gentlemen amateur performers in the eighteenth century; the flute would most likely have been the German or transverse flute, rather than the English flute, or recorder.

p. 41 *picquet*: A fashionable two-handed card game, played with a pack of 32 cards.

p. 41 *curiosity … Eve*: Though the Genesis account (Gen. 1:3) would attribute the Fall of Man to Eve's curiosity, the Enlightenment increasingly saw that curiosity as an indication of women's intellectual ability; jocular references to Eve's curiosity were commonplace, as in Hannah Cowley's comedy, *The Belle's Stratagem* (1780), published and performed in Dublin in 1781, in which Doricourt remarks 'Eve's curiosity was rais'd by the devil' (Act IV).

p. 42 *French military*: Between 1778 and 1782, Great Britain and Ireland were at war with France, which had signed a Treaty of Alliance with American colonists following the Declaration of Independence.

p. 43 *MAU VAIS HONTE*: i.e., *mauvaise honte*, bashfulness.

p. 43 *capital offence … blushing*: A contemporary medical writer, Seguin Henry Jackson (1750?–1816), noted that the passions and affections acted on the body in different ways and that 'SHAME causeth blushing, and the casting down of the eyes', *A Treatise on Sympathy* (London, 1781), p. 96; the reference to the 'casting down of the eyes' helps explain Louisa's subsequent reference to the French dancing-masters' instruction that will allow 'a Miss of fourteen years to come into a room full of company with a broad stare'.

p. 43 *fashionable mode of education*: Among others, Henry Home, Lord Kames, compared French female education unfavourably with that of Great Britain; see *Sketches of the History of Man*, 4 vols (1774; repr. Dublin, 1775), I, pp 194–5.

p. 43 *jaunt to England*: Louisa provocatively extends the perceived contrast between France and England to that between England and Ireland.

p. 43 *flirt*: A man who plays at courtship; in this non-derogatory sense, *OED* offers no example of the term earlier than 1779.

p. 43 *affectation*: Here, artificiality of manner.

p. 45 *Count de ROUSSILLON*: Though going back to the ninth century, the title of comte de Roussillon had been annexed to the French crown since the seventeenth century.

p. 45 *Montpelier*: Montpellier, in the south of France, had long enjoyed a reputation as a suitable refuge for invalids, especially consumptives, seeking respite from the cold, damp climates of Britain and Ireland.

p. 45 *chatteau*: i.e., *château*; the French word, usually denoting a country house, rather than a castle, had become anglicized in the mid-eighteenth century.

p. 45 *Mademoiselle Adelaide*: Gertrude's companion doubtless takes her name from Marie Adélaïde, known as Madame Adélaïde (1732–1800), one of the eleven children of Louis XV of France (1710–74).

p. 45 *pretty Irish woman*: The appellation by which Gertrude is known at Montpellier anticipates the description of Valeria O'Bryen, heroine of a slightly later Irish novel, who, first called 'la belle Angloise', becomes, at the insistence of her aunt's 'national pride', 'la belle Irlandoise'; see *The Fair Hibernian* (Dublin, 1790), p. 187.

p. 45 *Military Academy*: Following the War of the Austrian Succession, Louis XV founded the École Militaire (built 1751–80), which stands at one end of the Champ de Mars, in the 7th arrondissement of Paris.

p. 46 *Guitars*: The instruments popular in late-eighteenth-century France were still the older 5-course baroque guitars, soon to be superseded elsewhere by the 6-string guitar.

p. 46 *David Rizzio's most plaintive Scotch airs*: The airs attributed to David Riccio, or Rizzio (*c.*1533–66), musician and courtier, the favourite and alleged lover of Mary, Queen of Scots, enjoyed enormous popularity in the eighteenth century; the now-discredited attribution was first made by William Thomson in his collection, *Orpheus Caledonius* (Edinburgh, 1725), and, though later abandoned by him, the attribution proved tenacious. See also n. to p. 71 below, *"His passion's constant as the sun"*.

p. 46 *King at Versailles*: The French king in 1778 was Louis XVI (1754–93).

p. 46 *Count D'Artois' regiment*: The Compagnie de gardes suisses de Monsieur le comte d'Artois was created in 1773 by Louis XV for his second grandson, Charles-Philippe (1757–1836), comte d'Artois, the future King Charles X of France; service in the corps was considered a particular honour and one most unlikely to have been accorded a Protestant such as the Count of Rousillon.

p. 46 *Marquis de Bretagne*: Unidentified and probably fictional.

p. 48 *dinner-time*: In fashionable circles in late-eighteenth-century France, dinner was served in the late afternoon.

p. 48 *quadrille*: A four-handed card game, using a pack of 40 cards.

p. 49 *drawing*: Drawing was a polite accomplishment for both men and women in the eighteenth century.

p. 49 *uncharitable doctrines of Popery*: The Protestant Louisa Mortimer here gives expression to a view of Roman Catholicism that remained strong in the late-eighteenth century; that Louisa was not alone in demanding liberty, while denying it to Roman Catholics, is demonstrated by, for example, the work of Archibald Bruce (1748?–1816), a staunch defender of political and religious freedoms, even during the French Revolution, who, in *Free Thoughts on the Toleration of Popery* (Edinburgh, 1780), defended penal legislation on the grounds that the 'fixed and permanent' principles of Roman Catholicism 'will ever be at war with generous sentiments, and the best dispositions' (p. 229).

p. 50 *war breaking out*: See n. to p. 42 above, 'French military'.

p. 50 *regiment … America*: Though France sent an expeditionary force of 6,000 men to America in 1780, under the command of Jean-Baptiste Donatien de Vimeur, comte de Rochambeau (1725–1807), it did not include such élite units as the comte d'Artois's company.

p. 50 *now her own mistress*: i.e., had, under the terms of her father's will, reached the age of 16; see n. to p. 130 below, 'at age'.

p. 51 *17th Inst.*: i.e., instant, of the present month.

p. 51 *a little novel*: One of several self-reflexive moments in *The Triumph of Prudence over Passion* that draw attention to the work's status as novel.

p. 51 *delicacy*: Polite refinement.

p. 51 *Christian doctrine … done by*: The sentiments occur in Christ's sermon on the mount (Matt. 7:12), and are paraphrased elsewhere in the New Testament (Matt. 22:39; Luke 6:31), though they are to be found in many other cultures.

p. 51 *En Confidance*: i.e., *en confidence*, in confidence.

p. 52 *political affairs*: Eliza's comment suggests the gendered nature of contemporary personal correspondence, excluding women from political discourse, much to Louisa Mortimer's annoyance.

p. 52 *staunch patriot*: George Berkeley defined a patriot as 'one who heartily wisheth the public prosperity, and … doth endeavour to promote it', *Maxims concerning Patriotism* (Dublin, 1750), Maxim 21, p. 5. However, in the context of 1781, the term also had more specific connotations, referring to the 'patriot' party of Henry Flood (1732–91) and Henry Grattan (1746–1820) who, in the wake of the American revolution, sought, and in 1782–3 obtained, a greater degree of constitutional and economic freedom for the Irish parliament to legislate for Ireland, free from subordination to the parliament at Westminster.

p. 52 *tool of any Administration*: Samuel Johnson's *Dictionary* (1755) defined 'tool' as 'A hireling; a wretch who acts at the command of another'.

p. 52 *Senator*. Though employed attributively, to refer to a member of the Irish parliament, the term, as used in the context of her criticism of unmerited royal favour, also suggests Eliza's attachment to Roman republican values.

p. 52 *disgust*: i.e., displeasure.

p. 52 *easy behaviour*: i.e., unconstrained, informal behaviour.

p. 54 *gout in his stomach*: Though primarily a disease to which men were prone, chronic gout affecting internal organs in middle and old age was considered potentially fatal; see W[illiam] Black, *Observations Medical and Political*, pp 235–6.

p. 54 *set*: See n. to p. 31 above, 'sett'.

p. 54 *alteration of customs and manners*: Over the course of the eighteenth century late dining became a sign of social distinction, with dinner moving from the middle of the day to five or six in the evening, followed by a light supper taken at ten or eleven; provincial hours of dining generally remained earlier.

p. 55 *LE PETIT SOINS*: i.e., *les petits soins*.

p. 55 *teized*: i.e., teased.

p. 55 *passions ... reason*: The role of the reason in curbing or controlling the passions was a commonplace in eighteenth-century moral writing from Alexander Pope (1688–1744) to Mary Wollstonecraft (1759–97).

p. 55 *Harry Maunsel*: Maunsel, or Maunsell, is a name of both Scottish and English derivation, being found in the eighteenth century principally in Ulster and around Kilkenny; however, in 1780, one Eaton Maunsell was Mayor of Limerick, in Munster, with other Maunsels owning estates in Co. Clare in the same province, which is the home of Harry Maunsell, see p. 104.

p. 55 *Corke*: i.e., Cork.

p. 56 *turtle in love and constancy*: i.e., turtle dove.

p. 57 *shoping*: A comparatively new word that gained currency only around 1760.

p. 57 *Travel*: The desirability – and dangers – of travel for young gentlemen remained a lively topic of debate in the last decades of the eighteenth century, as it had been at least since John Locke's influential discussion in *Some Thoughts Concerning Education* (1693); Eliza holds modern views very similar to those expressed by the Revd Martin Sherlock: 'The great objects of travel are to form the manners, to acquire knowledge, to strengthen the judgment, and to refine and enrich the imagination ... Books give some knowledge. But clear and certain knowledge is not to be had but by experience', *Letters on Several Subjects*, 2 vols (London, 1781), II, pp 226, 230.

p. 58 *whey and hartshorn*: *whey*: The watery part of milk left after the separation of the curd by coagulation; *hartshorn*, the shavings of antlers, used to make spirit, oil, or salt of hartshorn (smelling salts); the preparation and use of these remedies, widely used in eighteenth-century medicine, is described in, for example, William Lewis, *The New Dispensatory* (4th rev. ed.; London, 1781), pp 161–2, 430–2.

p. 59 *of age*: After 1753, the age of marriage without parental consent was 21.

p. 59 *settlements*: The legal settling on property upon an individual.

p. 60 *in the horrors*: i.e., depressed; the colloquial phrase was a newish one, with *OED* giving 1768 as the date of first usage.

p. 60 *Belfast*: Arthur Young described the town to be 'very well built' and 'lively and busy', reckoning the population to be some 15,000 (in comparison to Dublin's population of over 150,000); see *A Tour in Ireland*, I, pp 205–6.

p. 61 *DIOGENES*: Greek philosopher (*c*.404–323 BC) renowned for his self-denial, as attested by the story that he chose to live at Athens in a wooden tub.

p. 66 *the delightful history of Henry and Louisa*: A mocking allusion to popular chapbook titles.

p. 66 *Patty*: A eighteenth-century diminutive of Martha.

p. 66 *Spa*: The small town of Spa, then in the Austrian Netherlands, now in Belgium, had been frequented for its health-giving waters since the middle ages.

p. 66 *some body has said actions have a language*: Louisa is perhaps thinking of Étienne Bonnet de Condillac who, in his *An Essay on the Origin of Human Knowledge* (1746; trans. London, 1756), defined a 'language of action' that 'produced every art proper to express our thoughts; such as gesture, dancing, speech, declamation, arbitrary marks for words or things, pantomimes, music, poetry, eloquence, writing, and the different characters of language'.

p. 67 *the college*: i.e., Trinity College Dublin.

p. 67 *drum*: A fashionable assembly held in the evening at a private house.

p. 68 *rubbers*: A set of games, here probably whist.

p. 68 *from the oldest families in England*: The Mortimers were of Norman French origin, settling in England and acquiring lands in Shropshire and Herefordshire, close to the Welsh border, shortly after the 1066 conquest; the family came to Ireland in 1308, and Roger Mortimer, 1st Earl of March (1287–1330) was made Lord-Lieutenant of Ireland by Edward II, whose son Edward III had Mortimer hanged at Tyburn for usurping royal power. Later Mortimers enjoyed great power and influence as earls of March and earls of Ulster, until the early fifteenth century.

p. 71 *"His passion's constant as the sun"*: A line from the fourth stanza of 'Ann thou were my ain Thing', in Allan Ramsay, *The Tea-table Miscellany* (Edinburgh, 1724), pp 136–7 (p. 137), set to music in William Thomson's *Orpheus Caledonius* (1725), which attributed seven of the songs, including this one, to David Rizzio (see n. to p. 46 above, 'David Rizzio's most plaintive Scotch airs'); among other composers who set this song was Francesco Geminiani (1687–1762) who lived intermittently in Ireland after 1737 and died in Dublin.

p. 74 *repine*: i.e., regret.

p. 74 *Platonic system*: i.e., Platonic love, based on affection rather than sexual desire; cf. 'Some ... have supposed that Enjoyment extinguishes Love, and that Love may be kept for ever alive and vigorous by Hope and Expectation; hence they would infer, that the Platonic System, which admits this fond Hope in all its Latitude, and shuts the Door against Fruition, is most likely to constitute a permanent undecaying Love. But this is a romantic Conclusion', Edward Long, *The Sentimental Exhibition; or, Portraits and sketches of the time* (London, 1774), pp 48–9.

p. 76 *in the dismals*: In low spirits.

p. 76 *Twiss*: The travel writer Richard Twiss (1747–1821) became notorious following the publication of *A Tour in Ireland in 1775* (London, 1776) which, though widely perceived by Irish readers as offensively critical of the country and its inhabitants, nevertheless reached its third Irish edition within a year. The passage to which Louisa refers reads: 'there are fewer old (repenting) maids in this than in any other country. The Irish single ladies are far from being disgustingly reserved, and as far from countenancing ill-bred familiarity; which renders them extremely engaging'; *Tour* (3rd ed. Dublin, 1777), p. 55.

p. 77 *a-pro-pos*: Fr. à propos; apropos.

p. 79 *Derry*: In 1781, Derry (or Londonderry), remained essentially confined to the small medieval walled town, dismissed by Richard Twiss as consisting 'chiefly of two streets, which cross each other, and an Exchange, called *Royal*, ... built in the centre'; *Tour*, p. 99. From a distance, however, Arthur Young thought the town 'the most picturesque to any place I have seen' and found the surrounding countryside well cultivated; *A Tour in Ireland*, I, pp 225–36 (236).

p. 79 *most beautifully improved*: i.e., characterized by typically eighteenth-century patterns of development and agricultural innovation, often including plantation, enclosure, and reclamation.

p. 79 *Popish purgatory*: In Roman Catholic theology, a place or state between heaven and hell, where the souls of those who die in a state of grace suffer according to their earthly sins, the torments differing from those of hell only in duration.

p. 80 *council*: i.e., counsel.

p. 83 *one of our female poets ... who*): Elizabeth Sheridan would certainly have known the poet to be Frances, or Fanny, Greville, *née* Macartney (1727?-1789), daughter of James Macartney, MP for Longford and Granard, and Catherine Coote. Probably born in Ireland, where she spent most of her last years, Frances Greville was the dedicatee of *The Critic* (London, 1781) by Richard Brinsley Sheridan, who declared his motive to be 'the gratification of private friendship and esteem' (p. i). The lines cited are taken from Greville's much-anthologized 'Prayer for Indifference', written in the mid-1750s, and were quoted in several novels of the period, including the Irish-published *Anna: a sentimental novel*, 2 vols (Dublin 1782), whose author writes: 'Yet do I concur with every sentiment of Mrs. Greville's beautiful ode, and think indifference the greatest calamity incident to the human heart' (II, p. 72), so indicating how variously the poem was understood by contemporary readers.

p. 83 *out*: i.e., ought.

p. 84 *lachrymals*: Weeping mood.

p. 85 *same end ... catastrophe*: Louisa here plays on two related but different meanings of 'catastrophe': the final event of a play, and an unhappy or disastrous conclusion; see also n. to p. 173 below, 'Eliza's novel ... matrimony'.

p. 85 *public prints*: i.e., newspapers.

p. 85 FREE TRADE: In 1779, the Dublin barrister, Richard Sheridan, published an angry *Letter to William Eden on the subject of ... the Irish Trade*, in which he concludes by arguing that 'A free trade, such as I have defined it to be, the people of Ireland do not ask of Great Britain as a *favour*, they demand it as a *right* ... When you speak then, of Ireland's being "a jewel in the British crown," you seem to forget that Ireland has a diadem of her own——plundered indeed it may have been by the usurped power of a foreign legislature [i.e., the Westminster parliament]; but, stripped and unadorned as it is, it can still confer power and dignity on the wearer. ——The HONOUR, Sir, of this diadem, is now guarded by FIFTY THOUSAND ARMED FREEMEN' (Dublin, 1779), pp 35, 37. In the same year, Charles Sheridan, then MP for Belturbet in Co. Cavan, made explicit comparison of 'illiberal' British policy towards America and Ireland in the pamphlet: *Observations on the doctrine laid down by Sir William Blackstone, respecting the extent of the power of the British Parliament, particularly with relation to Ireland* (Dublin, 1779), esp. pp 29–30. See also n. to p. 31 above, 'Nov. 4. 1779'.

p. 85 *America*: The Irish political events to which *The Triumph of Prudence over Passion* alludes are played out in the context of Great Britain's military involvement in north America, following the Declaration of Independence; see also n. to p. 31 above, 'Volunteers' and n. to p.52 above, 'staunch patriot'.

p. 87 *ancient custom*: See n. to p. 31 above, 'laudable custom'.

p. 87 *cloathed in her own housewifery*: Eliza's benevolent landlordism resonates with more ambitious contemporary schemes for improvement elsewhere on the island which saw the building of estate villages and the introduction of industry; the most ambitious such enterprise in the 1780s was the establishment by landowner Robert Brooke (1744–1811) of the village of Prosperous, Co. Kildare, as a cotton manufactory.

p. 87 *schooling*: Under legislation dating back to the reign of Henry VIII, the legal responsibility for educational provision in Ireland fell on the clergymen of the Church of Ireland, who were obliged to ensure the existence of a school in each parish. In practice, this provision was extremely limited and was augmented by a range of private and philanthropic efforts, while most children of the period were educated by Catholic school-masters in hedge schools, illegal according to the penal laws.

p. 87 *reading and writing*: Eliza's support for instruction in writing as well as reading, and her willingness to contemplate the social mobility of her tenants, distances her from more conservative views, waning but still vocal in the 1780s, that the ends of lower-class education were primarily moral and were satisfied once a child could read the Bible.

p. 88 *concessions abortive*: In 1780, the Prime Minister, Lord North, responded to Irish demands to address long-standing economic grievances by allowing Ireland free trade with the colonies and the right to export woollen goods.

p. 88 *men disapprove ... opinion on these subjects*: One such man was the Revd Vicesimus Knox who, in his extremely popular *Essays Moral and Literary* wrote: 'Of all subjects, politics seem the least adapted to the female character. Women are entirely excluded from legislative influence, and, it is well known, that public affairs are seldom treated with temper, either in writing or conversation', *Essays Moral and Literary* (2nd ed., corrected and enlarged; London, 1779), pp 363–4.

p. 90 *through Scotland*: The principal shipping route in the period was from Donaghadee on the Ards peninsula to Port Patrick, near Stranraer.

p. 90 *the Head*: i.e., Holyhead, on Anglesey in Wales.

p. 90–1 *home education ... men*: The relative merits of a public versus home education, both for boys and girls, were extensively and variously discussed in the late-eighteenth century; see, for instance, Charles Allen, *The Polite Lady: or, A Course of Female Education* (1760; 4th ed. Dublin 1779); John Duncombe, *A Lecture on Education: Humbly inscribed to Parents and Guardians; and such other persons who are, or may be concerned in the tuition of youth* (1775?); George Hawkins, *An Essay on Female Education: containing an Account of the present state of the Boarding Schools for Young Ladies in England* (1781), Percival Stockdale, *An Examination of the Important Question, whether education at a Great School, or by Private Tuition is Preferable?* (1782); William Coke, *A Poetical Essay on the Early Part of Education; to which is prefixed an Enquiry into the Discipline of the Ancients, with some Observations on that of our Public Schools* (1785); or *The Governess; or, The Boarding School Dissected: A Dramatic Original in Three Acts, wherein are exposed, in Dramatic Order, the Errors in the present Mode of Female Education* (1785).

p. 92 *"Oh! what pain it is to part"*: The opening line of Air XVII of John Gay's *The Beggar's Opera* (1728); the musical setting used the air 'Gin thou wert mine awn thing' (see n. to p. 71 above, *"His passion's constant as the sun"*).

p. 92 *Epicurism in Love*: Invoking the doctrines of the Greek philosopher Epicurus (342–270 BC) who taught that pleasure is the end of human existence, Louisa suggests that the pleasures of love are refined through absence.

p. 92 *his estate in England*: Although Charles Skeffington's primary loyalties are evidently to Ireland, Louisa makes the point that he is not an absentee landlord in England; absentee landlordism had, for over half a century, been seen as one of the besetting problems of Ireland, with Henry Grattan lamenting the fact that some £800,000 was remitted out of Ireland annually in the 1780s.

p. 93 *indolence*: The novel here notably anticipates the principal theme of Maria Edgeworth's *Ennui; or, Memoirs of the Earl of Glenthorn*, published as part of *Tales of Fashionable Life* (1809), whose opening sentence reads: 'Bred up in luxurious indolence, I was surrounded by friends, who seemed to have no business in this world but to save me the trouble of thinking or acting for myself; and I was confirmed in the pride of helplessness by being continually reminded, that I was the only son and heir of the Earl of Glenthorn' (p. 1).

p. 93 *sharping*: Swindling.

p. 94 *Holy-Days*: i.e., holidays.

p. 98 *Back-gammon*: The very ancient board-game was particularly popular in the mid-eighteenth century when Edmund Hoyle published *A Short Treatise on the Game of Back-Gammon* (1743).

p. 100 *to strike*: To lower the top-sail, as a sign of surrender.

p. 100 *devoirs*: Dutiful respects.

p. 101 *the language … Munster brogue*: Louisa's view stands in marked contrast to contemporary opinion that an Irish brogue was necessarily inferior to an English metropolitan accent. When Elizabeth Sheridan arrived in England from Ireland in 1784, she reported that an acquaintance 'upon hearing me speak accused me of having some brogue which my Father would by no means allow'; see *Betsy Sheridan's Journal*, ed. William LeFanu (London: Eyre and Spottiswoode, 1960), p. 23. Elsewhere in the journal, Elizabeth reported the case of an Irish physician who, at Bath, spoke French in public 'as he says "to *hide* his Brogue"' (p. 192).

p. 102 *knowing how to read … argue against it*: By this period only very exceptional objections were made to the desirability of a universal ability to read, although lower-class education was still understood in very restricted terms.

p. 103 *never despond*: An English version of the Latin *nil desperandum*; see Horace, *Odes*, I, vii, l. 27.

p. 105 *the fleeting forms of the night*: i.e., dreams.

p. 105 *skilful interpreters*: Among the best-known interpreters of dreams in the Bible are Joseph (Genesis 47:13–26), Daniel (Daniel 4:19–37), and the Wise Men (Matthew 2:12).

p. 105 *sons and daughters of affliction*: Louisa alludes to Matthew Henry's commentary on Job 2, which recommends visiting the sons and daughters of affliction; see *An Exposition of all the Books of the Old and New Testament*, 5 vols (1707–12; 4th ed. London, 1737), II, [np].

p. 106 *northern accent*: See above, n. to p. 101, 'the language … Munster brogue'.

p. 106 *to the play*: In the week of 14 January 1780 the Smock Alley theatre was performing *The Provoked Husband* (1728) by Sir John Vanbrugh (1664–1726) and Colley Cibber (1671–1757), and *The Jealous Wife* (1761) by George Colman (1732–1794).

p. 107 *Sussex*: A prosperous agricultural county in south-east England; the county returned 28 members of parliament, and had over 100 towns and villages holding licensed fairs in 1780; see [William Owen], *Owen's New Book of Fairs … in England and Wales* (1780).

p. 109 *quickened the clerks*: See John Gay, *The Beggar's Opera*, II.xii, 'Air XXXIII', 'If you at an office solicit your due,/And would not have business neglected;/You must quicken the clerk with the perquisite too./To do what his duty directed.' The song, to the tune of 'London Ladies' was well known not only through Gay's ballad opera but through the inclusion of the song in later editions of Allan Ramsay's *The Tea-Table Miscellany*, and other song books; see n. to p. 71, *"His passion's constant as the sun"*. In 1781, the verse was included in a satirical compilation, *Miniature Pictures: written originally by Mr. Gay, author of the Beggar's Opera, newly adapted to the most fashionable and public characters* (London, 1781), dedicated to Richard Brinsley Sheridan by 'An Admirer of Gay and Sheridan' (p. 12).

p. 109 *place at Court*: i.e., at Versailles.

p. 111 *the lower class of tenants … are none of them in want*: Eliza's anecdote offers an example of the difference between responsible and irresponsible landownership.

p. 112 *Eau de Luce*: A preparation of alcohol, ammonia and oil of amber, used as smelling salts.

p. 112 *Linen-Weaver, near Armagh*: Armagh was an important centre of linen weaving in the eighteenth century, and although the market fluctuated notably during the 1770s, Arthur Young described it as flourishing in the latter part of the decade; see Young, *A Tour in Ireland*, (Dublin: 1780), I, pp 166–9.

p. 113 *wise man's saying … 'house of mourning'*: Ecclesiastes: 7:2: 'It is better to go to the house of mourning, than to go to the house of feasting: for that is the end of all men; and the living will lay it to his heart'.

p. 113 *news-papers … distressed*: In one such notice, addressed to the 'Humane and Charitable', aid was sought on behalf of a tradesman of good character with a wife and five children, reduced through an illness of seven months 'to the lowest ebb of poverty'; benefactors willing to prevent the family 'sinking under a complication of miseries, the helpless victims of wretchedness and famine' were directed to the establishments of several tradesmen including that of William Hallhead, Bookseller, no. 63 Dame-Street, and 'the Printer hereof, who can testify the truth of the above', *Dublin Evening Post*, 15 Nov. 1780.

p. 114 *bedizening*: Dressing out.

VOLUME II

p. 119 *goût*: (French) taste, relish.

p. 120 *bride's-man*: A male friend who attends the bridegroom at a wedding.

p. 120 *till she has changed her mourning*: A period of mourning of one year was usual for widows at this period.

p. 120–1 *thousand a year ... four*: In the 1770s several squires entering parliament, including Richard Lovell Edgeworth, from Co. Longford, and Arthur Balfour of Co. Fermanagh, had incomes of approximately £2,500 a year, and an assessment of the incomes of 251 notables in counties Kilkenny, Tipperary and Waterford in 1775 indicates that only 19, most of whom were peers, had incomes in excess of £5,000 while 82 had less than £1,000 a year. By these standards, James is comfortably off while Emily is a very wealthy woman; see T.C. Barnard, *A new anatomy of Ireland: the Irish Protestants, 1649–1770* (New Haven and London: Yale University Press, 2003), pp 61–2.

p. 122 *crouding*: i.e., crowding.

p. 122 *not dazzled by titles*: In a letter of 1 July 1786, Elizabeth Sheridan speaks deprecatingly of titles, suggesting that her father is 'too apt to pay a hommage to fortune and titles' and of the 'unfeeling impertinence of many of our present titled people'; *Betsy Sheridan's Journal*, pp 91, 92.

p. 122 *gauze apron ... petticoat*: A fine, transparent cloth; here, probably of silk; *blond cap*: A cap made of silk lace of two threads, twisted and formed in hexagonal meshes (*OED*: 'blonde, blond', B.2.a); *robbins*: Trimmings in the form of a band or stripe; more usually *robins* or *robings* (see *OED*: 'robbing': 1.b); *very fine net tippet*: A narrow piece of cloth, worn as part of a head-dress or as a shawl; *brilliant pins*: i.e., diamond pins; *lay-lock*: i.e., lilac.

p. 122 *tabbinet*: 'A watered fabric of silk and wool resembling poplin: chiefly associated with Ireland'; see *OED*, 'tabinet'.

p. 122 *a woman ... very thoughtless indeed*: Louisa draws attention to the gravity of the marriage contract and its definitive consequences for the life of the bride.

p. 123 *garter and pins to dream on*: The young ladies will dream of their own future husband.

p. 124 *raking*: Living a dissolute life, like a rake.

p. 124 *Chair*: i.e., sedan chair.

p. 124 *duelling*: Though long decried, as in *Tatler*, 25 (7 June 1709), by Richard Steele, who had himself fought a duel in which his antagonist was severely wounded, the practice persisted. In 1772 Richard Brinsley Sheridan fought two duels with Capt. Thomas Mathews, whom Sheridan accused of defaming his future wife, Elizabeth Linley; the first duel, fought in London, ended in a victory for Sheridan but Mathews challenged him again and in the second duel, fought outside of Bath, Sheridan was dangerously wounded by his antagonist's sword.

p. 125 *Idol of the place*: Here, false god.

p. 125 *œconomy*: i.e., economy; a very different view of the Irish and English was offered by Philip Luckombe, who stressed the similarities between the two, when he wrote of Dublin in 1780 that 'Well-bred people of different countries approach much nearer to each other in manners, than those who have not seen the world', *A Tour through Ireland* (Dublin, 1780), p. 40.

p. 125 *Miss Freeman*: In contrast to other names in the novel, Miss Freeman's has obvious symbolic significance. In his *Dictionary*, Samuel Johnson defined 'freeman' as 'One not a slave; not a vassal' but while Englishmen prided themselves in being free, and while Irishmen and women of the period might regard themselves as 'slaves' to an oppressive England (see n. to p. 156 below), Miss Freeman will reveal herself to be enslaved by her ungovernable passions.

p. 125 *Jermyn-Street*: A street in the fashionable St James' district of London.

p. 126 *ASSA-FÆTIDA*: *Asafœtida* or assafetida, a gum with a strong odour, with various medicinal uses.

p. 126 *Sir Clement Cottrel*: Here, a general term for the master of ceremonies, after the courtier Sir Clement Cotterell (1686–1758), who had been appointed master of the ceremonies in 1710, being knighted a fortnight later.

p. 126 *awful*: i.e., solemn, awe-inspiring.

p. 127 *Adventures*: For eighteenth-century double-standards, compare with n. to p. 35, 'adventure'.

p. 128 *travel post*: To travel in the fastest way.

p. 128 *love of society*: The innate sociability of human beings was asserted by such eighteenth-century enlightenment thinkers as Adam Ferguson in his *Essay on the History of Civil Society* (1767), and became a commonplace of polite literature.

p. 130 *CARO-SPOSO*: (Italian), dear husband; the phrase, which Louisa uses jocularly, was most familiar from Italian opera.

p. 130 *at age*: The characters of the novel come of age variously according to the stipulations made in their fathers' wills.

p. 130 *sea-sickness*: Sea-sickness was considered a medical remedy in the eighteenth century for consumptives such as Miss Freeman, who might exhibit symptoms of impaired digestion; see, for example, *A Complete Collection of the Medical and Philosophical Works of John Fothergill, M.D.F.R.S. and S.A.* (London, 1781), pp 591–2.

p. 131 *widow-hood*: Mrs. Rochfort's apparent readiness to accept a proposal of marriage from Mr. Fitzgerald is especially comprehensible in the light of at least some contemporary estimates of widowhood; so, William Alexander opens his chapter 'Of Widowhood' thus: 'As the state of matrimony is of all others the most honourable, and the most desired by women, so that of widowhood is generally the most deplorable, and consequently the object of their greatest aversion', *The History of Women, from the Earliest Antiquity, to the Present Time* (Dublin, 1779), II, p. 374.

p. 132 *I should think ... against their consent*: See n. to p. 33 above, 'a child has a natural right to a negative voice'.

p. 132 *war*: The war between France and Britain began in July 1778 and would be ended by the Treaty of Paris and Treaties of Versailles in 1783.

p. 133 *CE CISBEO*: (Italian), *cicisbeo*; the acknowledged admirer of a married woman in Italy but not in Great Britain and Ireland, where the notion was considered scandalous, so that Louisa uses the term jocularly.

p. 134 *packets*: Packet-boats; mailboats.

p. 134 *this land of hospitality*: In the eighteenth century, the Irish were noted for their hospitality, to the extent that Richard Twiss thought it proper to remark that 'Hospitality and drinking went formerly hand in hand, but since the excesses of the table have been so judiciously abolished, hospitality is not so violently practiced as heretofore, when it might have been imputed to them as a fault', *A Tour in Ireland in 1775*, p. 8.; Arthur Young wrote much more favourably of the 'unbounded hospitality' of Ireland, where those he met were generous in their provision of the information he was seeking in his travels, *A Tour in Ireland*, I, p. ix.

p. 134 *turtle*: See also above n. to p. 56.

p. 137 *Rotunda*: The Rotunda, formerly the 'Round Room', was designed by John Ensor, and built between 1764 and 1767, to allow for musical and other entertainments, the profits of which went to support the charitable Dublin Lying-in Hospital, founded in 1745 by Dr Bartholomew Mosse; the name 'Rotunda' is now generally applied to the hospital itself.

p. 140 *borne away ... life!*: Louisa here pointedly reverses the usual gendered identification of men with reason and women with passion.

p. 140 *Will Lacky*: Will is the name of Aristippus's lackey in Richard Edward's *Damon and Pithius*, in *A Select Collection of Old Plays*, 12 vols (2nd ed; London, 1780), I, p. 172.

p. 140 *foster-brother*: In late-eighteenth-century Ireland, young male members of the gentry were frequently sent to live with neighbouring families.

p. 143 *Lucan*: A small town on the Liffey, west of Dublin.

p. 144 *mantua-maker*: Dressmaker.

p. 144 *garden*: The New Gardens were laid out behind the Dublin Lying-in Hospital built in 1757, and developed as a place of polite resort and as a musical venue in fine weather in the 1760s and 1770s.

p. 145 *wherry*: A light rowing boat, here used to take passengers to the ship bound for Holyhead.

p. 147 *Compte*: (French) comte; count

p. 150 *Harwick ... Helvoetsluys*: i.e., Harwich, in Essex, an important port, especially for travel to the Low Countries; *Helvoetsluys*: now more usually Hellevoetsluis, formerly an important port, near Rotterdam.

p. 151 *a reconciliation*: The London edition of *The Triumph of Prudence over Passion* was re-titled *The Reconciliation* (London: William Lane, 1783) but while the title may have seemed more enticing to contemporary novel readers, it is by no means as appropriate.

p. 153 *jilting ... female character*: 'Love is not to begin on your part; but is entirely to be the consequence of our attachment to you', John Gregory advised his daughters in his extremely popular *A Father's Legacy to his Daughters* (1774; repr. London, 1781), pp 80–1; in keeping with such notions of female propriety, particular censure attached to the agency assumed by any woman who encouraged but then rejected a man's attentions.

p. 154 *Comptesse Roussillon*: (French), countess.

p. 154 *valet de chambre*: A gentleman's personal attendant, especially in France or for those travelling on the continent.

p. 154 *Merrion-square*: The square was laid out in 1762, though developed piece-meal, with a single plot still unbuilt in 1818.

p. 155 *boarding-school*: See above, n. to pp 90–1, 'home education ... men'.

p. 156 *high and mighty Lords*: i.e., the Dutch, known formally as the High and Mighty Lords, the States General of the United Netherlands.

p. 156 *present Monarch*: Louis XVI (see above n. to p. 46) had become King of France in 1774.

p. 156 *daily loosening the bands of oppression and slavery*: Louisa's enthusiasm for liberty causes her to represent Louis XVI as a restorer of natural rights; in fact, as a weak monarch he was powerless to resist the assertiveness of his subjects.

p. 156 *our Rulers ... rivet the chains*: The language of slavery is to be found extensively in Irish patriot literature of the period; so, England uses every 'exertion and art' to 'forge and rivet our chain', C[harles] H[enry] Wilson, *A Compleat Collection of the Resolutions of the Volunteers, Grand Juries, &c. of Ireland* (Dublin, 1782), p. cxxxviii; see also *Reasons for a Repeal of the Act of Poyning* (Dublin, 1781), p. [5]; *A Scheme for a Constitutional Association* (Dublin, 1780), p. 25.

p. 157 *ach*: i.e., ache

p. 158 *small-pox*: One contemporary estimated that smallpox killed some 400,000 people a year in Europe by the end of the eighteenth century, at a rate of 1 in every 4 victims affected, with children being especially susceptible; see W[illiam] Black, *Observations Medical and Political, on the Small-Pox ... and on the Mortality of Mankind at every age in City and Country* (London, 1781), p. 109 and passim. The viral illness often resulted in severe scarring, as well as still more serious consequences such as blindness and infertility.

p. 158 *consumption*: Consumption, or pulmonary tuberculosis, was a major cause of mortality in the eighteenth century; in a much-reprinted work, the Scottish physician, John Gregory, argued for the mutual influence of mind and body stating that: 'It has been the misfortune of most of those who have study'd the Philosophy of the Human Mind, that they have been little acquainted with the structure of the Human Body, and the laws of the Animal Oeconomy; and yet the Mind and Body are so intimately connected, and have such a mutual influence on one another, that the constitution of either, examined apart, can never be thoroughly understood', *A Comparative View of the State and Faculties of Man with those of the Animal World* (London, 1765), p. 6.

p. 158 *Roussillon*: The area north-west of Montpellier.

p. 159 *external objects operating on the mind*: Louisa seems be thinking of John Locke's *Essay Concerning Human Understanding* (1690), II, 1.

p. 159 *many a true word*: Louisa refers to the assertion by Philip Dormer Stanhope, 4th earl of Chesterfield (1694–1773), that 'A man of fashion never has recourse to proverbs and vulgar aphorisms', *Letters to his son*, 4 vols (1774; Dublin, 1776), II, p. 261.

p. 159 *Lucretia*: The story, told by the historian Livy among others, of the rape of Lucretia by Sextus Tarquinius, son of Lucius Tarquinius Superbus, and of Lucretia's subsequent suicide, was very widely recounted in many forms in the eighteenth century, being understood both as an exemplary case of female virtue, and as an example of resistance to the arbitrary power of tyrants.

p. 159 *English ladies … few years*: Accounts of such cases are to be found in, for example, *A New and Compleat Collection of the Most Remarkable Trials for Adultery, &c. from the time of Henry VIII to the Present Period*, 2 vols (London, 1780).

p. 160 *Geneva*: The city of Geneva was an independent, Protestant republic from 1536, loosely connected with the Swiss Confederation after 1584, until 1798.

p. 160 *Dukes … Marquisses*: The proliferation of titles among the French nobility was a matter of considerable comment and amusement to British and Irish travelers; compare Tristram Shandy's account of his travels to the south of France: 'they are all Dukes, Marquisses, and Counts, there——the deuce a Baron, in all Avignion'; Laurence Sterne, *The Life and Opinions of Tristram Shandy, Gentleman*, 9 vols (1759–67), VII, xli.

p. 161 *gout*: See above, n. to p. 54.

p. 161 *not near so populous as England or Ireland*: In the late-eighteenth century the respective populations of England and Ireland were much more equivalent than has been the case since the mid-nineteenth century; in 1780, the population of England was between 7 and 8 million while that of Ireland was moving towards 4.5 million.

p. 161 *buried in Convents*: The socially and economically damaging consequences of Roman Catholic practices in continental Europe was a common topic of censure among British and Irish Protestants.

p. 161 *depopulate, and consequently impoverish the country*: The dissolution of monasteries and convents was ordered by the French General Assembly in 1790, shortly after the outbreak of the French Revolution.

p. 161 *Spain and Portugal*: After a first attempt to close the monasteries of Spain by Joseph I, brother to Napoleon Bonaparte, in 1812, the government of Juan de Mendizábal finally suppressed all monasteries and convents in 1835, two years after the dissolution of monasteries in Portugal.

p. 161 *phrenzy*: i.e., frenzy.

p. 164 *reconciliation*: See above, n. to p. 151.

p. 165 *"We only can taste … at ease"*: A much-quoted line from a song from Thomas Arne's incidental music to *The Sacrifice of Iphigenia*, first published in *The London Magazine* (1750).

p. 166 *act of oblivion*: Legislation whereby a government extends an amnesty to those who have engaged in sedition or treason; by 12 Charles II c. 11 (1660) the newly restored Charles II extended indemnity to those republicans who had fought in the civil war (1642–51).

p. 167 *high crimes and misdemeanors*: The phrase appears in parliamentary impeachments; it was first used in 1386 in the impeachment of Michael de la Pole, 1st earl of Suffolk, King's Chancellor, but may have been in Louisa's mind because of the notorious 1780 impeachment and court-martial of Admiral Viscount Augustus Keppel following the first Battle of Ushant in which Keppel, defended by Whigs including Richard Brinsley Sheridan and Edmund Burke, was eventually acquitted. The reference highlights Louisa's characteristic tendency to consider the personal in political terms.

p. 167 *faculty*: Although, as she admits, Louisa is talking 'nonsense', her joke has a point, since Montpellier had one of the most celebrated medical faculties in Europe in the eighteenth century.

p. 168 *blush still mantling*: A reminiscence of the line 'No mantling blush ensues', in Richard Brinsley Sheridan's song, 'When a tender maid', from the hugely popular comic opera, *The Duenna* (1775), to music chiefly by Thomas Linley.

p. 168 *marrying and giving in marriage*: The phrase recalls Matt. 24:38 but is also a noteworthy anticipation of the closing line of Mary Wollstonecraft's autobiographical *Mary: a fiction* (London, 1788), concerning the heroine, brought close to death by her experience of, among much else, a deeply unhappy marriage: 'She thought she was hastening to that world *where there is neither marrying*, nor giving in marriage' (p. 187).

p. 169 *pour passer le tempts*: (French), *pour passer le temps*; to pass the time.

p. 171 *linen and haberdashery*: Conduct book literature of the period often enjoined female servants to use money saved in service to enter into business with their husbands on marriage; married women were notably involved in textile trades, especially linen, in eighteenth-century Ireland.

p. 171 *faite me … le Compte*: (French) *faites mes baisemens à Monsieur le Comte*, give my best respects to the Count.

p. 173 *Eliza's novel concluded … catastrophe, matrimony*: See also n. to p. 85, 'same end … catastrophe'.

p. 173 *obey*: Explicit objections to the words of the marriage ceremony are very rare in the eighteenth century; a forceful objection was, however, articulated by Mary, Lady Chudleigh in her poem 'To the Ladies' (1703) which cautioned that 'When she the word *obey* has said,/ And man by Law supreme has made,/ Then all that's kind is laid aside,/ And Nothing left but State and Pride'.

p. 174 *most horrid custom, duelling*: See n. to p. 124, 'duelling', above.

p. 174 *French stile*: In Great Britain and Ireland, the 1780s saw a move towards much greater informality in young children's clothing, such as white muslin dresses, while French clothes for children remained generally imitative of adult models.

p. 174 *I kiss your hands*: Louisa translates literally the French salutation 'Je vous baise les mains'.

p. 175 *Emeline: A Moral Tale*: the title page of *The Triumph of Prudence over Passion* indicates the novel to be by the 'authoress of *Emeline*', published in 1780; both fictions would be published in London by William Lane in 1783 under different titles, in this case: *The Fairy Ring; or, Emeline: a Moral Tale*.

p. 177 *The Tutor*: A novel by the Killarney-born Hugh Kelly (1739–77), playwright, poet, miscellaneous writer and novelist, whose best-known prose fiction was *Memoirs of a Magdalen; or, The History of Louisa Mildmay* (1767).

List of emendations

The text of the present edition respects that of the first edition of *The Triumph of Prudence over Passion* in all matters, including spelling and punctuation, with the exception of the use of modern conventions for denoting direct speech, and the emendations listed below.

VOLUME I

p. 33, l. 2up Mrs.] Mr.

p. 38, l.3 12] 25

p. 51, l. 12up: penetration] denetration

p. 56, l. 6up: here.] here..

p. 58, l. 14: any] any any

p. 60, l. 19up: discourage] dscourage

p. 64, l. 20up: subject] jubject

p. 66, l. 6up: surprised] susprised

p. 67, l. 5up: account of] account of of

p. 68, l.8: descended] descend-ded

p. 69, l. 14: Harry] Harrry

p. 71, l. 1: idea] indea

p. 71, l. 10: I] I I

p. 72, l. 7: institution] instituion

p. 73, l. 4: narrative] na-rative

p. 73, l. 11: symptom] sympton

p. 79, l. 14up: do not] do not not

p. 83, l. 12: one] some

p. 84, ll. 13up: to] to to

p. 85, l. 12: be sorry] be be sorry

p. 86, l. 3up: an unmerciful] an an unmerciful

p. 87, l. 2: Miss FITZGERALD, to Miss MORTIMER.] Miss MORTIMER, to Miss FITZGERALD.

p. 88, l. 9up: trifles] triflles

p. 90, l. 8: part from him] part him

p. 90, l. 14up: mother's] mother'

p. 92, l. 12: ignorance,] ignoranc,

p. 94, l. 20: neither] either

p. 100, l.5: depend] de-spend

p. 101, l.7: he had] he he had

p. 105, l. 2: Miss MORTIMER, to Miss FITZGERALD.] Miss FITZGERALD, to
Miss MORTIMER.

p. 107, l. 14up: preference] prefernce

p. 109, l. 5: unusual] unsual

p. 111, l. 7up: saw] say

p. 114, ll. 10–11up: a material difference in] a material in

p. 115, l. 9up: is not] is is not

VOLUME II

p. 124, l. 13: specious] spacious

p. 124, l. 15up: scarcely] scarely

p. 133, l. 1up: LOUISA] . LOUISA

p. 137, l. 13: found] sound

p. 145, l. 18up: added] ad-ed

p. 151, l. 20up: Mrs.] Mr.

p. 151, l. 7up: intention] Intention

p. 155, l. 8: They] they

p. 155, l. 14: O'Neil] O'Neil

p. 157, l. 7: the reason] the the reason

p. 158, l. 12up: reins] reigns

p. 160, l. 9up: I quite eclipse] [ ] quite eclipse

p. 162, l. 16up: thoroughly] thouroghly

p. 162, l. 12up: forgiveness.] forgiveness,

p. 163, l. 13: Skeffington] Sheffington

p. 167, l.13: Skeffington] Skeffigton

p. 167, l. 9up: pantomime] pantomine

p. 168, l. 8up: than] their

p. 170, l. 13: bowers.] bowers,

p. 171, ll. 3–2up: *Monsieur le Compte*] *Monsieur La Compte*

p. 174, l. 17: happy] happpy

Select bibliography

PRIMARY TEXTS

a) Works by Elizabeth Sheridan

[Elizabeth Sheridan]. *The Fairy Ring; or, Emeline. A Moral Tale. By a Lady.* London: Printed for William Lane, 1783.

—. *The Triumph of Prudence over Passion: or, The History of Mss Mortimer and Miss Fitzgerald. By the Authoress of Emeline*, 2 vols. Dublin: Printed (for the Author) by S. Colbert, 1781.

—. *The Reconciliation; or, History of Miss Mortimer, and Miss Fitzgerald. An Hibernian Novel ... By an Irish Lady*, 2 vols. London: Printed for W. Lane, 1783.

—. *Betsy Sheridan's Journal: Letters from Sheridan's sister 1784–1786 and 1788–1790*, edited by William LeFanu. London: Eyre & Spottiswoode, 1960.

—. *The India Voyage ... by Mrs. H. Lefanu, daughter of the late Thomas Sheridan, M.A.*, 2 vols. London: Printed for G. and J. Robinson, 1804.

—. *The Sister: A Tale*, 2 vols. London: Richards and Co. 1810.

b) Other Sources

Alicia Le Fanu, *Memoirs of the Life and Writings of Mrs. Frances Sheridan.* London, 1824.

Thomas Moore, *Memoirs of Richard Brinsley Sheridan*, 2 vols. London: Longman, 1825.

William Fraser Rae, *Sheridan: a biography*, 2 vols. London: Richard Bentley & Son, 1896.

SECONDARY TEXTS

Armstrong, Nancy. *Desire and Domestic Fiction: A Political History of the Novel.* Oxford: Oxford University Press, 1987.

Backscheider, Paula R. and Catherine Ingrassia (eds). *A Companion to the Eighteenth-Century English Novel and Culture.* Oxford: Blackwell, 2005.

Douglas, Aileen. 'The Novel before 1800', in John Wilson Foster (ed.), *The Cambridge Companion to the Irish Novel.* Cambridge: Cambridge University Press, 2006. Pp 22–38.

——. 'Dublin in the Fiction of the Later Eighteenth Century', in Gillian O'Brien and Finola O'Kane (eds), *Georgian Dublin*. Dublin: Four Courts Press, 2008. Pp 135–44.

——. '"Whom gentler stars unite": Fiction and Union in the Irish Novel', *Irish University Review*, 41:1 (2011), 183–95.

Fitzer, Anna M. 'Introduction' to Alicia Lefanu, *Strathallan* [1816]. London: Pickering & Chatto, 2008. Pp vii–xxiii.

Gallagher, Catherine. *Nobody's Story: The Vanishing Acts of Women Writers in the Marketplace, 1670–1820*. Oxford: Clarendon Press, 1994.

Hammond, Brean and Shaun Regan. *Making the Novel: Fiction and Society in Britain, 1660–1789*. Basingstoke: Palgrave, 2006.

Haslett, Moyra. *Pope to Burney, 1714–1779*. Basingstoke: Palgrave Macmillan, 2003. Esp. 1, 3, 'Female communities'. Pp 138–72.

Kennedy, Catriona A. '"What Can Women Give But Tears": Gender, Politics and Irish National Identity in the 1790s'. Unpublished PhD dissertation, University of York, 2004.

Kilfeather, Siobhán. '"Strangers at Home": Political Fictions by Women in Eighteenth-Century Ireland'. Unpublished PhD dissertation, Princeton University, 1989.

Le Fanu, T.P. *Memoir of the Le Fanu Family*. Manchester: Privately Printed, 1924.

McCarthy, B.G. *The Female Pen: Women Writers and Novelists, 1681–1818*, with a preface by Janet Todd. 1944–7; repr. Cork: Cork University Press, 1994.

O'Dowd, Mary. 'The Women in the Gallery: Women and Politics in Eighteenth-Century Ireland', in Sabine Wichert (ed.), *From United Irishmen to Twentieth-Century Unionism: a festschrift for A.T.Q. Stewart*. Dublin: Four Courts Press, 2004. Pp 35–47.

——. 'Women and Patriotism in Eighteenth-Century Ireland', *History Ireland* 14:5 (2006), 25–30.

O'Toole, Fintan. *A Traitor's Kiss: the Life of Richard Brinsley Sheridan*. London: Granta, 1997.

Raven, James. *Judging New Wealth: Popular Publishing and Responses to Commerce in England, 1750–1800*. Oxford: Clarendon Press, 1987.

Ross, Ian Campbell. '*The Triumph of Prudence over Passion*: Nationalism and Feminism in an Eighteenth-Century Irish Novel', *Irish University Review*, 10:2 (1980), 232–40.

——. 'Fiction to 1800', in Seamus Deane, with Andrew Carpenter and Jonathan Williams (eds). *Field Day Anthology of Irish Writing*, 3 vols. Derry: Field Day, 1991. Vol. I. Pp 682–59.

Schellenberg, Betty A. *The Professionalization of Women Writers in Eighteenth-Century England*. Cambridge: Cambridge University Press, 2005.

Stewart, Carol. *The Eighteenth-Century Novel and the Secularization of Ethics*. Farnham: Ashgate, 2010.

Todd, Janet. *The Sign of Angellica: Women, Writing, and Fiction 1660–1800*. London: Virago, 1987.

Watson, Nicola J. *Revolution and the Form of the English Novel, 1790–1825: intercepted letters, interrupted seductions*. Oxford: Clarendon Press, 1994.

Webster, Mary D. *Francis Wheatley*. London: Paul Mellon Foundation for British Art in association with Routledge & Kegan Paul, 1970.

Wright, Julia M. '"All the Fire-Side Circle": Irish Women Writers and the Sheridan-Lefanu Coterie', *Keats-Shelley Journal*, 55 (2006), 63–72.

BIBLIOGRAPHY

Garside Peter, James Raven et al. *The English Novel, 1770–1829: a bibliographic survey of prose fiction published in the British Isles*, 2 vols. Oxford: Oxford University Press, 2000.

Loeber, Rolf and Magda Loeber, with Anna Mullin Burnham. *A Guide to Irish Fiction, 1650–1800*. Dublin: Four Courts Press, 2006.